The Ideal of Equalit

The Ideal of Equality

Edited by

Matthew Clayton
Lecturer in Government
Brunel University

and

Andrew Williams
Lecturer in Politics and Philosophy
University of Reading

Published 2002 by
PALGRAVE MACMILLAN
Houndmills, Basingstoke, Hampshire RG21 6XS and
175 Fifth Avenue, New York, N. Y. 10010
Companies and representatives throughout the world

PALGRAVE MACMILLAN is the global academic imprint of the Palgrave Macmillan division of St. Martin's Press, LLC and of Palgrave Macmillan Ltd. Macmillan® is a registered trademark in the United States, United Kingdom and other countries. Palgrave is a registered trademark in the European Union and other countries.

First edition 2000
Reprinted with corrections 2002

ISBN 0–333–68695–5 hardback (*outside North America*)
ISBN 0–312–23017–6 hardback (*in North America*)
ISBN 0–333–97119–1 paperback (*worldwide*)

This book is printed on paper suitable for recycling and made from fully managed and sustained forest sources.

A catalogue record for this book is available from the British Library.

The Library of Congress has cataloged the hardcover edition as follows:
The ideal of equality / edited by Matthew Clayton, Andrew Williams.
     p. cm.
     Includes bibliographical references and index.
     ISBN 0–312–23017–6 (cloth)
     1. Equality. I. Clayton, Matthew, 1966– II. Williams, Andrew, 1963–
HM821 .I33 2000
305—dc21
                                                          99–049744

10   9   8   7   6   5   4   3   2   1
11   10   09   08   07   06   05   04   03   02

Printed and bound in Great Britain by
Antony Rowe Ltd, Chippenham and Eastbourne

Contents

List of Contributors

Richard Arneson is Professor of Philosophy at the University of California, San Diego.

Matthew Clayton is Lecturer in Government at Brunel University.

G. A. Cohen is Chichele Professor of Social and Political Theory, and a Fellow of All Souls College, at the University of Oxford.

Ronald Dworkin is Professor of Law at New York University and Quain Professor in Jurisprudence at University College London.

Thomas Nagel is Professor of Philosophy and Law at New York University.

Derek Parfit is a Senior Research Fellow at All Souls College, University of Oxford.

John Rawls is Emeritus Professor of Philosophy at Harvard University.

T. M. Scanlon is Alford Professor of Natural Religion, Moral Philosophy, and Civil Polity at Harvard University.

Larry Temkin is Professor of Philosophy at Rutgers University.

Andrew Williams is Lecturer in Politics and Philosophy at the University of Reading.

Acknowledgements

The editors gratefully acknowledge the following permissions to reprint essays in this volume:

John Rawls, 'Reply to Alexander and Musgrave', sections I–III, V–VII, originally appeared in the *Quarterly Journal of Economics*, 88:4 (MIT Press Journals: November, 1974), pp. 633–43, 646–55. © 1974 by the President and Fellows of Harvard College. Reprinted with permission of The MIT Press.

T. M. Scanlon, 'The Diversity of Objections to Inequality' was delivered as the Lindley Lecture at the University of Kansas, 22 February 1996. © Copyright 1997 by Department of Philosophy, University of Kansas. Reprinted with permission of the author and the Department of Philosophy, University of Kansas.

Thomas Nagel, 'Equality' was delivered as a Tanner Lecture on Human Values at Stanford University, 1977. Printed with permission of the author and the Tanner Lectures on Human Values, a Corporation, University of Utah, Salt Lake City, Utah.

Derek Parfit, 'Equality or Priority?' was delivered as the Lindley Lecture at the University of Kansas, 21 November 1991. © Copyright 1995 by Department of Philosophy, University of Kansas. Reprinted with permission of the author and the Department of Philosophy, University of Kansas.

Larry Temkin, 'Equality, Priority, and the Levelling Down Objection'. © Larry Temkin, 1998. Printed with permission of the author.

G. A. Cohen, 'The Pareto Argument for Inequality', sections I–IV and two paragraphs from the conclusion, originally appeared in *Social Philosophy and Policy*, 12 (1995), pp. 160–75, 184. © 1995 Social Philosophy and Policy Foundation. Reprinted with permission of the author and Cambridge University Press.

Richard Arneson, 'Liberalism, Distributive Subjectivism, and Equal Opportunity for Welfare', originally appeared in *Philosophy and Public Affairs*, 19 (1990), pp. 158–64, 174–79, 183–93. © 1990 by Princeton University Press. Reprinted with permission of the author and Princeton University Press.

Ronald Dworkin, 'Justice in the Distribution of Health Care', was delivered as the McGill Lecture in Jurisprudence and Public Policy on 17 March 1993 at the Faculty of Law, McGill University, and originally appeared in the *McGill Law Journal*, 38 (1993), pp. 883–98. © Ronald Dworkin 1993. Reprinted with permission of the author.

The editors apologize for any errors or omissions in the above list. If contacted they will be pleased to rectify these at the earliest opportunity.

All royalties from the sale of this book go to Oxfam.

1

Some Questions for Egalitarians

Matthew Clayton and Andrew Williams

I. Introduction

How should benefits and burdens be distributed between people? This is one of the fundamental questions of distributive ethics. The ideal of equality is one long-standing answer to that question. Nevertheless, in recent years the nature and defence of the egalitarian ideal have become the subject of renewed philosophical debate. Two questions figure prominently in the debate. First, Derek Parfit asks the question, 'Equality or Priority?'[1] Should those with a concern for equality value a diminution of the *gap* between the better and worse off for its own sake. Or should they attach priority to benefiting the badly off, even if this *increases* the gap between them and the better off? The second question is Amartya Sen's: 'Equality of What?'[2] If we are to distribute benefits and burdens equally, what dimensions of people's lives should be compared in order to establish whether one person is worse off than another: should egalitarian interpersonal comparison be conducted in terms of wealth and income, or a wider set of resources, or the extent to which people are satisfied with their lives, or certain opportunities to acquire or do certain things in life, or something else again?

These two questions may seem far removed from the debates about equality which arise in everyday discussions of social and economic policy. Such debates often centre on whether some proposed policy change, ranging from pension or welfare reform to the restructuring of education or the health service, serves the cause of equality. In some cases we can assess the worth of a policy change from an egalitarian point of view without delving too deeply into the questions raised above. For instance, the commonly held view that the

1

Thatcher governments in Britain between 1979 and 1990 impeded
the realization of equality can be defended without asking whether
we should be concerned to reduce the gap between the rich and
the poor, or whether our fundamental concern should be to reduce
the absolute disadvantage of the least advantaged. If real income is
taken as a plausible indicator of advantage, neither goal was fur-
thered: between 1979 and 1990/1 the number of individuals with
real incomes (allowing for family circumstances and housing costs)
below 40 per cent of the average rose from 1.7 million to 7.7 million
while the real income (after housing costs) of the bottom tenth of
the population is estimated to have fallen by 14 per cent.[3]

In other cases, however, we may need to scrutinize the ideal of
equality more deeply. Consider, for example, educational justice.
We may think that equality justifies targeting above average educational resources on economically disadvantaged children to compensate them for their worse start in life. On the other hand, we
may think that equality favours enhancing the education of those
with more productive potential, notwithstanding their social advantages, on the grounds that a more prosperous economy can
benefit the poor to a greater extent. Or, in the case of health care,
we may be unsure about whether equality supports or condemns
the rationing of scarce medical resources according to a policy which
exhibits a bias in favour of the interests of the young rather than
the elderly. Faced with uncertainty in these matters, there seems
no alternative but to confront fundamental issues about how the
ideal of equality must be characterized if it is to serve as a plausible guide to political change.

This collection addresses those issues, which are now central to
distributive ethics. Its aim is to survey some of the main disputes
involved in characterizing the ideal of equality. Of course, some
deny that equality has any importance. Others might deny that
any distributive pattern can be better or worse from the point of
view of political morality.[4] These objections, while serious, are rejected by the contributors to this volume. They agree about the
importance of distributive ethics and, furthermore, that equality
has some role within that field. They disagree, however, about how
best to construe the egalitarian impulse. Although this is by no
means an exhaustive categorization, we employ the questions raised
by Parfit and Sen to illustrate some of the debates.

II. Parfit's Question

The question 'equality or priority?' asks us to consider a distinction between two conceptions of egalitarian justice. In the first, *strict*, sense of the term, egalitarians claim that an unequal distribution of benefits and burdens across different people is, in itself, unjust or morally bad. Consequently, a diminution of the gap between the advantaged and disadvantaged would be an improvement. On a less strict interpretation, egalitarians do not regard the gap between the better and worse off as having ethical significance in itself. Instead, what matters is that the interests of the worse off should be given greater weight when we are assessing social and economic policy. Strict egalitarians are concerned about how people fare *compared* to others; they value the reduction of *relative* deprivation. The less strict view is concerned with the *absolute* level of advantage that people enjoy: the less well off a person is, the more urgent morally it is to benefit her. Parfit calls egalitarians of this kind *non-relational egalitarians* or *prioritarians*. One of the main claims of Parfit's paper is that left-wing thinkers have often confused equality and priority, which is unfortunate because these ideals rest on different foundations, have different implications, and are susceptible to different kinds of objection.[5]

To illustrate the difference we might consider Rawls's second principle of justice: that 'social and economic inequalities are to meet two conditions: they must be (a) to the greatest expected benefit of the least advantaged (the maximin criterion [or difference principle]); and (b) attached to offices and positions open to all under conditions of fair equality of opportunity.'[6] The first part of this principle is often understood as the priority view applied to the distribution of wealth and income.[7] Rawls's claim is that when deciding the shape of tax policy and benefit arrangements our first concern should be to maximize the wealth of those in the group with least wealth. Once this has been achieved our concern should be to maximize the wealth of the next least wealthy, and so on, until, finally, we should be concerned to maximize the prospects of the most wealthy. In short, priority should always be given to raising the wealth of those with less, even when we can raise their wealth to a lower degree than we can that of the more wealthy. Understood in this way, the difference principle mandates economic inequality because the prospect of a greater than average level of wealth may encourage the productive to work harder than they otherwise would and, thereby, produce more wealth which can be redistributed to the least advantaged. Thus, the difference principle's concern for the least well off may lead us in a different direction than that proposed by strict egalitarians.

The second part of Rawls's principle of social and economic justice relates to fair equality of opportunity. This is the familiar idea that differences in life-prospects – in terms of educational and occupational attainment and the enjoyment of wealth and income – are unjust to the extent that they are produced by differences in social backgrounds. The upshot of this is that justice favours a reduction of the gap in life-prospects between those born into deprived backgrounds and those who have more privileged backgrounds. This ideal is egalitarian in the strict sense.[8] So, Rawls's conception of justice exhibits both egalitarian and prioritarian concerns. Inequalities that benefit the worst off are permissible provided that the competition for unequal rewards ensures that everyone has equal opportunity to acquire positions of relative advantage.

III. Equality

Sometimes the achievement of strict equality will be a by-product of the successful pursuit of some distinct goal. Under some circumstances choosing an equal distribution might, for example, coincide with maximizing the prospects of the least advantaged. One could therefore prefer an equal distribution even if one did not value equality. Strict egalitarians, however, do not have a merely coincidental preference for equality. They claim that equality is an important value which we should *aim* to achieve. Nevertheless they may still value equality in different ways. So, in order to assess their claim, it is important to distinguish the various ways in which equality might be of value.

In doing so, it is useful to draw two distinctions.[9] First, equality might either be instrumentally valuable because of its effects, or intrinsically valuable for reasons other than its effects. *Instrumental egalitarians* might aim for equality in order, for example, to secure the self-respect of the least advantaged or reduce certain forms of social antagonism. *Intrinsic egalitarians* display a less contingent commitment to equality. To understand their view a second distinction is relevant. Those who are *derivative egalitarians* value equality as a constitutive element of some wider ideal. This view is articu-

lated by Scanlon among others.[10] An attractive ideal of social cooperation, he claims, involves public knowledge that everyone is
an equal. Unlike instrumental and derivative egalitarians, *non-derivative
egalitarians* attach ultimate value to the achievement of equality.
For example, they might think it regrettable that some are unavoid-
ably worse off than others even though they are unaware of their
relative disadvantage. Temkin defends this view, though he accepts
that other goods, such as benefiting people, have ultimate value,
and the good of equality must be weighed against such goods in
order to arrive at a judgement concerning what is best all things
considered.

These various conceptions of the value of equality are liable to
different types of criticism. Some are sceptical about the instrumental
or derivative benefits of equality, but perhaps the most politically
influential and philosophically interesting anti-egalitarian argument
applies to non-derivative egalitarians: *the levelling down objection*.[11]
Since these egalitarians value a reduction of the gap between the
better and worse off for its own sake, they are committed to regarding a worsening of the condition of the better off as, in some
respect, valuable *even when this does not benefit the worse-off at all*.
Many find this counter-intuitive: how can a move from one state
to another be in any respect better if it is better for no one and
worse for some? Temkin's paper is primarily devoted to clarifying
and rebutting this objection. He argues that the ideal of equality is
similar in many respects to certain other commonly held ideals,
such as punishing people according to their deservingness. Since
the value of these ideals does not necessarily rest on anyone being
benefited by their application, we need not worry if the ideal of
equality fails to exhibit this feature as well. If Temkin is right, critics of equality must either abandon their appeal to the levelling
down objection to equality or give up various other beliefs which
they typically hold.

IV. Priority

The ideal of equality tends to attract people who are concerned
about the plight of the badly-off. If such individuals are also persuaded by the levelling down objection they may embrace a
non-relational construal of the ideal to accommodate their concern, thereby converting to prioritarianism. Since attaching priority

to the interests of the worse-off does not value the reduction of inequality for its own sake, but only as a by-product or as a means of raising the level of the worse-off, it escapes the levelling down objection.

Defence of the priority view is associated with the various forms of contractualism articulated by Rawls, Nagel, and Scanlon. Rawls's conception of *justice as fairness* appeals to the idea that principles of social justice are principles which would be agreed to in a hypothetical context, the *original position*, where individuals are deprived of information that may jeopardize the fairness of their agreement. In this position individuals are uncertain of the probability of occupying any particular position in society, and are duty-bound to agree only to principles which they can abide by, and to respect certain other constraints on their choice.[12] Rawls argues that, placed in such a situation, rational self-interested individuals would adopt the maximin rule, which prefers social arrangements that attach priority to benefiting the least advantaged, rather than utilitarianism, which seeks to maximize the sum of benefits which individuals enjoy.

Rawls's view has, of course, been subject to wide-ranging criticism. Some critics claim that even if Rawls is right in theorizing justice in terms of the kind of hypothetical choice he describes, maximin is a defective principle of rational choice. Some argue that, at best, his hypothetical choice situation supports the adoption of utilitarianism constrained by the maintenance of some social minimum.[13] Others, however, are sceptical about some of the constraints Rawls places on the information available to individuals within the original position. For example, Nagel questions whether justice requires the choice of principles to be made without any information concerning the probability of enjoying different levels of advantage.[14]

Despite, and in part because of, these criticisms, Rawls's view has motivated alternative versions of contractualism. For Nagel, the original position is appealing because it attempts to ensure that we place ourselves in everyone else's shoes and assess whether social arrangements are acceptable to each individual. He argues that this leads naturally to the ideal of seeking principles which can achieve free and unanimous agreement or, in Scanlon's version, principles which no one can reasonably reject. This, in turn, leads to an alternative defence of prioritarian thinking. If we value everyone's endorsement of principles of justice then those principles must attend in the first instance to the fate of the worst-off since, because they fare worst from the operation of social arrangements, their complaints are, other things being equal, strongest: the worse off you are, the greater is your legitimate complaint and, therefore, the greater is the *moral* urgency to benefit you.[15]

For this reason, Nagel proposes attaching priority to the interests of the worse-off. However, his ideal of unanimous endorsement is not unequivocally prioritarian. He claims that although one's level of disadvantage is an important determinant of the strength of one's complaint, a possibly competing determinant is how much one loses from the prevailing arrangements compared to another member of the feasible set of arrangements. For this reason, he claims that the ideal of unanimity may support giving greater benefits to people who are already well off rather than lesser benefits to people who are badly off. Thus, unlike Rawls's difference principle, Nagel's view does not give *absolute* priority to the worse-off. If Nagel is right, there is further work to be done in terms of quantifying the weight of the different determinants of the strength of an individual's complaint.

A third defence of prioritarian justice appeals to the ideals of equality and efficiency. Roughly, the argument rests upon the prima facie appeal of equality and the claim that the introduction of certain inequalities may be *Pareto superior*, that is, better for some and worse for no one. The latter is the case, because the presence of unequal financial rewards attached to different occupations can act as an incentive for the productive to take more socially beneficial jobs or to work harder. The consequence of such incentives is beneficial to everyone: while the productive gain from higher than average earnings, the less productive benefit from the greater benefits that the productive create. Moreover, if departures from equality are constrained by the difference principle, any inequality must maximize the advantage of the worst-off and, consequently, the gap between the better- and worse-off will be narrower than alternative Pareto-superior departures from equality. Thus, Rawls asserts that the difference principle selects the Pareto efficient distribution closest to equality.[16]

Various problems beset the Paretian egalitarian argument for prioritarian justice. For instance, it has been argued that different ways of combining equality with Pareto efficiency – depending on which ideal, if either, has priority – produce different results. Thus, without further elucidation the view is indeterminate.[17] In addition, while not objecting to the ideal as such, Cohen argues that the widely held view that Paretian egalitarianism supports the offer of inequality-generating incentive payments to the productive is unsound.[18] If Cohen's argument succeeds then, practically, there may be far less at stake in the choice between equality and priority than is commonly thought.

V. Sen's Question

In formulating their competing views of distributive justice, egalitarians and prioritarians face certain common tasks. The most widely debated involves specifying a standard of interpersonal comparison applicable to issues of distributive justice. Such standards specify the conditions under which some individuals are worse off than others. They enable egalitarians to establish whether inequality exists, whilst prioritarians employ them to identify those individuals whose claims are morally most urgent. We shall refer to the question of how to characterize the relevant standard as *Sen's Question*, after the author of the classic essay 'Equality of What?'.[19]

Defending the appropriate answer to Sen's Question involves addressing various issues. For illustration of one such issue, suppose two individuals have access to the same goods but one attains fewer goods due to factors which lay within his control. In asking whether an inequality exists, or whether priority should now be attached to benefiting one individual, should our standard of comparison focus upon *achievement* or only upon *access*? Some egalitarians favour the latter position. They emphasize that in opposing only *involuntary* inequalities their view escapes the familiar conservative criticism that egalitarianism is blind to personal responsibility. It can, for example, distinguish the claims of the involuntarily unemployed from those who have chosen not to work. There is, however, a price to be paid for avoiding such a criticism.

Imagine that Cautious Carl and Daring Dan could both lead equally secure lives, but Dan becomes paralysed in some risky sport, for which he is uninsured. It appears that access egalitarianism does not require that Carl finance health care or a mobility allowance for Dan. Yet many think that justice, and not merely charity, demands at least some publicly funded redistribution even in cases where individuals bring disaster upon themselves. Conceding that equality is not the only important distributive principle, they could defend that conviction by appeal to some non-egalitarian concern, perhaps expressed by a sufficiency principle. However, if they wish to defend it on egalitarian grounds, it seems they cannot attend exclusively to access in making interpersonal comparisons.

Access versus achievement, however, is not the only important issue addressed within the debate over Sen's Question. Another even more complex problem concerns the *goods* upon which a plausible standard of interpersonal comparison should focus. Here, it is common to distinguish *welfare, resources* and *capability* as the main alternatives, although hybrid views combine various elements and are common.[20] One way to understand the range of answers, and their accompanying difficulties, is to begin with a deliberately simple resourcist form of interpersonal comparison.[21] Consider the claim that justice requires the equal distribution of wealth, construed as *impersonal resources* such as natural assets, or manufactured goods and services. No individual should, therefore, be able to acquire resources which possess a higher market value than those available to any other individual.

Various problems might beset such a proposal. Perhaps the most obvious of these relates to the narrowly economic standard the proposal involves. Why on earth, a critic might ask, should egalitarians, or prioritarians, focus simply on wealth? As Sen himself has frequently argued, that proposal appears doubly defective. First, it is obviously *incomplete* insofar as it can treat two individuals as equal even if one has a severe physical disability the other lacks. Many, however, are convinced that justice requires compensation for at least some disabilities even if their victims are no worse off than others in financial terms. Second, and less obviously, the simple proposal appears strikingly *superficial*. After all, in our personal decision-making we care about wealth insofar as it enables us to improve the quality of our lives. Surely then when distributing wealth to others we should care about it in a similarly derivative manner. We should focus ultimately upon the extent to which individuals attain, or can achieve, what they care about or, perhaps, what they have reason to care about.

VI. Welfare

A number of competing answers to Sen's Question can be construed as attempts to avoid one, or both, of these worries. Consider first welfarist accounts of interpersonal comparison, which focus upon the extent to which individuals' personal preferences are satisfied. In giving a central role to subjective satisfaction rather than monetary reward, such metrics appear to escape the charge of superficiality. However, they soon encounter their own distinctive problems. Anti-welfarists argue that welfare is completely *irrelevant*, whilst hybrid-welfarists argue that welfare, like impersonal resources, is an *incomplete* metric. To sample just a few of their arguments, we shall initially consider the problems of *malformed, expensive,* and *cheap* tastes.

The problem of malformed tastes arises because some individuals might exhibit the same level of preference satisfaction as others because subconscious psychological processes have tailored their preferences to their modest circumstances.[22] Yet it seems quite unjust to treat such individuals as no worse off than others merely because they show similar levels of satisfaction. Thus, any plausible and complete welfarist metric requires an account of authentic preference formation in order to escape worries about malformed tastes.[23] Whilst this preliminary objection might be overcome, the two remaining problems – related to expensive and cheap tastes – create a more profound threat to welfarist metrics: the *anti-welfarist dilemma.*[24]

To understand the dilemma's source, note that in order to equalize actual welfare it will be necessary to allocate more resources to individuals with especially costly ambitions. Many find such pandering to expensive tastes unfair. They deny that individuals are entitled to any more resources than others merely because their ambitions are more costly to achieve. If so, they must reject forms of egalitarianism which focus upon actual welfare. Welfarists can, however, escape this difficulty by claiming that their reluctance to subsidize expensive tastes is appropriate only because such tastes are voluntarily acquired. When tastes are involuntarily acquired, their bearers have fewer opportunities for welfare than others, and so are entitled to more resources.

By shifting from a metric of achievement to one of access, welfarists can escape the problem of expensive tastes. In doing so, however, they then face the related problem of cheap tastes. Imagine some individuals require fewer resources than others in order to enjoy the same access to welfare. Due to natural or social luck they have preferences which, though not malformed, are nevertheless relatively easy to satisfy. Access to welfare metrics treat those individuals as the beneficiaries of good fortune, and so deny that they are, ceteris paribus, entitled to as many impersonal resources as others.[25] Anti-welfarists, however, claim that such denial is unfair. They conclude that since welfare metrics must either pander to those with expensive tastes or penalize those with cheap tastes, welfare should play no role whatsoever in interpersonal comparison. The force of the anti-welfarist dilemma remains debatable.[26] Even if the dilemma is inconclusive, however, others have argued for the irrelevance of welfare on distinct grounds, or for the less radical conclusion that welfare is not the only relevant consideration in interpersonal comparison.[27] We now turn to the most influential version of that latter criticism.

VII. Capabilities

Recall the claim that it is unfair to disregard an individual's disability even if she is as wealthy as others. Some argue it is also unfair to do so even if her welfare is as high. They appeal to the common conviction that certain disabilities are, in themselves, grounds for entitlement. For that reason no metric of advantage can be plausible unless it also incorporates information about additional goods. The resulting focus upon what Sen has termed individual *functioning* and *capability*, is one of the main rivals to both pure welfarist and resourcist accounts of interpersonal comparison. It has gained many adherents, and plays an important role in measuring poverty in developing countries.[28]

Like welfarist proposals, capability metrics are a natural response to the earlier charge of superficiality levelled against simple resourcist metrics. Yet, unlike such proposals, they do not focus only upon what specified individuals care about, but instead employ a less subjective account of need. Sen, for example, refers not only to being happy, but also to functionings such as escaping morbidity, mortality, and malnutrition, as well as achieving self-respect and participating in community life.[29] According to their critics, however, capability accounts have their own peculiar problems. For example, some critics claim that without appealing to perfectionist ideals of personal well-being it is impossible to explain why certain capabilities have moral relevance whilst others do not, or to establish the relative importance of differing capabilities. Those ideals, they suggest, give content to the capability approach by identifying the manner in which differing functions impact upon an individual's quality of life.[30] Welfarists, who are frequently sceptical about the validity of any perfectionist ideals, might reject the capability approach for that reason.[31] Other anti-perfectionist critics grant that such ideals may well be acceptable guides to personal conduct but still question their role within *political* morality. Rawlsian anti-perfectionists, for instance, claim that respect for basic civil liberties is inevitably accompanied by deep divisions over what makes life worth living, even amongst reasonable individuals who accept the fundamental values of liberal democracy. Since in their view an adequate conception of justice must be capable of winning the allegiance of those individuals, they object to capability metrics which rely upon perfectionist assumptions unable to pass that test.[32]

The welfarist and anti-perfectionist objections raise perennial questions within moral and political philosophy. Thus, the criticisms canvassed so far are likely to remain the subject of debate. The same may be true of a less familiar objection which was first directed against welfarism but can be generalized to capability metrics.[33] This objection asserts that capability metrics sometimes give implausible results because they are blind to individuals' own attitude to their disabilities. To understand the anti-welfarist form of the objection imagine some individuals experience feelings of intense guilt which result in their enjoying considerably lower levels of welfare than others. Nevertheless, because they regard those feelings as the appropriate response to their own failings, they much prefer their presence to their absence. Even some of those drawn to welfarism accept that individuals who do not regard their luck as *mis*fortune are not relevantly worse off than others, and so cannot claim compensation.[34] There appears then to be a case for revising welfarist metrics to accommodate such convictions.

If that case is sound, the objection can be extended to capability metrics. After all, any disability which could be thought relevant to interpersonal comparison might be welcomed by some individuals. For example, even if most women would regret being infertile, some might welcome liberation from the risk of involuntary conception. Where a disability is welcomed should we accept the individual's own apparent judgement that it does not constitute a disadvantage? If we answer 'no', we allow that individuals may legitimately claim compensation for conditions about which they themselves are perfectly happy, but accepting such a conclusion seems counter-intuitive. If we answer 'yes', we might be tempted to revert to a suitably revised form of welfarism. However, we might, instead, return to resourcism, and ask whether any of its more sophisticated variants prove acceptable. In answering that question the natural starting point is Rawls's social primary goods metric.

VIII. Resources

Rawls now grants that, under realistic circumstances, his list of social primary goods is an incomplete metric. His solution is to suggest that the list should be supplemented by an account of those capabilities essential to be a 'normally cooperating member of society'.[35] Unfortunately, it is difficult to assess Rawls's resource-capability hybrid since its details are left unspecified. Rawls's solution also appears open to the type of objection often directed at sufficiency principles. It is silent once the relevant capability threshold is crossed but provides no reason to deny that inequalities in capabilities might still be morally relevant even after that point. After all, the difference principle is itself premised upon the importance of inequalities in earning potential between normal cooperators, and aims to ensure they work to everyone's benefit. Why then shouldn't other differences in personal endowment also be regarded as important?

In the absence of an answer, it might be worth considering alternative resourcist proposals, of which Dworkin's is the leading example. Like Rawls, Dworkin denies the need to make interpersonal welfare comparisons between individuals who differ in their personal endowment. Yet, despite this affinity, their two views exhibit important philosophical differences. For example, information about individuals' preferences plays an important role in Dworkin's view. Thus, the requirement that nobody prefer any other individual's endowment to her own is fundamental to his defence of an equal distribution of impersonal resources. This *envy test*, as economists have misleadingly dubbed it, can naturally be extended to circumstances in which individuals vary in their *personal* resources.[36] Without any reference to ideal-based accounts of human need, the resourcist can claim that personal resources are unequal where some prefer the opportunities which others enjoy in virtue of their physical and mental capabilities. Dworkin employs such a claim in explaining why, under realistic conditions, justice demands more than an equal distribution of wealth.[37]

Although Dworkin conceives inequalities in impersonal and personal resources similarly, his response to them is dissimilar. In the former case, impersonal resources can be redistributed until each individual's share has the same competitive value. However, Dworkin rejects radical proposals to redistribute personal resources or to distribute impersonal resources until each individual's comprehensive endowment, encompassing both types of resource, has the same value. Instead he defends compensatory redistribution that mimics the operation of a fair insurance market in which each individual faces the same risk of suffering bad luck.[38] He concedes that his proposal does not fully satisfy the envy test.[39] However, like its competitors, Dworkin's proposal is open to objections. Some focus upon alleged deficiencies in his account of the insurance market's operation.[40] Others challenge envy elimination as an adequate interpretation of the egalitarian aim.

Opponents of perfectionist and welfarist metrics are drawn to the envy test because it enables interpersonal comparison to shun appeal to ideals without succumbing to the anti-welfarist dilemma. But those unmoved by such considerations may fail to see the appeal of the test, or may find it counter-intuitive. They might claim that the existence of envy is neither necessary nor sufficient for inequality. For illustration, consider two cases which involve variation in reproductive endowments. Suppose it is more costly in a host of ways to *bear* than to *beget* children. In those respects, it is more burdensome for women than for men to exercise their procreative capability. Many women, however, attach great value to child-bearing. Though they might prefer its costs to be reduced, they do not regret being born with their reproductive endowment rather than the masculine alternative.[41] Under such conditions envy over differing reproductive endowments appears to be absent. Nevertheless, many are convinced that justice to women demands that they should be compensated for having to bear so high a burden in exercising their procreative capability. For that reason they regard envy as unnecessary for distributive injustice. Now consider a less familiar, though not completely unrealistic, scenario. Imagine that a man regrets that he cannot bear children and would prefer to have been born with a female reproductive endowment. Even so, unless he can appeal to something more than his mere preference for an alternative endowment, many deny the existence of any morally relevant inequality. If their conviction is sound, then unredressed envy does not even suffice for injustice.

These cases seem to show that individuals can be more needy than others even if they do not prefer the others' resources or less needy yet still prefer those resources. Under such conditions the claims of envy elimination and of need diverge. Finding a satisfactory answer to Sen's Question depends in part on establishing which claim, if any, to honour. But that is a task for another occasion.[42]

Notes

1 D. Parfit, 'Equality or Priority?' in this volume. See also D. McKerlie, 'Equality and Priority', *Utilitas*, 6 (1994), pp. 25–42.
2 Sen, 'Equality of What?', in S. McMurrin (ed.), *The Tanner Lectures on Human Values*, I (Salt Lake City: University of Utah Press and Cambridge: Cambridge University Press, 1980); rpr. *Choice, Welfare and Measurement* (Oxford: Blackwell, 1982).
3 J. Hills et al., *The Future of Welfare: A Guide to the Debate* (York: Joseph Rowntree Foundation, 1993), pp. 34–8. Hills notes that the latter estimate includes the self-employed who, it is sometimes argued, have a greater tendency to underreport their income compared to other groups. If this group is excluded, the real income of the bottom 10 per cent is estimated to have fallen by 6 per cent.
4 See, for example, R. Nozick, *Anarchy, State, and Utopia* (Oxford: Blackwell, 1974), part 2, esp. pp. 149–50.
5 Parfit, 'Equality or Priority?', esp. sections VII, IX–XIII.
6 J. Rawls, 'Reply to Alexander and Musgrave', in this volume, section III.
7 For an alternative interpretation, see T. Pogge, *Realizing Rawls* (Ithaca: Cornell University Press, 1989), p. 197. For further discussion of the relationship between Rawls's position and the priority view, see the Appendix to Parfit's chapter in this volume.
8 See *A Theory of Justice* (Cambridge, Mass.: Harvard University Press, 1971), p. 73. Note, however, that Rawls's final statement of fair equality of opportunity on p. 303 appears more prioritarian.
9 We owe these distinctions to Joseph Raz. See p. 177 of his book *The Morality of Freedom* (Oxford: Clarendon Press, 1986), ch. 9 of which contains a brilliant discussion of the value of equality.
10 T. Scanlon, 'The Diversity of Objections to Inequality', in this volume, sections I and III. See also D. Miller, 'Equality and Justice' and R. Norman 'The Social Basis of Equality', both of which appear in A. Mason (ed.) *Ideals of Equality* (Oxford: Blackwell, 1998).

16 *Matthew Clayton and Andrew Williams*

11 For statements and discussion of this objection see Parfit, 'Equality or
    Priority?' sections V and XII; and L. Temkin, 'Equality, Priority, and
    the Levelling Down Objection'.
12 See *A Theory of Justice*, ch. 3.
13 See, for example, J. Waldron, 'John Rawls and the Social Minimum',
    Journal of Applied Philosophy 3 (1986), pp. 21–33. The social minimum
    is a so-called *sufficiency principle*, which asserts that no one should be
    allowed to fall below a particular threshold of advantage. Some argue
    that sufficiency principles are an alternative to egalitarian and prioritarian
    principles. See H. Frankfurt, 'Equality as a Moral Ideal', *Ethics*, 98 (1987),
    pp. 21–43. However, even if it is true that satisfying sufficiency is one
    of the most morally pressing demands of political morality, it does not
    follow that, once satisfied, justice has been done. Equality or priority
    may remain important objectives above the relevant threshold.
14 T. Nagel, 'Equality', in this volume, section VII; 'Rawls on Justice', re-
    printed in N. Daniels (ed.) *Reading Rawls* (Stanford: Stanford University
    Press, 1989), pp. 10–12.
15 See Nagel, 'Equality', sections VI–IX, and his book *Equality and Partial-
    ity* (New York: Oxford University Press, 1991); Scanlon, 'Contractualism
    and Utilitarianism', in A. Sen and B. Williams (eds), *Utilitarianism and
    Beyond* (Cambridge: Cambridge University Press, 1982).
16 Rawls, 'Reply to Alexander and Musgrave', in this volume, section IV.
    For further discussion, see R. Martin, *Rawls and Rights* (Lawrence: University
    Press of Kansas, 1985), ch. 5.
17 For criticism along these lines, and the objection that paretian egali-
    tarianism has difficulty in meeting certain minimal formal requirements
    of principles of justice, see A. Williams, 'The Revisionist Difference Prin-
    ciple', *Canadian Journal of Philosophy*, 25 (1995), pp. 257–82.
18 See G. A. Cohen, 'The Pareto Argument for Inequality', *Social Philos-
    ophy and Policy*, 12 (1995), pp. 160–85, an abridged version of which is
    reprinted in this volume. For Cohen's critique of Rawlsian defences of
    inequality more generally see his 'Incentives, Inequality, and Commu-
    nity', in G. Peterson (ed.) *The Tanner Lectures on Human Values*, 13 (Salt
    Lake City: University of Utah Press, 1992), pp. 262–329; and 'Where
    the Action Is: On the Site of Distributive Justice', *Philosophy and Public
    Affairs*, 26 (1997), pp. 3–30.
19 See S. McMurrin (ed.), *The Tanner Lectures on Human Values*, I (Cam-
    bridge: Cambridge University Press, 1980), and rpr. in S. Darwall (ed.),
    Equal Freedom (Ann Arbor: University of Michigan Press, 1995).
20 For example, in 'On the Currency of Egalitarian Justice', *Ethics* 99 (1989),
    pp. 906–44, Cohen defends *access to advantage*, which combines all three
    elements.
21 Few resourcists recommend such a proposal, though Hillel Steiner's left-
    libertarianism came close to doing so, prior to its inclusion of children's
    genetic information within the common pool of resources. See, for
    example, 'Three Just Taxes', in P. Van Parijs (ed.), *Arguing for Basic In-
    come* (London: Verso, 1992). Other resourcists focus upon goods additional
    to wealth. Thus, Rawls initially proposed a list of social primary goods,

which includes 'basic liberties', 'freedom of movement and free choice of occupation against a background of diverse opportunities', 'powers and prerogatives of offices or responsibility in the political and economic institutions of the basic structure' and 'the social bases of self-respect', as well as 'income and wealth'. See *Political Liberalism*, p. 181 (New York: Columbia University Press, 1993). As discussed later, Rawls also now regards a 'normal' set of capabilities as relevant. Dworkin focuses upon two types of resources. As he explains, 'Personal resources are qualities of mind and body that affect people's success in achieving their plans and projects; physical and mental health, strength, and talent. Impersonal resources are parts of the environment that can be owned and transferred: land, raw materials, houses, television sets and computers and various legal rights and interests in these.' See 'Foundations of Liberal Equality', in G. Petersen (ed.), *The Tanner Lectures on Human Values*, XI (Salt Lake City: Utah University Press, 1989), p. 37, and S. Darwall (ed.), *Equal Freedom*, p. 224.

22 On the importance of *adaptive preference formation*, see J. Elster, 'Sour Grapes – Utilitarianism and the Genesis of Wants', A. Sen and B. Williams (eds) *Utilitarianism and Beyond*.

23 Note that the problem also applies to resourcist views insofar as they rely upon preference information in order to identify inequalities. For Dworkin's discussion of the principle of authenticity employed in equality of resources, see 'What is Equality? Part Three: The Place of Liberty', *University of Iowa Law Review* (1987), sec. V.A.

24 For a thorough treatment of the dilemma, see R. Dworkin, 'What is Equality? Part I: Equality of Welfare', *Philosophy and Public Affairs* 10 (1981), sec. VIII.

25 Arneson's *equality of opportunity for welfare* appears to deny that individuals with cheap tastes who initially enjoy equal access to welfare but then willingly cultivate more expensive tastes are entitled to any more resources to finance their new ambitions. Cohen's equality of access to advantage grants them more resources than Arneson's metric since it includes a resource as well as a welfare component. However, it still denies them as many resources as others enjoy, even if they do not themselves regard their greater capacity to convert resources into welfare as a piece of good fortune.

26 For further discussion, see R. Arneson, 'Liberalism, Distributive Subjectivism, and Equal Opportunity for Welfare', in this volume, pp. 190–2.

27 For example, as well as employing the problem of expensive tastes, Rawls objects to welfarist metrics by appealing to the need for 'a practicable public basis of interpersonal comparisons based on objective features of citizens' social circumstances open to view'. Scanlon argues that 'the strength of a person's preferences, insofar as this is taken to be independent of value judgments about there is reason to prefer, lacks sufficient connection with the idea of what is good for a person – what makes his or her life better'. See, respectively, *Political Liberalism*, p. 181 and 'The Moral Basis of Interpersonal Comparison', J. Elster and J. Roemer (eds), *Interpersonal Comparisons of Well-being* (Cambridge: Cambridge University Press, 1991), p. 38.

18   *Matthew Clayton and Andrew Williams*

28 See M. Nussbaum and J. Glover (eds), *Women, Culture and Development* (Oxford: Clarendon Press, 1995), and United Nations Development Programme, *Human Development Report, 1997* (New York: Oxford University Press, 1997).

29 See 'Capability and Well-Being', M. Nussbaum and A. Sen (eds), *The Quality of Life* (Oxford: Clarendon Press, 1993), pp. 36–7.

30 For the most sophisticated statement of perfectionism, both as a political morality and conception of well-being, see J. Raz, *The Morality of Freedom.*

31 See Arneson, 'Equality and Equal Opportunity for Welfare', *Philosophical Studies* 56 (1989), sec. V.

32 Note, however, that some argue that ideal-based capability metrics can be constructed which satisfy the relevant anti-perfectionist constraints. Rawls, for example, points out that his list of primary goods is justified by means of an ideal-based account of citizens' needs rather than simply an empirical description of the content of preferences. But, more recently, he also stresses that the relevant ideal is a 'political' conception of person's capacities and interests, which can be endorsed by individuals who hold competing conceptions of the good. See 'Social Unity and Primary Goods' in Sen and Williams (eds) *Utilitarianism and Beyond*, and *Political Liberalism*, ch. V.

33 See Scanlon, 'Equality of Resources and Equality of Welfare: a Forced Marriage?', *Ethics* 97 (1989), pp. 116–17.

34 See Cohen, 'On the Currency of Egalitarian Justice', sec. V.A.

35 'See *Political Liberalism*, ch. V, sec. 3, where Rawls conjectures that 'a sufficiently flexible index can be devised in that it gives judgments as just or fair as those of any political conception we can work out' and adds that 'as Sen urges, any such index will consider basic capabilities, and its aim will be to restore citizens to their proper role as normal cooperating members of society' (p. 186). For application to the case of health, Rawls refers to 'Social Unity and Primary Goods', p. 168, and Norman Daniels's work on health care.

36 Note the test has little to do with envy as a psychological phenomenon. For further discussion see 'What is Equality? Part Two: Equality of Resources', pp. 285–6, and C. Arnesperger's excellent survey 'Envy-Freeness and Distributive Justice', *Journal of Economic Surveys*, 8 (1994), pp. 155–86.

37 See 'What is Equality? Part Two: Equality of Resources', pp. 292–3.

38 See 'What is Equality? Part Two: Equality of Resources', sec. III, and 'Justice in the Distribution of Health Care', in this volume.

39 It does, nevertheless, escape objections to the forcible transfer of bodily parts and the so-called *slavery of the talented*. For the latter objection, see 'What is Equality? Part Two: Equality of Resources', pp. 311–12.

40 See, for example, J. Roemer, 'Equality of Talent', *Egalitarian Perspectives* (Cambridge: Cambridge University Press, 1994). For further objections, and an alternative resource-egalitarian approach to Dworkin's, see P. Van Parijs, *Real Freedom for All* (Oxford: Oxford University Press), ch. 3, esp. secs. 3.4–3.5.

41 Because bearing the relevant costs is not in itself valuable to the women concerned, they differ from the guilt-afflicted individuals previously mentioned.

42 For helpful discussion we thank J. Burley, P. Casal, K. Watson and participants in a seminar on *Equality and its Critics* at Yale's Ethics, Politics and Economics Program.

Editorial introduction to Rawls's chapter

In this chapter Rawls responds to the papers by S. S. Alexander and R. A. Musgrave in the *Quarterly Journal of Economics*, 88 (1974) which discussed his book *A Theory of Justice*. Rawls's reply provides a compendious statement of his conception of *justice as fairness* and defends his two principles of justice. His account of the ideal of a well-ordered society, which is central to his recent book *Political Liberalism*, illustrates the continuity in his thought. The reply is also of interest because Musgrave's paper, 'Maximin, Uncertainty, and the Leisure Tradeoff', contained an early statement of the view that inequality-generating incentives might be morally problematic, and explored lump-sum ability taxes as an alternative to such incentives. The problem of incentives is discussed in greater depth in G. A. Cohen's chapter in this volume, but Rawls offers some interesting observations about this type of criticism in section VI. – Eds

2
Reply to Alexander and Musgrave*

John Rawls

The papers by Alexander and Musgrave raise many fundamental issues about the views presented in *A Theory of Justice*, far more in fact than I can consider in this reply. To discuss their criticisms point by point, even if it were possible, would not, I think, be the most useful way to proceed. For I believe that it is first necessary to set out certain basic matters that will be needed later. Thus, I shall begin with a sketch of the main outline of justice as fairness (as I shall refer to the theory) and try to cast it in a somewhat different and sharper perspective. Having done this, I shall take up several of what I believe to be Alexander's and Musgrave's most important objections.

I. The notion of a well-ordered society

The aim of a theory of justice is to clarify and to organize our considered judgments about the justice and injustice of social forms. Thus, any account of these judgments, when fully presented, expresses an underlying conception of human society, that is, a conception of the person, of the relations between persons, and of the general structure and ends of social cooperation. Now there

* I should like to thank S. S. Alexander and R. A. Musgrave for their papers, and the editors of this *Journal* for the opportunity to reply. I am indebted to Robert Cooter for advice and comments that enabled me to make many improvements; and to Ariel Pakes for discussion about the argument in section [V in this volume], where I have adopted several of his suggestions for clarifying its assumptions; and to Burton Dreben for a number of revisions, particularly in section I.

21

are, I believe, rather few such conceptions; and these are sharply distinct so that the choice between them is a choice between disparate things: one cannot continuously vary their basic features so as to pass gradually from one to another. Thus, to formulate a theory of justice, we must specify its underlying conception in a particular though still abstract way. Justice as fairness does this by bringing together certain general features of any society that it seems one would, on due reflection, wish to live in and want to shape our interests and character. The notion of a well-ordered society is the result: it embodies these features in a definite way and indicates how to describe the original position, which is introduced in the next section. I begin by enumerating the features of such a society.[1]

First of all, a well-ordered society is defined as one that is effectively regulated by a public conception of justice. That is, it is a society in which:

(1) Everyone accepts, and knows that others accept, the same principles (the same conception) of justice.

(2) Basic social institutions and their arrangement into one scheme (the basic structure of society) satisfy, and are with reason believed by everyone to satisfy, these principles.

(3) The public conception of justice is founded on reasonable beliefs that have been established by generally accepted methods of inquiry.

It is assumed second that the members of a well-ordered society are, and view themselves as, free and equal moral persons. More specifically, they may be described as follows:

(4) They each have, and view themselves as having, a sense of justice (the content of which is defined by the principles of the public conception) that is normally effective (the desire to act on this conception determines their conduct for the most part).

(5) They each have, and view themselves as having, fundamental aims and interests (a conception of their good) in the name of which it is legitimate to make claims on one another in the design of their institutions.

(6) They each have, and view themselves as having, a right to equal respect and consideration in determining the principles by which the basic structure of their society is to be regulated.

In addition, a well-ordered society is said to be stable with respect to its conception of justice. This means that, viewing the society as a going concern, its members acquire as they grow up a sufficiently strong and effective sense of justice, one that usually overcomes the temptations and stresses of social life. Thus:

(7) Basic social institutions generate an effective supporting sense of justice.

Since we are interested in a theory of justice, we shall restrict our attention to well-ordered societies that exist under circumstances that require some conception of justice and give point to its peculiar role. Although natural resources and the state of technology are assumed to be such so as to make social cooperation both possible and necessary, and mutually advantageous arrangements are indeed feasible; nevertheless, the benefits they yield fall short of the demands that people make. Therefore:

(8) Conditions of moderate scarcity exist.

But also, we assume that persons and groups have conceptions of the good that incline them in contrary directions and make claims and counterclaims on one another (see (5) above). Furthermore, people have opposing basic beliefs (religious, philosophical, and moral) and different ways of assessing evidence and arguments in many essential cases, and so:

(9) There is a divergence of fundamental interests and ends, and a variety of opposing and incompatible basic beliefs.

As for the usefulness of social institutions, we assume that the arrangements of a well-ordered society are productive; they are not, so to speak, a zero-sum game in which one person's (or group's) gain is another's loss. Thus:

(10) The scheme of basic institutions is a more or less self-sufficient and productive scheme of social cooperation for mutual good.

Given these circumstances of justice ((8)–(10)), we can delineate the role and subject of justice. Since many of their fundamental aims and beliefs stand in opposition, the members of a well-ordered society are not indifferent as to how the greater benefits produced by their cooperation are distributed. Hence a set of principles is required for adjudicating between social arrangements that shape this division of advantages. We express this by:

(11) The role of the principles of justice (the public conception) is to assign rights and duties in the basic structure of society and to specify the manner in which it is appropriate for institutions to influence the overall distribution of benefits and burdens.

To which we add finally:

(12) The members of a well-ordered society take the basic structure of society (that is, basic social institutions and their arrangement

into one scheme) as the primary subject of justice (as that to which the principles of justice are in the first instance to apply). Thus the principles of social justice are macro and not necessarily micro principles.

This enumeration of conditions shows that the notion of a well-ordered society under circumstances of justice is extremely complicated. It may help to observe that the various conditions go together. Thus, (1)–(7) specify the notion of a well-ordered society: (1), (2), and (3) characterize publicity; (4), (5), and (6) fill in the idea of free and equal moral persons; and (7), stability, concludes this part of the list. Conditions (8), (9), and (10) characterize the circumstances of justice, which restrict the class of relevant cases in the way appropriate for a theory of justice; and (11) and (12) describe the role and subject of justice.

The notion of a well-ordered society articulates a formal and abstract conception of the general structure of a just society, much as the notion of general equilibrium in price theory describes the structure of markets in the economy as a whole. The analogy with the theory of general equilibrium must, however, be used with discretion; otherwise, it may mislead us as to the nature of the theory of justice. To illustrate: the relations between members of a well-ordered society are not like the relations between buyers and sellers in competitive markets. A closer analogy is to think of a pluralistic society, divided along religious, ethnic, or cultural lines, in which the various groups and associations have managed to reach a consensus on a scheme of principles to govern their political institutions and to regulate the basic structure of society. Although there is public agreement on this framework and citizens are attached to it, they have profound differences about other things. While their inclination to press their cause makes a certain vigilance against one another necessary, their public conception of justice and their affirmation of it makes their secure association together possible. It is far better to regard the notion of a well-ordered society as an extension of the idea of religious toleration than of the idea of a competitive economy.

Clearly the value of the notion of a well-ordered society, and the force of the reasoning based upon it, depends on the assumption that those who appear to hold incompatible conceptions of justice will nevertheless find conditions (1) to (7) congenial to their moral convictions, or at least would do so after consideration. Otherwise, there would be no point in appealing to these conditions in deciding between different principles of justice. But we should recognize that they are not morally neutral (whatever that would be) and certainly they are not trivial. Those who feel no affinity for the notion of a well-ordered society, and who wish to specify the underlying conception in a different form, will be unmoved by justice as fairness (even granting the validity of its argument), except of course as it may prove a better way to systematize their judgments of justice.

II. The role of the original position

The idea of the original position arises in the following way. Consider the question: Which conception of justice is most appropriate for a well-ordered society, that is, which conception best accords with the above conditions? Of course, this is a vague question. One can sharpen it by asking which of a few representative conceptions, drawn from the tradition of moral philosophy, is the closest fit. Assume, then, that we have to decide between but a few conceptions (for example a variant of intuitionism and of utilitarianism, and certain principles of justice). Justice as fairness holds that the particular conception that is most suitable for a well-ordered society is the one that would be unanimously agreed to in a hypothetical situation that is fair between individuals conceived as free and equal moral persons, that is, as members of such a society. Alternatively, the conception that is most appropriate for a society is the one that persons characteristic of the society would adopt when fairly situated with respect to one another. This hypothetical situation is the original position. Fairness of the circumstances under which agreement is reached transfers to the fairness of the principles agreed to; and since these principles serve as principles of justice, the name 'justice as fairness' seems natural.

We assume that in the original position the parties have the general information provided by natural science and social theory. This meets condition I (3). But in order to define the original position as fair between individuals conceived as free and equal moral persons, we imagine that the parties are deprived of certain morally irrelevant information. For example, they do not know their place in society, their class position or social status, their fortune in the distribution of natural talents and abilities, their deeper aims and interests, or finally, their particular psychological makeup. And to insure fairness between generations, we must add that they do not know to which generation they belong and thus information about natural resources, the level of productive techniques, and the like, is also forbidden to them. Excluding this knowledge is necessary if no one is to be advantaged or disadvantaged by natural contingencies and social chance in the adoption of principles. Since all are similarly situated, and the parties do not know how to frame principles to favor their peculiar condition, each will reason in the same way. There is no need to have a binding vote, and any agreement reached is unanimous. (Thus, being in the original position is always to be contrasted with being in society.)

The description of the original position must satisfy two conditions: first, it is to be a fair situation, and second, the parties are to be conceived as members of a well-ordered society. Thus, this description contains elements drawn from the notion of fairness, for example, that the parties are symmetrically situated and subject to the veil of ignorance. It also includes features drawn from the nature and relations of persons in a well-ordered society: the parties view themselves as having final aims and interests in the name of which they think it legitimate to make claims on one another; and that they are adopting what is to serve as a public conception of justice and must, therefore, assess principles in part by their publicity effects. They must also check for stability. So long as each part of the description of the original position has a legitimate pedigree, or we are prepared to accept certain conditions in view of their implications, everything is in order.

The aim of the description of the original position is to put together in one conception the idea of fairness with the formal conditions expressed by the notion of a well-ordered society, and then to use this conception to help us select between alternative principles of justice. A striking feature of the preceding account is that we have not said anything very specific about the content of the principles of justice in a well-ordered society. We have simply combined certain rather formal and abstract conditions. One possibility is that these conditions determine unambiguously a unique conception of justice. More likely the constraints of the original position only narrow down the class of admissible conceptions; but this is still significant if it turns out that some ostensibly plausible moral conceptions are ruled out.

Finally, that the original position is hypothetical poses no difficulty. We can simulate being in that situation simply by reasoning in accordance with the stipulated constraints. If we accept the values expressed by these constraints, and therefore the formal values embodied in the notion of a well-ordered society, the idea of fairness, and the rest, we must accept the resulting limitations on conceptions of justice and reject those principles that are excluded. The attempt to unify the more formal and abstract elements of moral thought so as to bring them to bear on questions of lesser generality is characteristic of Kantian theory.

III. The first pair-wise comparison: two principles of justice vs. the principle of utility

What alternative conceptions are available in the original position? We must avoid the general case where the parties are to decide between all possible conceptions of justice, since one cannot specify this class in a useful way. We need to simplify greatly if we are to gain an intuitive understanding of the combined force of the conditions that characterize the original position. Thus we imagine that the parties are to choose from a short list of conceptions drawn from the tradition of moral philosophy. Actually, I shall at this point discuss only one pair-wise comparison. Doing this serves to fix ideas and enables me to note a few points that will be required as we proceed.

Now one aim of contract theory has been to give an account of justice that is both superior to utilitarianism and a more adequate basis for a democratic society. Therefore, let us imagine a choice between (α), a conception defined by the principle that average utility (interpreted in the classical sense) is to be maximized, and (β), a conception defined by two principles that express on their face, as it were, a democratic idea of justice. These principles read as follows:

(1) Each person has an equal right to the most extensive scheme of equal basic liberties compatible with a similar scheme of liberties for all.

(2) Social and economic inequalities are to meet two conditions: they must be (a) to the greatest expected benefit of the least advantaged (the maximin criterion); and (b) attached to offices and positions open to all under conditions of fair equality of opportunity.

The first of these principles is to take priority over the second; and the measure of benefit to the least advantaged is in terms of an index of social primary goods. These I define roughly as rights, liberties, and opportunities, income and wealth, and the social bases of self-respect; they are things that individuals are presumed to want whatever else they want, or whatever their final ends. And the parties are to reach their agreement on this supposition. (I shall come back to primary goods below.) I assume also that everyone has normal physical needs so that the problem of special health care does not arise.

Which of these two conceptions (α) or (β), would be agreed to depends, of course, on how the persons in the original position are conceived. Since they represent free moral persons, as earlier defined, they regard themselves as having fundamental aims and interests, the claims of which they must protect, if this is possible. It is partly in the name of these interests that they have a right to equal consideration and respect in the design of society. The religious interest is a familiar historical example; the interest in the integrity of the person is another (freedom from psychological oppression and physical assault belong here). In the original position the parties do not know what particular form these interests take. But they do assume that they have such interests; and also that the basic liberties necessary for their protection are guaranteed by the first principle. Here it is essential to note that basic liberties are defined by a certain list of liberties; prominent among them are freedom of thought and liberty of conscience, freedom of the person and political liberty. These liberties have a central range of application within which they can be limited and adjusted only because they clash with other basic liberties. None of these liberties, therefore, is absolute, since they may conflict with one another; but, however they are adjusted to form one's system, this system is to be the same for all. Liberties not on the list, for example, the right to own property and freedom of contract as understood in the doctrine of laissez faire are not basic: they are not protected by the priority of the first principle.

To consider the above pair-wise comparison, we must first say how one is to understand the principle of average utility. It is to be taken in the classical sense, which permits (by definition) interpersonal comparisons of utility that can at least be assessed at the margin; and utility is to be measured from the standpoint of individuals in society (and not from the standpoint of the original position) and means the degree of satisfaction of their interests. If accepted, this is how the principle will be understood and applied in society. But then it might sometimes lead, when consistently applied over time, to a basic structure securing the basic liberties; but there is no reason why it should do so in general. And even if this criterion often insures the necessary freedoms, it would be pointless to run the risk of encountering circumstances when it does not. The two principles of justice, however, will protect these liberties; and since in the original position the parties give a special priority to their fundamental interests (which they assume to be of certain general kinds), each would far rather adopt these principles (at least when they are the only alternative).

One must also take into account other special features of a well-ordered society. For example, the principles adopted are to serve as a public conception, and this means that the effects of publicity must be assessed. Particularly important are the effects on the social bases of self-respect; for when self-respect is lacking, we feel our ends not worth pursuing, and nothing has much value. Now it would seem that people who regard themselves as free and equal moral persons are much more likely to find their self-esteem supported and confirmed by social institutions satisfying the two principles of justice than by those answering to the standard of average utility. For such institutions announce by the principles they are publicly known to satisfy the collective intent that all should have equal basic liberty and that social and economic inequalities are to be regulated by the maximin criterion. Obviously this reasoning is highly speculative; but it illustrates the kind of considerations introduced by the publicity conditions of a well-ordered society.

The reasoning that favors the two principles can be strengthened by spelling out in more detail the notion of a free person. Very roughly, the parties regard themselves as having a highest-order interest in how all their other interests, including even their fundamental ones, are shaped and regulated by social institutions. They do not think of themselves as inevitably bound to, or as identical with, the pursuit of any particular complex of fundamental interests that they may have at any given time, although they want the right to advance such interests (provided they are admissible). Rather, free persons conceive of themselves as beings who can revise and alter their final ends and who give first priority to preserving their liberty in these matters. Hence, they not only have final ends that they are in principle free to pursue or to reject, but their original allegiance and continued devotion to these ends are to be formed and affirmed under conditions that are free. Since the two principles secure a social form that maintains these conditions, they would be agreed to. Only by this agreement can the parties be sure that their highest-order interest as free persons is guaranteed.

I shall conclude this section with a few remarks about primary goods. As noted earlier these are things that, from the standpoint of the original position, it is reasonable for the parties to assume that they want, whatever their final ends. For the description of the original position to be plausible, this motivation assumption must be plausible; and the (thin) theory of the good is intended to support it. In any case, an essential part of a conception of justice is the rules governing its application by members of a well-ordered society. When the parties adopt a conception, the understanding about these rules must be made explicit. Thus while the motivation of the persons in the original position is different from the motivation of individuals in society, the interpretation of the principles agreed to must be the same.

Now an important feature of the two principles is that they assess the basic structure in terms of certain primary goods: rights, liberties, and opportunities, income and wealth, and the social bases of self-respect. The latter are features of the basic structure that may reasonably be expected to affect people's self-esteem in important ways. In the maximin criterion (part (a) of the second principle) the measure of benefits is an index of these goods. Certainly there are difficulties in defining a satisfactory index,[2] but the points to stress here are (a) that primary goods are certain objective characteristics of social institutions and people's situation with respect to them, and therefore the index is not a measure of overall satisfaction or dissatisfaction; and (b) that the same index of these goods is used to compare everyone's social circumstances. Interpersonal comparisons are based on this index; and to apply the maximin rule its ordinal ranking suffices. In agreeing to the two principles, the parties agree that in making judgments of justice, they are to use such an index. Of course, the precise weights can hardly be determined in the original position; these may be determined later, for example, at the legislative stage.[3] What can be settled initially is certain constraints on these weights, as illustrated by the priority of the first principle.

Implicit in the use of primary goods is the following conception. We view persons as able to control and to adjust their wants and desires in the light of circumstances and who are to be given the responsibility for doing so (assuming that the principles of justice are fulfilled). Society on its part assumes the responsibility for maintaining certain basic liberties and opportunities and for providing a fair share of primary goods within this framework, leaving it to individuals and groups to form and to revise their aims and preferences accordingly. Thus there is an understanding among members of a well-ordered society that as citizens they will press claims only for certain kinds of things and as allowed for by the principles of justice. Strong feelings and zealous aspirations for certain goals do not, as such, give people a claim upon social resources or the design of public institutions. It is not implied that those with the same index have equal well-being, all things considered; for their ends are generally different and many other factors are relevant. But for purposes of social justice this is the appropriate basis of comparison. The theory of primary goods is a generalization of the notion of needs, which are distinct from aspirations and desires. So we could say: as citizens the members of a well-ordered society collectively take responsibility for dealing justly with one another on the basis of a public measure of (generalized) needs, while as individuals and members of associations they take responsibility for their preferences and devotions. [. . .]

IV. Second pair-wise comparison: interpretation of maximin, and risk aversion as a consequence, not as an assumption

It is tempting at first sight to suppose that the maximin criterion is based on an extreme and arbitrary assumption about risk aversion. I wish to show that this is a misapprehension. As a way of arriving at the conception that underlies maximin, let us consider a second pair-wise choice. Suppose that we substitute the principle of average utility (as earlier defined) for maximin in the two principles of justice. In the resulting conception the standard of utility is constrained in the same way as maximin and regulates social and economic inequalities.

We can find a natural interpretation for maximin as follows: the principles of equal liberty and fair equality of opportunity are common to both alternatives in the second pair-wise comparison, and so some form of democracy obtains when either alternative is realized. Because we are dealing with well-ordered societies, the conceptions will be public in both cases: citizens view themselves as free and equal persons, and social institutions are willingly complied with and recognized as just.

Assume, however, that certain social and economic inequalities exist, either as requirements for maintaining social arrangements or as incentives satisfying the relevant standard of justice, or whatever. Individuals' life-prospects are bound to be significantly affected by their family and class origins, by their natural endowments and by the chance contingencies of their nurture, as well as by other accidents of fortune over the course of their lives. We must ask: in the light of what principle can free and equal moral persons, living under democratic institutions, permit their relations to be affected by social chance and the natural lottery? Since individuals do not deserve their place in the distribution of talents, nor their starting place in society, desert is not an answer. Yet free and equal citizens want the effects of chance to be regulated by some principle, provided a reasonable principle exists.

Now when the maximin criterion is followed, the natural distribution of abilities is viewed in some respects as a collective asset. While an equal distribution of these abilities might seem more in keeping with the equality of free moral persons, at least if the distribution were a matter of choice, this is not a reason for eliminating natural variations, much less for destroying unusual talents. To the contrary, natural variations are recognized as an opportunity for mutual advantage, especially as they are generally complimentary and form a basis for social ties. Institutions may make use of the full range of abilities provided that the inequalities are no greater than necessary to yield corresponding advantages for the less fortunate, and the scheme of equal democratic liberties is not adversely affected. The same constraint holds for inequalities between social classes. Thus, at first sight the distribution of natural assets and the social contingencies of life-expectations threatens the relations between free and equal moral persons. But when the maximin criterion is satisfied, these relations may be preserved: no one benefits from natural accidents and social contingencies except in ways that are to everyone's advantage (recall that inequalities are assumed to exist) and, in particular, the least favored.[4]

This shows, I think, that maximin has at least one natural interpretation. It is the criterion that would be adopted to regulate inequalities if the parties were moved by the principle that none should benefit from certain undeserved contingencies with deep and long-lasting effects, such as class origin and natural abilities, except in ways that also help others. And this might seem particularly appropriate in a society that already affirms the other parts of the two principles: it would extend to the regulation of these inequalities the democratic conception already implicit in the basic structure. Moreover, it is not correct, I think, that maximin gives no weight to efficiency. It imposes a rule of functional contribution among inequalities; and since it applies to social arrangements that are mutually advantageous, some weight is given to efficiency. This is illustrated clearly in the case where there are only two relevant classes; here maximin selects the (Pareto) efficient point closest to equality. Thus, in this instance at least, it has another interpretation as a natural focal point between strict equality and maximizing average benefits (measured in primary goods).[5]

Now in *A Theory of Justice* I noted the first of these interpretations of the maximin criterion and its connection with democratic conceptions, but I did not want to attribute to persons in the original position an acceptance of moral notions, although I granted that this might be done. Instead, my argument was that the conditions defining the original position already require any reasonable individual, conceived as a free and equal moral person, to acknowledge the two principles of justice (with maximin) in both the pair-wise comparisons we have discussed. As we have seen, such an argument is satisfactory provided that these conditions have an independent philosophical justification or we find their implications sufficiently compelling on reflection. It is at this point that risk aversion comes in, to which both Alexander and Musgrave take exception. I did not, however, simply postulate that the parties have some peculiar or special aversion to risk; that would indeed have been no argument at all.[6] Rather, the features of the original position, when one considers their combined force, would lead reasonable people to choose as if they were highly risk-averse. Or put another way: a conservative decision is the only sensible one, given the list of alternatives available. Thus such a choice is imposed, as Alexander says; still, it is not imposed arbitrarily but via the constellation of weaker and more basic conditions on the original position, each with its appropriate pedigree or justification.

To be more specific: I said that the veil of ignorance is complete in the sense that it imposes these three conditions: (a) the parties do not have any knowledge of their desires and ends (except what is contained in the thin theory of the good, which supports the account of primary goods), and so no conception of their choice functions in society; (b) they do not know, and a fortiori cannot enumerate, the social circumstances in which they may find themselves or the array of techniques their society may have at its disposal; and (c) even if they could enumerate these possibilities, they have no grounds for relying on one probability distribution over them rather than another, and the principle of insufficient reason is not a sound way around this limitation. If one accepts the formal moral constraints that stand behind the veil of ignorance (e.g., the idea of fairness and the Kantian interpretation), then one must accept also the choices to which they lead.[7]

I held that the two principles must be agreed to in the few pairwise choices that I considered. My argument was at best intuitive, although it may not be impossible to find a formal proof. Arrow and Hurwicz have recently shown that if complete ignorance is taken to mean the permissibility of column deletion for social states with similar outcomes, then from other plausible restrictions on choice functions, the decision is determined by an ordering of ordered pairs consisting of the maximum and the minimum outcomes of the representatives of states with similar outcomes. Thus the choice depends only on the maximum and the minimum of states, and the difference between them.[8] Of course, Arrow and Hurwicz assume more information than the original position allows, since the parties have no way of estimating the maximum and the minimum outcome. Perhaps the stronger constraints on information in the original position force the decision to depend on the minima alone, defined in some suitably general sense (exemplified by the maximin criterion).

Even though such formal proofs are suggestive, they should be viewed with caution. We must check whether their premises are sound and really express conditions that should characterize the original position. I mention the possibility here only to rebut the criticism that a particular and even extreme attitude towards risk was simply postulated as part of the description of the original position. Any such attitude is the consequence of other assumptions. Moreover, there is at present so much disagreement about the meaning and interpretation of probability that arguments relying on the complete ignorance condition are perhaps best used to support the argument from the strains of commitment, which I take up next.

V. The contract condition and the strains of commitment

The argument from the strains of commitment has an important place in justice as fairness, and the concept of a contract (agreement) is essential to it. Alexander doubts that this concept has any role; he holds that the concept of a choice is the only one required. I wish to show why this supposition is incorrect.

To begin with, the concept of a contract appears in justice as fairness in at least three places: first, it reminds us (although other notions might do so as well) of the significance of the distinctions between free and equal persons who regard themselves as entitled to make claims on one another; individuals are not container-persons, mere places to locate levels of satisfaction. Thus, the classical utilitarian procedure of conflation is suspect from the start.

Second, the contract conception introduces the publicity conditions, which have wide and intricate ramifications. Indeed, this is one of the most characteristic aspects of contract theory. As noted before, these conditions require the parties to evaluate conceptions of justice in the light of their publicity effects, and important here are the consequences for the social bases of self-respect.

Third, the concept of a contract (the contract condition) introduces a further constraint on the parties in the original position. The belief that it does not may arise as follows: the agreement in the original position is to be unanimous and yet everyone is situated so that all are willing to adopt the same principles. Why, then, the need for an agreement when there are no differences to negotiate? The answer is that reaching a unanimous agreement without a binding vote is not the same thing as everyone's arriving at the same choice, or forming the same intention. That it is an undertaking people are giving may similarly affect everyone's deliberations so that the agreement that results is different from the choice everyone would otherwise have made. It is only because the contract condition governs the parties' reflections from the outset that their willingness to acknowledge the same principles can give rise to the illusion that this condition is redundant.

In general, the class of things that can be agreed to is included within, and is smaller than, the class of things that can be rationally chosen. We can decide to take a chance and at the same time fully intend that, should things turn out badly, we shall do what we can to retrieve our situation. But if we make an agreement, we have to accept the outcome; and therefore to give an undertaking in good faith, we must not only intend to honor it but with reason believe that we can do so. Thus the contract condition is a significant further constraint.

Now the reason for invoking the concept of a contract in the original position lies in its correspondence with the features of a well-ordered society. These features require, for example, that everyone accepts, and knows that the others accept, the same principles of justice (I(1)); therefore the citizens of such a society, whatever their social position, all find its arrangements acceptable to their conception of justice. None should view their situation as humiliating or degrading, nor should they be subject to circumstances they cannot help but resent and acquiesce in only from timidity and fear of reprisal (I(7)). To accept or to honor the principles agreed to means to apply them willingly as the public conception of justice, and to affirm their implications in our thought and conduct. These and other aspects of a well-ordered society are incorporated into the description of the original position by the contract condition.

Thus the concept of contract leads to the argument from the strains of commitment.[9] The idea is this: since everyone is to give an undertaking in good faith, and not simply to make the same choice, no one is permitted to agree to a principle if they have reason to doubt that they will be able to honor the consequences of its consistent application. This limitation will similarly affect everyone's deliberations, particularly since they must keep in mind that the undertaking is final, binds them and their descendants in perpetuity, yields a public conception of justice to apply to the basic structure of society, and so on. Thus consider any two conceptions: if, given some possible circumstances, the first would permit, or require, social positions that one could not accept, whereas the second results in arrangements that everyone can honor in all circumstances, then the second must be agreed to. I argued that, in view of the highest-order interest in securing the basic liberties and other considerations, the two principles of justice have to be acknowledged in a pair-wise contest with the principle of average utility. The two principles always secure acceptable conditions for all, while the utility criterion may not. This test is not so clear when the utility principle is substituted for maximin, as in the second pair-wise comparison; but I believe that once we introduce more refined considerations based on publicity and stability, and the like, this test still has force.[10]

We should note two assumptions of this argument. First, how do the parties know that the circumstances facing their society do not preclude all the available conceptions of justice (those on the list for comparison) from insuring social positions acceptable to all? The stipulation concerning the circumstances of justice (particularly moderate scarcity and the productivity of cooperation, I(8), I(10)), is meant to guarantee that some conception of justice will indeed insure social positions that everyone can honor, at least as long as the two principles of justice are on the list. Thus, the circumstances of justice serve, in part, as an existence assumption.

Second, on what grounds is it held that different people would find the same social positions acceptable, and so evaluate basic structures similarly? For if they do not, a conception ruled out for one person may not be ruled out for another, so that a maximin solution is not defined. At this point, one uses the index of primary goods: for theoretical purposes this index serves as a common standard. If anyone would find the worst-off position acceptable, then all would, and a fortiori everyone would find the other positions acceptable. In this respect the index resembles a shared choice function. It is not implied, however, that people have the same desires and final ends; in fact, these are assumed to be diverse and conflicting. But, as noted before, society is not responsible for citizens' preferences and aims, so long as they are admissible and compatible with an effective sense of justice necessary for stability.

Two brief observations on this argument. Plainly it excludes a certain kind of randomizing: one cannot accept a principle if there is a chance, however small, that one will not be able to honor it. At this point the implications of complete ignorance come into play, for these require the persons in the original position to consider the worst eventualities and to regard them as real possibilities. Even if it might be rational to take great risks, the contract condition imposes the stronger requirement: the parties must decline all risks each possible outcome of which they cannot agree in good faith to accept.

Finally, the strains of commitment must be estimated in the following way. Given a certain conception of justice, we have to decide whether there are circumstances under which the realization of that conception would lead to any unacceptable social positions. We do not consider the strains of commitment that might result from some people having to move from a favored position in an unjust society to a less favored position (either absolutely or relatively, or both) in this just society. Rather, one is to ask what strains arise from the ongoing conditions of the society one is putting to test. Thus, we must try to assess whether the corresponding well-ordered society could be honored by all in stable equilibrium, so to speak; and which ones are better or worse on this score. The strains of commitment test applied to cases of hypothetical transition from unjust societies is irrelevant.[11]

VI. Musgrave on leisure trade-off: maximin not merely second best

Unhappily, space allows me only a few comments on Musgrave's paper. Since my preceding remarks address the points he queries in the first part of his discussion, I shall limit my remarks to the second part about the leisure trade-off.

The question is this: elsewhere I noted that the maximin criterion would conform to the precept cited by Marx, 'From each according to his abilities, to each according to his needs,' if society were to impose a lump sum tax on natural assets and those better endowed have to pay a higher tax.[12] In this way inequalities of income and wealth could be greatly reduced if not eliminated. Marx seems to have thought that this precept would apply only when the circumstances of justice are surpassed; for it belongs to a fully developed socialist society when work itself is life's principal need (*das erste Lebensbedürfnis*) and the limitations of moderate scarcity no longer hold. Thus, in a sense, it is not a precept of justice, but one for a society beyond justice.

But Musgrave believes, I think, that it is a precept of justice in the strict sense, and the notion of a lump sum tax on natural abilities (potential earning capacity) shows, theoretically at least, how it could be applied in circumstances of justice. Everyone recognizes the enormous practical difficulties of such a scheme; ability may be impossible to measure, and individuals will have a strong motive to conceal their talents. I had mentioned that there is another difficulty, namely, the interference with liberty. By that I meant, although I did not explain, interference with the basic liberties (as earlier defined). To influence by taxation the trade-off between leisure and income, say, is not an interference with liberty until it infringes upon the basic liberties, although a fuller account of these is necessary in order to decide when this happens.

Thus I have no initial objection to Musgrave's scheme viewed from a theoretical standpoint. While the notion of leisure seems to me to call for clarification, there may be good reasons for including it among the primary goods and therefore in the index as Musgrave proposes, and doing this may be compatible with the basic liberties. Whether leisure should be included among the primary goods depends on a better understanding of these goods and the feasibility of counting leisure among them. I would add only that an index of primary goods is not, as Musgrave's discussion sometimes suggests, a measure of welfare; but this has been noted earlier and requires no further comment.

Nevertheless, I suspect that the idea of a lump sum tax on natural abilities is subject to more than merely practical difficulties. It seems doubtful, in fact, whether natural abilities even exist in a form that could be measured, even theoretically, for purposes of lump sum taxation. If an ability were, for example, a computer in the head with a measurable and fixed capacity, and with definite and unchanging social use, this would not be so. But intelligence, for example, is hardly any one such fixed native ability. It must have indefinitely many dimensions that are shaped and nurtured by different social conditions; even as a potential, as opposed to a realized, capacity it is bound to vary significantly in little understood and complex ways. And among the elements affecting these capacities are the social attitudes and institutions directly concerned with their training and recognition. Thus potential earnings capacity is not something independent from the social forms and the particular contingencies over the course of life, and the idea of a lump sum tax does not apply. All this is bad enough, but the situation is even worse if we ask at what time of life the tax is to be assessed. None of this affects, I think, the interpretation of maximin: we can still say that whatever people's natural endowments are and the influence on them of their social circumstances, no one benefits from these contingencies except in ways that contribute to everyone's advantage.

We cannot conclude, however, that all forms of taxation in the direction of Musgrave's scheme are ruled out. Other possibilities might prove workable. But at least some degree of inequality will presumably still exist. I would only add that if the remarks above are correct, and the lump sum tax version of maximin is theoretically inapplicable, it would, I think, be misleading to regard maximin (as previously defined) as merely a second best precept of justice. Instead, Marx would probably be right: the precept he invoked presupposes a society beyond justice; and even given just institutions, it may take much more than any feasible system of taxation to put it into effect.

Notes

1 The advantage of beginning the exposition with the notion of a well-ordered society was suggested to me by Ronald Dworkin's discussion in 'The Original Position,' *Chicago Law Review*, XL (1973), esp. 519–23.

2 K. J. Arrow ('Some Ordinalist-Utilitarian Notes on Rawls' Theory of Justice,' *Journal of Philosophy*, LXX (1973), p. 254) has noted that special health needs, which I assume here not to arise, will be a particularly difficult problem. This question requires a separate discussion.

3 See *A Theory of Justice* (Cambridge, Mass.: Harvard University Press, 1971), pp. 198f. At this stage we have much more information and within the constraints can adjust the index to existing social conditions.

4 For a criticism of maximin when interpreted in this way, see Robert Nozick, 'Distributive Justice', *Philosophy and Public Affairs* (Fall 1973), esp. pp. 107–25.

5 See the comments of E. S. Phelps, 'Wage Taxation for Economic Justice,' this *Journal*, LXXVII (Aug. 1973), 334–7; A. B. Atkinson, 'How Progressive Should Income-Tax Be?' in *Essays in Modern Economics*, M. Parkin, ed. (London: Longmans, 1973), pp. 105–8. I do not know, however, whether the focal point can be defined sufficiently clearly to sustain the second interpretation suggested above when there are three or more relevant classes. The problem is that we need a measure of equality. If we use the maximin criterion itself as a measure, the interpretation is true by definition; but with an independent measure, the interpretation would certainly not hold in general. I am indebted to Partha Dasgupta for clarification on this point.

6 See *A Theory of Justice*, p. 172.

7 See *A Theory of Justice*, pp. 152–6. For the Kantian interpretation, see Sec. 40.

8 See K. J. Arrow and Leonid Hurwicz, 'An Optimality Criterion for Decision Making Under Ignorance', in *Uncertainty and Expectation in Economics*, C. F. Carter and J. L. Ford, eds (Oxford, Basil Blackwell, 1972), pp. 1–11.

9 See *A Theory of Justice*, pp. 175ff.

10 See my remarks in 'Some Reasons for the Maximin Criterion', *American Economic Review*, LXIV (May 1974), 143f.

11 I am afraid that I misled Alexander on this point by not being clear myself. The bottom lines of *A Theory of Justice*, p. 176, are incorrect.

12 See my paper, 'Some Reasons for the Maximin Criterion', p. 145. For the precept itself, See *Critique of the Gotha Program*, May 1875. Marx probably has in mind a passage that Louis Blanc added to his *Organisation du Travail* for the 9th edition (Paris, 1850). The relevant sentence reads: 'L'egalité n'est donc que le proportionnalité, et elle n'existera d'une manière véritable que lorsque chacun, d'après la loi écrite ou quelque sorte dans son organisation par Dieu lui-même, PRODUIRA SELON SES FACULTÉS ET CONSOMMERA SELON SES BESOINS,' p. 72.

3

The Diversity of Objections to Inequality

T. M. Scanlon

I believe that equality is an important political goal. That is to say, virtually every society is marked by forms of inequality the elimination of which is a political objective of the first importance. But when I ask myself why I think it so important that these inequalities should be eliminated, I find that my reasons for favoring equality are in fact quite diverse, and that most of them can be traced back to fundamental values other than equality itself. The idea that equality is, in itself, a fundamental moral value turns out to play a surprisingly limited role in my reasons for thinking that many of the forms of inequality which we see around us should be eliminated.

When I say that the idea of equality plays surprisingly little role in my thinking here, I have in mind an idea of substantive equality – that it is morally important that people's lives or fates should be equal in some substantive way: equal in income, for example, or in overall welfare. This is in contrast to a merely formal notion of equal consideration, as stated for example in the principle that the comparable claims of each person deserve equal respect and should be given equal weight. This is an important principle. Its general acceptance represents an important moral advance, and it provides a fruitful – even essential – starting point for moral argument. But taken by itself it is too abstract to exercise much force in the direction of substantive equality. As Thomas Nagel and Amartya Sen have both pointed out,[1] even a rights theorist such as Robert Nozick, who would not normally be counted an egalitarian, could accept this principle, since he holds that everyone's rights deserve equal respect. My hypothesis is that the bare idea of equal consideration leads us to substantively egalitarian consequences only via other more specific values that I will enumerate, most of which are not essentially egalitarian.

In saying this I do not mean to attack equality or to 'unmask' it as a false ideal. My aims, rather, are clarification and defense: clarification, because I believe that we can understand familiar arguments for equality better by seeing the diversity of the considerations on which they are based; defense, because I think that the case for pursuing particular forms of equality is strengthened when we see how many different considerations point in this direction. Opponents of equality seem most convincing when they can portray equality as a peculiarly abstract goal – conformity to a certain pattern – to which special moral value is attached.[2]

I will begin by distinguishing what seem to me to be the fundamental moral reasons lying behind our objections to various forms of inequality. I will then illustrate these ideas by showing how they figure in various ways in Rawls's views about distributive justice. Finally, I will return to examine one of these values – the one which seems the most purely egalitarian – in more detail. Let me turn, then, to an enumeration of our reasons for finding the pursuit of equality a compelling political goal.

I

In some cases our reason for favoring the elimination of inequalities is at base a humanitarian concern – a concern, for example, to alleviate suffering. If some people are living under terrible conditions, while others are very well off indeed, then a transfer of resources from the better to the worse off, if it can be accomplished without other bad effects, is desirable as a way of alleviating suffering without creating new hardships of comparable severity.

The impulse at work here is not essentially egalitarian. No intrinsic importance is attached to narrowing or eliminating the gap between rich and poor; this gap is important only because it provides an opportunity – a way of reducing the suffering of some without causing others to suffer a similar fate – and the strength of this reason for moving toward greater equality is a function of the urgency of the claims of those who are worse off, not of the magnitude of the gap which separates them from their more fortunate neighbors.[3]

In characterizing this first reason, I have spoken of 'the alleviation of suffering' in order to present this reason in its strongest form, but its force may still be felt in cases where, although the term 'suffering' would be inappropriate, those who are 'worse off' are still living under conditions which we regard as seriously deficient. This force fades away, however, as we imagine the situation of both rich and 'poor' to be greatly improved, while the difference between them is held constant (or even increased). We may still feel, even in this improved state, that the difference between richer and poorer ought to be reduced or eliminated. Our reason for thinking this will not, however, be the humanitarian concern I am presently concerned with, but some different reason, perhaps a more truly egalitarian one.

(2) One possible reason for objecting to these differences would be the belief that it is an evil for people to be treated as inferior, or made to feel inferior. Social practices conferring privileges of rank or requiring expressions of deference are objectionable on this ground, for example. So also is the existence of prevailing attitudes of superiority (e.g. racial superiority) even when these are not expressed in or taken to justify economic advantage or special social privileges. Large differences in material well-being can be objectionable on the same ground: when the mode of life enjoyed by some people sets the norm for a society, those who are much worse off will feel inferiority and shame at the way they must live.

The egalitarian character of this objection is shown by the fact that it provides a reason specifically for the elimination of the differences in question rather than for the improvement of the lot of the worse off in some more general sense. This is obviously so where the differences are purely ones of status. But even where the basis of inferiority is a difference in material well-being, the aim of avoiding stigmatization can in principle provide a reason for eliminating the benefits of the better off (or for wishing that they had never been created) even if these cannot be transferred to the worse off. If simply eliminating these benefits seems wrong (perhaps even perverse), this judgment reflects a willingness to sacrifice the aim of equality (in the sense under consideration) for the sake of material benefit. This aim – the ideal of a society in which people all regard one another as equals – has played a more important role in radical egalitarian thinking than the idea of distributive justice which dominates much discussion of equality in our own time. This ideal may seem utopian, however, and there are interesting difficulties about how it should be understood. I will return to these matters later in my lecture, after some other reasons for favoring equality have been considered.

(3) A third reason for the elimination of inequalities is that they

give some people an unacceptable degree of control over the lives of others. The most obvious example is economic power. Those who have vastly greater resources than anyone else not only enjoy greater leisure and higher levels of consumption but also can often determine what gets produced, what kinds of employment are offered, what the environment of a town or state is like, and what kind of life one can live there. In addition, economic advantage can be translated into great political power – for example into the kind of power that the recent Campaign Financing Laws were intended to curb.

This example brings me to a fourth reason for pursuing equality, which overlaps with the one just mentioned but should be listed separately. Some forms of equality are essential preconditions for the fairness of certain processes, and the aim of making or keeping those processes fair may therefore give us a reason to oppose inequalities of these kinds, at least when they are very large. So, for example, in the case just mentioned, instead of speaking of unacceptable degrees of political power (thus appealing to the value of political liberty) we might have spoken instead of preserving the fairness of the political process. These two forms of argument overlap in this particular case, but they are in fact distinct. When inequality of starting points undermines the fairness of a process, domination of those who are placed at a disadvantage does not always result, since the process may confer no power but only honor or the opportunity for a more pleasant and rewarding life. Unfairness remains, however, and can take several forms: some people can simply be excluded from competition, or background conditions such as inequalities in training and resources can render the competition unfair. So the idea of equality of opportunity – as expressed in the familiar metaphors of a 'fair race' or 'a level playing-field' – provides a familiar example of this fourth reason for objecting to inequality: inequalities are objectionable when they undermine the fairness of important institutions.

As the common contrast between 'equality of opportunity' and 'equality of results' indicates, this idea is generally seen as only weakly egalitarian, since it can be compatible with large inequalities provided that they result from a fair process and do not disrupt the fairness of ongoing competition. But, as I will now argue, the idea of a fair procedure can also provide another kind of reason for insisting on equality of outcomes. (This is my fifth reason for objecting to inequalities.)

Suppose that the members of a group have equal claims to a certain form of benefit, such as the wealth produced by their combined efforts. If a distributive procedure is supposed to be responsive to these claims, then it will be unfair if (absent some special reason) it gives some of these people a higher level of benefit than others. This provides, in schematic form, an argument which leads us to a prima facie case for equality in a certain dimension of benefit. Its starting points include an idea of fairness together with substantive premises about the claims that the people in question have to this benefit and about the function of a particular procedure. To generate a particular egalitarian conclusion we need to fill in the relevant premises, and the force of this conclusion will depend on how plausible these premises are. We might, for example, begin with the idea that, other things equal, all individuals have equal claims to welfare. This sounds like quite a strong claim, but it might be a fairly weak one: much depends on how many things there are that might not be equal. A natural first step in specifying this would be to make explicit the fact that one class of relevant differences are differences in the choices people have made. This yields the principle that people ought to be equal in the levels of welfare they enjoy apart from differences in welfare resulting from their own free choices.[4] I have not included an 'other things equal' clause in the statement of this principle, but I assume that it is still only one moral idea among others, which might have to be sacrificed or balanced for the sake of other values.

These values enter in when we begin to specify the other premise mentioned above, that is, to ask what range of actions might be thought of as part of a 'procedure' which is supposed to be responsive to these equal claims. It would not be very plausible, for example, to claim that all of our actions have this function (or must be thought of as part of a 'procedure' with this aim). It does not seem that in general we are under even a 'prima facie' duty to promote the equal welfare of all. A more plausible claim would be that the state, or in Rawls's phrase 'the basic institutions of society' should be understood in this way, that is, as an institution whose function it is to respond to the (equal) claims to welfare of all of its subjects (equal, that is, apart from differences arising from individual choice). This is what might be called the 'parental' conception of the state. I choose that term because it seems to me that the claim of unfairness to which this conception gives rise is similar to the one raised by a child who protests the fact that a sibling has received some benefit by saying 'That's not fair!' The similarity rests in the fact that both claims are grounded in an idea that the agent to whom it is addressed is under an equal duty to promote the welfare of each of the parties in question.

As this description no doubt suggests, I do not myself find this conception of the state altogether compelling. A more plausible conception, and hence a more plausible case for equality, can be obtained if we view the citizens not merely as beneficiaries but rather as participants. It might be said, for example, that the basic institutions of a society should be seen as a cooperative enterprise producing certain benefits, and that citizens, as free and equal participants in this process, have (at least prima facie) equal claim to the benefits they collectively produce. (It is worth emphasizing that this premise does not lead to the conclusion that people should be equal in all respects, but only in their shares of these socially produced benefits. It therefore provides a plausible basis for some form of 'equality of resources'.)

This claim to equal outcomes is not indisputable. It might be maintained, for example, that insofar as social institutions are seen as cooperative undertakings for mutual benefit the claims of participants to its products are not equal but proportional to their contributions. My task here is not, however, to offer a full defense of the argument I have sketched, but rather to identify it as one among several sources of egalitarianism.

To summarize, I have identified five reasons for pursuing greater equality. The elimination of inequalities may be required in order to:
(1) Relieve suffering or severe deprivation
(2) Prevent stigmatizing differences in status
(3) Avoid unacceptable forms of power or domination
(4) Preserve the equality of starting places which is required by procedural fairness.
In addition,
(5) Procedural fairness sometimes supports a case for equality of outcomes.

At least two of these reasons, (1) and (3), are based on powerful moral ideas that are not fundamentally egalitarian. The ideas behind (2), on the other hand, are more clearly egalitarian, but while they are certainly important they do not seem to have as much moral force as the humanitarian ideals expressed in (1). Reason (4) is only weakly egalitarian, since the idea of procedural fairness which supports it is compatible with great inequalities of some kinds as long as these do not undermine the fairness of the continuing process. This leaves (5) and (2) as the clearest expressions of egalitarianism. Reasons of type (5) are at least as powerful as those to which (2) appeals, but these reasons come in a variety of forms, which vary in strength. The idea which they have in common is not that all men and women are created equal but rather that *if* all the members of a certain group have prima facie equal claim to benefit in a certain way then a fair procedure for distributing such benefits must (in the absence of special justification) result in equal benefits. I imagine that everyone would agree to the truth of this conditional statement, but its uncontroversial character is purchased by packing a great deal into its antecedent. The egalitarian thrust of (5) arises from the claim that this antecedent is true in an important range of cases – e.g. that participants in many cooperative ventures do have prima facie equal claims to the benefits produced, and, specifically, that this is so in the case of the basic institutions of a society.

Are there further reasons for favoring equality which I have omitted? The main possibility is a straightforward moral ideal of substantive equality, that is to say, the idea that a society in which people are equally well off (as determined by some appropriate measure) is for that reason a morally better society. This is certainly an intelligible and even an appealing idea. But how much of a role does it actually play in our moral thinking? Reasons (1) through (5) above are not, I think, derived from this idea. They are much more specific and have independent moral force. Once the distinctness of these reasons is recognized, how much force does the substantive ideal just mentioned retain? My own sense is that it may have the status of one appealing social ideal among others, but that it lacks the particular moral urgency which the idea of equality seems to have in ordinary political argument, a force which derives, I believe, from the other reasons I have listed.

II

To illustrate these five reasons for pursuing equality, I want now to consider how they figure in Rawls's theory of justice and account for much of the egalitarian content of his view. It may seem at first that Rawls's Difference Principle, which calls for us to maximize the expectations of the worst off, draws on the first of the reasons I mentioned: a humanitarian concern with the fate of the worst off. The argument for the use of the maximin rule, for example, seems to appeal to a first-person version of this concern insofar as it relies on the idea that there are certain outcomes 'that one could hardly accept', and that it is rational, under the circumstances of the Original Position, to be primarily concerned with avoiding these outcomes, in comparison with which other gains are relatively insignificant.[5] Like the humanitarian case for equality mentioned above, this reason for the Difference Principle would diminish in force if the possible positions of the worst off were to become more and more bearable, holding constant the distance between these positions and those of the better off.

But the case for the Difference Principle is not primarily 'humanitarian'. That is to say, it is not primarily based in sympathy for the worst off. Rawls's central idea lies, rather, in his emphasis on seeing the basic structure of society as a fair system of cooperation, and on taking the question of justice to be that of how the benefits of such cooperation are to be shared. The case for the Difference Principle then rests on an appeal to reasons (4) and (5) above: the need for equality of starting points as a precondition of procedural fairness, and the appeal of equal outputs as a fair mode of distribution. Consider the latter first. This argument for the Difference Principle can be put in two steps. The first step is the prima facie case for equal shares as a fair way to distribute the fruits of cooperation among those who have participated in producing them. The second step is the idea that departures from equality which leave everyone better off cannot reasonably be objected to, as long as (a) the positions to which greater rewards are attached are 'open to all under conditions of fair equality of opportunity' and (b) these inequalities do not give rise to unacceptable stigmatization of some members of the society as inferior.

Rider (a) incorporates the fourth idea mentioned above, that a sufficient degree of equality in starting places has to be preserved as a precondition for procedural fairness. At least it incorporates this idea if, as is clearly Rawls's intent, 'fair equality of opportunity' is understood to include more than the mere absence of legal restrictions and discriminatory practices.[6] The fact that this idea – of the importance of preserving at least approximate equality of starting positions – occurs only in a rider, as a constraint on permissible inequalities and a way of warding off possible objections, should not be allowed to obscure the central role it plays in the positive case *for* the Difference Principle. This centrality is shown in the fact that this idea is the basis of one of the main objections which Rawls levels against alternatives to his conception of distributive justice.[7] For example, his objection to the *laissez faire* conception of justice that he calls 'the system of natural liberty' is that the operation of this system over time can lead to great differences in family wealth with the result that individuals born into different positions in the society will have vastly different opportunities for education and for entry into economic life, as well as different dispositions to make use of the opportunities they do have. An important part of the case for Rawls's Two Principles is the fact that institutions which satisfy them will not be subject to this objection, and that, more generally, these principles guarantee the kind of background necessary for a system of pure procedural justice.

Alongside of this argument, and complementary to it, is the idea that the system of natural liberty should be rejected because it allows people's life prospects to be determined by factors, such as fortunate family circumstances, which are 'arbitrary from a moral point of view'. This might be understood as a restatement of the objection that I have just summarized: the system is unacceptable because it allows life prospects to be determined by competition under 'arbitrary' conditions, rather than under conditions of 'background fairness'. But it can also be seen as an appeal to type (5) unfairness: a system of natural liberty is unfair because outcomes which are sensitive to the 'accidents of birth' are not responsive to the equal claims of 'free and equal cooperating members of society'.

Because the distributive shares assigned to members of one generation are a large part of what determines the starting places of the next, considerations of these two kinds (equality of starting places and equality of distributive shares) tend to converge. Insofar as the focus is on fair sharing of what individuals *have produced* as free and equal members of a cooperative scheme, (5) seems to be particularly central; when the focus is on fairness to individuals born into certain social positions, their productive lives still lying ahead, (4) comes into play. Rawls certainly appeals at various points to reasons of both types. They are complementary but may differ in dialectical strength.

As I mentioned above, the force of the idea that fairness demands equal distributive shares depends on a prior claim that as participants in a cooperative scheme the individuals in question have equal claim to the fruits of their cooperation. This is an appealing moral idea, but a controversial one to take as *the starting point* for an argument in support of a particular conception of justice. By contrast, appeals to (4) rest, in the first instance, on the more broadly shared idea that the legitimacy of holdings is undermined when the process through which they are gained is unfair. The controversy in this case is over conditions of fairness: What kind of initial conditions must be provided in order for a process to be one whose outcomes cannot be complained of? There is certainly wide disagreement on this question,[8] but there may also be more scope for internal argument (about how best to extrapolate from shared examples, and so on).[9]

Let me return now to the idea of 'stigmatization'. I incorporated this idea as a rider on my restatement of Rawls's Difference Principle: economic inequalities are unjust if they give rise to unacceptable stigmatization of some as inferior. Rawls did not, of course, deal with this problem through a separate rider. Instead, his measure of what it is for the lot of the worst off to be improved includes, as one component, 'the social bases of self-respect'. His formulation thus allows, at least formally, for the possibility that loss in this dimension of well-being might be compensated for by other advantages. I do not believe that this difference in formulation will make much difference in practice, but I leave that question open.[10] What is important for present purposes is that Rawls took it to be an important feature of his conception of justice that it provided a more secure protection for individual self-respect than did alternative conceptions such as utilitarianism or the 'system of natural liberty'. He stresses that this protection is provided not only by the Difference Principle but also by his First Principle, which requires that the equal status of all citizens should be secured by their having equal civil and political rights and liberties.

The equality demanded by this principle is, on its face, rather formal: it demands that all citizens have the most extensive system of equal basic liberties. This is formal insofar as it deals only with what the laws and constitution specify. But Rawls also asserts, as an important advantage of his Difference Principle, that by assuring nearly equal economic shares it guarantees what he calls the 'fair value' of these rights and liberties. The idea, then, is that the Difference Principle will be sufficiently egalitarian to insure the fairness of the political process (an instance of (4)) and thus to prevent some from exercising an unacceptable degree of power over others (3).

To conclude this brief discussion of Rawls: his argument for his Two Principles of justice, in particular for the second of these principles, appeals directly or indirectly to at least four of the grounds for equality mentioned above, namely numbers (2) through (5), and perhaps to (1) as well. But (4), or a combination of (4) and (5), appears to play the most central role. This emphasis on the claims of citizens qua participants in a fair procedure helps to explain the fact that the Difference Principle is concerned with individuals' shares of 'primary social goods' (i.e., the fruits of their cooperation) rather than with their levels of overall welfare.

III

The second reason that I presented, in Section I, for objecting to inequality was based on the idea that 'it is an evil for people to be treated as inferior, or made to feel inferior'. I want now to consider, at least in a preliminary way, some of the difficulties involved in determining more exactly how this objection is to be understood. My initial statement of this objection was cautiously ambivalent. It consisted of two parts, the first of which suggests that what is objectionable is a certain form of treatment (being *treated* as inferior, or not being 'treated as an equal') and the second suggests that the evil is an experiential one (being made to *feel* inferior). More needs to be said both about how this 'experiential' component is to be understood and about how it is supposed to be related to the underlying forms of treatment in order to give rise to the objection in question.

The experiential evil involved here can be characterized in several different ways – indeed, there are several different kinds of experience that one might have in mind. Let me distinguish two broad categories. The first, more 'individualistic', characterization emphasizes what might be called damage to individuals' sense of self-worth: such things as feelings of inferiority and even shame resulting from the belief that one's life, abilities or accomplishments lack worth or are greatly inferior to those of others.[11] The second category emphasizes damage to the bonds between people: what might be called the loss of fraternity resulting from great differences in people's material circumstances, accomplishments and the social importance accorded to them. Unlike the first, this is a loss suffered by the better off and worse off alike, and perhaps it is the more fully egalitarian of the two. Much more could be said by way of characterization of these two classes of experiential evils, but I will not pursue these questions here. My concern will instead be with the independence of these evils from other objections to inequality and with the particular difficulty of avoiding them. I will concentrate on evils of the first of the two kinds just distinguished, but I believe that the same points apply as well to evils of the second sort.

It is of course quite possible that someone might suffer from these forms of undesirable consciousness (such as a sense of inferiority and worthlessness) simply from psychological causes that have nothing to do with the actual facts of one's society. This would be a misfortune, but not the basis of an objection to social institutions. Such objections arise only when institutions *cause* people to have these undesirable feelings. Let me consider three ways that institutions might do this.

First, they might do it by depriving some people (but not others) of basic rights: denying them the right to move freely in public, the right to participate in politics, or the right to compete for other valued positions in the society. People treated in these ways would certainly not be treated 'as equals'. But the main objection in such a case would be to these forms of treatment themselves, not to their experiential consequences. So I will set this case aside.

Second, institutions which were not *otherwise* unjust might nonetheless treat some people in ways that could only be understood as intended to express the view that they were inferior. This might be done by, say, attaching special 'dishonorific' titles to their names, or by requiring them to defer to members of other groups whenever they met in public. These signs of status are clearly objectionable, and our reasons for objecting to them depends on the fact that those subject to these forms of treatment could reasonably feel shamed and humiliated by them.

But the same objection would apply to institutional arrangements that, while they did not have the aim of *expressing* inferiority, nonetheless had the effect of giving rise to feelings of inferiority on the part of most reasonable citizens. This is my third case. The obvious examples are economic institutions which yield such great disparities of wealth and income so that some people experience shame and humiliation because they must live in a way that is far below what most people in the society regard as minimally acceptable. There are also non-economic examples, such as a society in which almost everyone places great value and importance on certain forms of accomplishment, forms that many, but not all, can attain, and in which it is regarded as a great misfortune not to be 'successful' in these ways. These views imply that those whose accomplishments do not measure up are inferior in important ways. In this respect this case is like my second one; but it is not the *point* of these practices (as it was of those in the previous case) to mark some out as inferior. That is merely the side effect of the recognition of what is seen as valuable accomplishment and good fortune. While these two cases may be different, I will not make much of this difference here, but will suppose that both the second and the third cases I have just distinguished give rise to the objection to inequality that I earlier called 'stigmatizing differences in status'. My focus in the remainder of this lecture will be on the question of whether and how these objections can be met or avoided.

Consider first a familiar example of objectionable inequality, the phenomena of racial and sexual discrimination in our societies. Women and African Americans have for many years been denied opportunities for forms of achievement which are most recognized and valued in society, including political leadership, positions of economic power and high status, positions recognizing accomplishment in academic, intellectual and even many parts of artistic life. As in the first of the three cases I just considered, this denial is itself a form of unfairness: the process through which these positions and the rewards connected with them were awarded was unfair because women and blacks were not given the chance to compete. But this unfairness is not the only evil involved, and not the one I want to focus on. It is unfair, and wounding, to be denied important opportunities because of one's race or gender. But one thing that makes this particularly wounding is the fact that race and gender are commonly taken to be signs of the lack of substantive qualification: stigmatization is added to unfairness when there is the (perhaps unstated) supposition that because you are not a white male you are less able to contribute to society and its culture in those ways that are regarded as particularly valuable and important.

Suppose now that all the underlying unfairness in this case were removed, and that everyone had a chance to compete on 'equal terms'. Assuming that the number of desired positions remained the same, and the number of competitors for them did not decrease, some people (a racially and sexually diverse group, let us suppose) would still be denied these rewards, and while they would not be excluded 'from the start' by being ruled out of the competition they would, in an important sense, be denied rewards on the same grounds that women and blacks were: they will be judged to lack the relevant abilities and attainments. I will suppose that this meritocratic discrimination is not unfair: (1) it is not based on unfounded assumptions about differences in ability but on actual, demonstrated differences, and (2) it is not unnecessary but serves important social goals. Nonetheless, as Thomas Nagel has pointed out,[12] the resulting differences in status and treatment are still to be regretted as objectionable inequalities. The evil involved is the one we have been considering: though not unfair, this meritocracy can be expected to deprive some people of a secure sense of self-worth – of the sense of their own value and the belief that their lives and accomplishments are worthwhile.

This evil, being deprived of important grounds for a sense of self-worth, is, as I have said, one of the important evils underlying the forms of discrimination with which we are familiar. In the case we are imagining these forms of discrimination have been removed, but the relevant experiential evil may remain and may even be aggravated in two respects. First, the inferiority would not be a matter of prejudice, but would be established by the outcome of fair competition. Second, if this fair meritocracy has been reached through a process of overcoming discrimination this history is likely to have the effect of dramatizing the value of the rewards and accomplishments in question and belittling the value of a life lived without them. In order to rouse the oppressed to battle and kindle sympathy and guilt in others, one would naturally emphasize not only the unfairness of discrimination but also the importance of the opportunities and forms of accomplishment and recognition in question, and the great value of a life with these things as compared to one without them. This has the effect of condemning the lives which victims of discrimination have had to lead, and hence also the lives which others will continue to lead once this discrimination is overcome. Overcoming it may represent a gain in fairness, but there may be no decrease, and perhaps even an increase, in objectionable consequences of inequality of the particular kind I am presently discussing.

I am not urging the fatalist thesis that people should 'stay in their places' since inequality cannot be eliminated but only shifted around. I am all in favor of the elimination of discrimination and the reduction of inequality. My aim here is to understand the diversity of the evils which it involves. An egalitarianism which decries the evil I am characterizing may seem hopelessly utopian, because it may seem that the distinctions which give rise to it can never be avoided. Trying to eliminate them may seem to involve unacceptable costs not only in economic efficiency and the quality of the products of a culture but also in individual fulfillment. One thing individuals naturally and reasonably want is to develop their talents and to exercise these realized abilities. Given an uneven distribution of talents, one result of this is that some will inevitably be distinguished from others in ways that generate the problem I have been discussing. Rousseau[13] can be read as suggesting that this is an inevitable and even tragic conflict. Even if one does not hold out much hope for eliminating this conflict, however, it is possible to conceive of some ways of at least reducing it.

The degree to which the accomplishment and rewards of some people undermine the grounds of other people's sense of self-worth depends upon the degree to which particular forms of ability and accomplishment are regarded as having pre-eminent importance. Even a highly differentiated meritocratic system of offices and rewards might not undermine the self-respect of those who are not successful in it if the attainments which it recognizes and rewards are regarded as less important indices of self-worth than good moral character, conscientiousness as a citizen, and devotion to the well-being of one's family and friends. A society which accorded these qualities their proper value might be able to enjoy the benefits of rewarding accomplishment without suffering the consequences which I am here decrying.[14]

A second strategy is diversification. If there are many different forms of accomplishment and distinction no one, or no few, of which dominate as *the* socially important measures of success in life, then the threat to people's sense of self-worth will be mitigated. This solution has been proposed, in different forms, by both Rawls and Michael Walzer. Walzer has suggested[15] that if there are many forms of inequality, each confined to its own 'sphere', they will to some extent cancel each other out, and their effects will be acceptable – even appropriate and desirable. Rawls, on the other hand, has spoken of the partition of society into what he calls 'noncomparing groups':

> the plurality of associations in a well-ordered society, each with its own secure internal life, tends to reduce the visibility, or at least the painful visibility, of variations in men's prospects. For we tend to compare our circumstances with others in the same or in a similar group as ourselves, or in positions that we regard

as relevant to our aspirations. The various associations in society tend to divide it into so many noncomparing groups, the discrepancies between these divisions not attracting the kind of attention which unsettles the lives of those less well placed.[16]

Each of these proposals may seem unsatisfactory when understood as a general response to inequality; but there is much to be said for them when they are seen, in a more limited way, as a response merely to the aspect of inequality which I am presently discussing. Walzer, for example, advocates 'complex equality' as a general solution to the problem of inequality. He argues that inequalities in wealth, power, fame and other goods are acceptable as long as each good is distributed on the grounds appropriate to it, and no one good is allowed to 'dominate' the others as, for example, when wealth is used to buy power, fame, medical care and so on. In addition, he couples this view with a denial that there are general standards of justice which every society must satisfy. Both of these doctrines – his doctrine of 'spheres' and his relativistic thesis – have been widely criticized. But the idea of complex equality is more appealing if we view it merely as a way of mitigating the conflict between the protection of self-worth and the necessity of recognizing differences in ability and accomplishment. There is considerable plausibility to the claim that this problem is best approached not by trying to minimize differences but rather by fostering a healthy multiplicity of distinctions and by trying to insure that no one (or no few) of these 'dominates' the others by becoming established as *the* form of distinction that really matters.

Similarly, Rawls's idea of noncomparing groups may be criticized because it is seen as a way of making unacceptable inequalities seem acceptable by hiding them. But Rawls is supposing that the inequalities in question already satisfy principles of justice: they are justified in the way that the Difference Principle requires, and conditions of fair equality of opportunity are assumed to obtain. The point could be put by saying that people are owed more than fairness in the distribution of concrete goods: they are also owed a concern for the maintenance of their sense of self-worth (in his terms, self-respect) and this is, as I argued above, importantly a matter of the character of their experience. Whether they reasonably feel a loss of self-worth is a function not only of the inequalities which they know exist but of the way in which those inequalities figure in their lives. As far as this concern goes, then, the device of noncomparing groups may be a perfectly appropriate one.

I suggested earlier that the particular egalitarian concern which I have been discussing in this section – the problem of stigmatizing differences in status – is a source of strong motives for opposing inequality and a source which is more purely egalitarian than most of the others I have enumerated. About its motivational strength there seems to me to be no doubt. The instinct to preserve the grounds of one's self-esteem and to oppose what threatens it is a powerful force in the world today, supporting not only struggles for greater equality but also, I would argue, forms of nationalism and nativism, religious fundamentalism and racial and religious bigotry. It is commonly said, for example, that many white males see doctrines of racial and gender equality as a threat to their sense of standing and self-worth.

What has to be claimed is that these reactions, however real they may be, are not reasonable and therefore do not support objections of the kind I have been discussing. In other cases, reasonable feelings of loss of self-esteem may be deserved, hence again not objectionable.[17] What should be claimed, then, is that a regime of equality would be one that protected its members adequately against *reasonable* and undeserved feelings of loss of self-esteem.

To conclude: relief of suffering, avoidance of stigmatizing differences in status, prevention of domination of some by others, and the preservation of conditions of procedural fairness are basic and important moral values. Within the framework of the principle of equal consideration they provide strong reasons for the elimination of various inequalities. Taken together these values account for at least a large part of the importance that equality has in our political thinking. They may account for all of this importance, or there may be an important role to be played by a further moral idea of substantive equality. But it remains unclear exactly what that idea would be.

Notes

1 See Thomas Nagel, 'Equality' in *Mortal Questions* (Cambridge: Cambridge University Press, 1979) [reprinted in this volume], and Amartya Sen, *Inequality Reexamined* (Cambridge, Mass.: Harvard University Press, 1992), p. 13.
2 See, for example, Robert Nozick's objections in Chapters 7 and 8 of *Anarchy, State and Utopia* (New York: Basic Books, 1974). I was led to the basic ideas of this lecture in the course of working on a review of

Nozick's book. Some of these ideas were briefly stated in that review, 'Nozick on Rights, Liberty and Property', *Philosophy & Public Affairs* 6 (1976).

3   A point made by Derek Parfit in his 1991 Lindley Lecture, 'Equality or Priority?' [reprinted in this volume]. Harry Frankfurt has gone further, suggesting that we replace concern for equality with concern for 'sufficiency'. He writes, 'What is important from the moral point of view is not that everyone should have *the same* but that each should have *enough*. If everyone had enough, it would be of no moral consequence whether some had more than others.' See Frankfurt, 'Equality as a Moral Ideal', in *The Importance of What We Care About* (Cambridge University Press, 1988), pp. 134–5. In the present lecture I will be investigating whether, contrary to what Frankfurt says in this last sentence, there are further reasons for caring about equality beyond the one I have so far identified.

4   See Richard Arneson, 'Equality and Equal Opportunity for Welfare', *Philosophical Studies* 55 (1989).

5   *A Theory of Justice* (Cambridge, Mass.: Harvard University Press, 1971), p. 154.

6   That this is Rawls's intent is made clear in *A Theory of Justice*, esp. pp. 83–9. It is natural to think of 'equality of opportunity' solely in terms of the competition for economic advantage and positions of special status. In order for the considerations mentioned under (4) above to be fulfilled, however, it is essential to preserve the fairness of competition in the political realm. Rawls clearly believes and considers it important that this condition (what he calls 'the fair value of political liberty') will be met when his Two Principles are satisfied (see *A Theory of Justice*, pp. 224–7), but he does not make this an explicit condition on the inequalities permitted by the Difference Principle.

7   See *A Theory of Justice*, pp. 72–3.

8   I defend the claim that this is the best way to understand the disagreement between Rawls and Nozick in Lecture 2 of 'The Significance of Choice', *The Tanner Lectures in Human Values VII*, S. McMurrin, ed. (Cambridge: Cambridge University Press, 1988).

9   The more controversial character of appeals to (5) may seem to reflect the fact, mentioned above, that (5) represents a stronger egalitarian idea, since (4) appears at first to be compatible with wide inequality of output. This apparent difference may turn out to be illusory, however, once it is noticed how the benefits assigned to members of one generation affect the starting places of the next. Rawls's version of (4) is not the familiar, weak idea of equal opportunity, and the degree of equality required to secure fairness of starting places seems likely to be very great indeed. But the degree to which this observation makes the egalitarian consequences of (4) more stringent is precisely the area of disagreement over the interpretation of 'fair grounds of competition' which was mentioned above.

10 Russ Shafer-Landau pointed out in the discussion following this lecture that Rawls's inclusion of the 'social bases of self-respect' in the list of primary social goods (i.e. the measure of distributive shares) represents

an integration of my (2) into (5). The result is a focus not on 'stigmatization' in general but on equality in the distribution of those social indicators of status that it is the business of basic institutions to define and distribute.

11 See Rawls, *A Theory of Justice*, p. 440.

12 In 'Equal Treatment and Compensatory Discrimination,' *Philosophy and Public Affairs* 2 (1973), reprinted as 'The Policy of Preference' in *Mortal Questions*. My thought experiment also has obvious similarities to Michael Young's famous fable, *The Rise of the Meritocracy, 1870–2033* (Harmondsworth: Penguin Books, 1963).

13 In his *First and Second Discourses*. But it seems likely that his concern was more with what might be called a loss of fraternity than with what I have here termed a blow to individual self-respect.

14 It might be countered (as Richard De George pointed out in the discussion following this lecture) that since people are bound to be unequal in these 'moral attainments' a society which gave them pre-eminent place would be just another form of meritocracy, admirable in some respects, perhaps, but just as damaging (maybe even more damaging) to the self-respect of those whom it condemns. The reply, I suppose, is that these feelings of loss of self-respect, if deserved, would not be objectionable.

15 In his book, *Spheres of Justice* (New York: Basic Books, 1983).

16 *A Theory of Justice*, pp. 536–7.

17 See note 13 above.

4

Equality

Thomas Nagel

I

It is difficult to argue for the intrinsic social value of equality without begging the question. Equality can be defended up to a point in terms of other values like utility and liberty. But some of the most difficult questions are posed when it conflicts with these.

Contemporary political debate recognizes four types of equality: political, legal, social, and economic. The first three cannot be defined in formal terms. Political equality is not guaranteed by granting each adult one vote and the right to hold public office. Legal equality is not guaranteed by granting everyone the right to a jury trial, the right to bring suit for injuries, and the right to counsel. Social equality is not produced by the abolition of titles and official barriers to class mobility. Great substantive inequalities in political power, legal protection, social esteem and self-respect are compatible with these formal conditions. It is a commonplace that real equality of every kind is sensitive to economic factors. While formal institutions may guarantee a minimum social status to everyone, big differences in wealth and income will produce big distinctions above that – distinctions that may be inherited as well.

So the question of economic equality cannot be detached from the others, and this complicates the issue, because the value of the other types of equality may be of a very different kind. To put it somewhat paradoxically, their value may not be strictly egalitarian. It may depend on certain rights, like the right to fair treatment by the law, that must be impartially protected, and that cannot be protected without a measure of substantive equality. Rights are in an extended sense egalitarian, because everyone is supposed to have them; but this is not a matter of distributive justice. The equal protection of individual rights is usually thought to be a value independent of utility and of equality in the distribution of advantages. Later I shall comment on the relation among these values, but for now let us assume their distinctness. This means that the defense of economic equality on the ground that it is needed to protect political, legal, and social equality may not be a defense of equality *per se* – equality in the possession of benefits in general. Yet the latter is a further moral idea of great importance. Its validity would provide an independent reason to favor economic equality as a good in its own right. If, *per impossibile*, large economic inequalities did not threaten political, legal, and social equality, they would be much less objectionable. But there might still be something wrong with them.

In addition to the arguments that depend on its relation to other types of equality, there is at least one nonegalitarian, instrumental argument for economic equality itself, on grounds of utility. The principle of diminishing marginal utility states that for many goods, a particular further increment has less value to someone who already possesses a significant amount of the good than to someone who has less.[1] So if the total quantity of such a good and the number of recipients remains constant, an equal distribution of it will always have greater total utility than a less equal one.

This must be balanced against certain costs. First, attempts to reduce inequality may also reduce the total quantity of goods available, by affecting incentives to work and invest. For example, a progressive income tax and diminishing marginal utility make it more expensive to purchase the labor of those whose services are most in demand. Beyond a certain point, the pursuit of equality may sacrifice overall utility, or even the welfare of everyone in the society.

Second, the promotion of equality may require objectionable means. To achieve even moderate equality it is necessary to restrict economic liberty, including the freedom to make bequests. Greater equality may be attainable only by more general coercive techniques, including ultimately the assignment of work by public administration instead of private contracts. Some of these costs may be unacceptable not only on utilitarian grounds but because they violate individual rights. Opponents of the goal of equality may argue that if an unequal distribution of benefits results from the free interactions and agreements of persons who do not violate each other's rights, then the results are not objectionable, provided they do not include extreme hardship for the worst off.

II

So there is much to be said about the instrumental value and disvalue of equality; the question of its intrinsic value does not arise in isolation. Yet the answer to that question determines what instrumental costs are acceptable. If equality is in itself good, then producing it may be worth a certain amount of inefficiency and loss of liberty.

There are two types of argument for the intrinsic value of equality, communitarian and individualistic. According to the communitarian argument, equality is good for a society taken as a whole. It is a condition of the right kind of relations among its members, and of the formation in them of healthy fraternal attitudes, desires, and sympathies. This view analyzes the value of equality in terms of a social and individual ideal. The individualistic view, on the other hand, defends equality as a correct *distributive* principle – the correct way to meet the conflicting needs and interests of distinct people, whatever those interests may be, more or less. It does not assume the desirability of any particular kinds of desires, or any particular kinds of interpersonal relations. Rather it favors equality in the distribution of human goods, whatever these may be – whether or not they necessarily include goods of community and fraternity.

Though the communitarian argument is very influential, I am going to explore only the individualistic one, because that is the type of argument that I think is more likely to succeed. It would provide a moral basis for the kind of liberal egalitarianism that seems to me plausible. I do not have such an argument. This essay is a discussion of the form such an argument would have to take, what its starting points should be, and what it must overcome.

A preference for equality is at best one component in a theory of social choice, or choice involving numbers of people. Its defense does not require the rejection of other values with which it may come into conflict. However, it is excluded by theories of social choice which make certain other values dominant. Egalitarianism may once have been opposed to aristocratic theories, but now it is opposed in theoretical debate by the adherents of two nonaristocratic values: utility and individual rights. I am going to examine the dispute in order to see how equality might be shown to have a value that can resist these to some extent, without replacing them.

Though I am interested in the most general foundation for such a principle, I shall begin by discussing a more specialized egalitarian view, the position of John Rawls.[2] It applies specifically to the design of the basic social institutions, rather than to distributive choices, and perhaps it cannot be extended to other cases. But it is the most developed liberal egalitarian view in the field, and much debate about equality focuses on it. So I will initially pose the opposition between equality, utility, and rights in terms of his position. Later I shall explain how my own egalitarian view differs from his.

Rawls's theory assigns more importance to equal protection of political and personal liberties than to equality in the distribution of other benefits. Nevertheless it is strongly egalitarian in this respect also. His principle of distribution for general goods, once equality in the basic liberties is secure, is that inequalities are justified only if they benefit the worst-off group in the society (by yielding higher productivity and employment, for example).

This so-called Difference Principle is used not to determine allocation directly, but only for the assessment of economic and social institutions, which in turn influence the allocation of goods. While it is counted a good thing for anyone to be made better off, the value of improving the situation of those who are worse off takes priority over the value of improving the situation of those who are better off. This is largely independent of the relative quantities of improvement involved, and also of the relative numbers of persons. So given a choice between making a thousand poor people somewhat better off and making two thousand middle class people considerably better off, the first choice would be preferred. It should be added that people's welfare for these purposes is assessed in terms of overall life prospects, not just prosperity at the moment.

This is a very strong egalitarian principle, though it is not the most radical we can imagine. It is constructed by adding to the general value of improvement a condition of priority to the worst off. A more egalitarian position would hold that some inequalities are bad even if they benefit the worst off, so that a situation in which *everyone* is worse off may be preferable if the inequalities are reduced enough. So long as the argument remains individualistic such a position could seem attractive only for reasons stemming from the connection between economic and social equality.[3]

Later I shall discuss Rawls's arguments for the view, and offer some additional ones, but first let me say something about the two positions to which it is naturally opposed, and against which it has to be defended. They are positions that do not accord intrinsic value to equality but admit other values whose pursuit or protection may require the acceptance of considerable inequality. Those values, as I have said, are utility and individual rights.

From a utilitarian point of view, it does not make sense to forgo greater benefits for the sake of lesser, or benefits to more people for the sake of fewer, just because the benefits to the worst off will be greater. It is better to have more of what is good and less of what is bad, no matter how they are distributed.

According to a theory of individual rights, it is wrong to interfere with people's liberty to keep or bequeath what they can earn merely in order to prevent the development of inequalities in distribution. It may be acceptable to limit individual liberty to prevent grave evils, but inequality is not one of those. Inequalities are not wrong if they do not result from wrongs of one person against another. They must be accepted if the only way to prevent them is to abridge individual rights to the kind of free action that violates no one else's rights.

Both types of theory point out the costs of pursuing distributive equality, and deny that it has independent value that outweighs these costs. More specifically, the pursuit of equality is held to require the illegitimate sacrifice of the rights or interests of some individuals to the less important interests of others. These two theories are also radically opposed to one another. Together with egalitarianism they form a trio of fundamentally different views about how to settle conflicts among the interests of different people.

III

What is the nature of the dispute between them? The units about which the problem arises are individual persons, individual human lives. Each of them has a claim to consideration. In some sense the distinctness of these claims is at the heart of the issue. The question is whether (a) the worst off have a prior claim, or (b) the enforcement of that claim would ignore the greater claim of others not among the worst off, who would benefit significantly more if a less egalitarian policy were adopted instead, or (c) it would infringe the claims of other persons to liberty and the protection of their rights.

Now this looks like a dispute about the value of equality. But it can also be viewed as a dispute about *how* people should be treated equally, not about whether they should be. The three views share an assumption of moral equality between persons, but differ in their interpretations of it. They agree that the moral claims of all persons are, at a sufficiently abstract level, the same, but disagree over what these are.[4]

The defender of rights locates them in the freedom to do certain things without direct interference by others. The utilitarian locates them in the requirement that each person's interests be fully counted as a component in the calculation of utility used to decide which states of affairs are best and which acts or policies are right. The egalitarian finds them in an equal claim to actual or possible advantages. The issue remains acute even though most social theories do not fall squarely into one of these categories, but give primacy to one interpretation of moral equality and secondary status to the others.

All three interpretations of moral equality attempt to give equal weight, in essential respects, to each person's point of view. This might even be described as the mark of an enlightened ethic, though some theories that do not share it still qualify as ethical. If the opposition of views about distributive equality can be regarded as a disagreement about the proper interpretation of this basic requirement of moral equality, that provides a common reference against which the opposing positions may be measured. It should be possible to compare the quality of their justifications, instead of simply registering their mutual incompatibility.

What it means to give equal weight to each person's point of view depends on what is morally essential to that point of view, what it is in each of us that must be given equal weight. It also depends on how the weights are combined. And these two aspects of the answer are interdependent. Let us consider each of the positions from this point of view.

IV

The moral equality of utilitarianism is a kind of majority rule: each person's interests count once, but some may be outweighed by others. It is not really a majority of *persons* that determines the result, but a majority of interests suitably weighted for intensity. Persons are equal in the sense that each of them is given a 'vote' weighted in proportion to the magnitude of his interests. Although this means that the interests of a minority can sometimes outweigh the interests of a majority, the basic idea is majoritarian because each individual is accorded the same (variable) weight and the outcome is determined by the largest total.

In the simplest version, all of a person's interests or preferences are counted, and given a relative weight depending on their weight for him. But various modifications have been suggested. One doubt voiced about utilitarianism is that it counts positively the satisfaction of evil desires (sadistic or bigoted ones, for example). Mill employed a distinction between higher and lower pleasures, and gave priority to the former. (Could there be a corresponding distinction for pains?) Recently, Thomas Scanlon has argued that any distributive principle, utilitarian or egalitarian, must use some objective standard of interest, need, or urgency distinct from mere subjective preference to avoid unacceptable consequences. Even if the aim is to maximize the total of some quantity of benefit over all persons, it is necessary to pick a single measure of that quantity that applies fairly to everyone, and pure preference is not a good measure. 'The fact that someone would be willing to forgo a decent diet in order to build a monument to his god does not mean that his claim on others for aid in his project has the same strength as a claim for aid in obtaining enough to eat (even assuming that the sacrifices required of others would be the same).'[5]

Even if a standard of objectivity is introduced, the range of morally relevant interests can still be quite broad, and it will vary from person to person. The individual as moral claimant continues to be more or less the whole person. On the other hand, anyone's claims can in principle be completely outvoted by the claims of others. In the final outcome a given individual's claims may be met hardly at all, though they have been counted in the majoritarian calculation used to arrive at that outcome.

Utilitarianism takes a generous view of individual moral claims and combines them aggregatively. It applies the resulting values to the assessment of overall results or states of affairs, and derives the assessment of actions from this as a secondary result. One is to do what will tend to promote the results that appear best from a point of view that combines all individual interests. The moral equality of utilitarianism consists in letting each person's interests contribute in the same way to determining what in sum would be best overall.

V

Rights are very different, both in structure and in content. They are not majoritarian or in any other way aggregative, and they do not provide an assessment of overall results. Instead, they determine the acceptability of actions directly. The moral equality of persons under this conception is their equal claim against each other not to be interfered with in specified ways. Each person must be treated equally in certain definite respects by each other person.

In a sense, these claims are not combined at all. They must be respected individually. What anyone may do is restricted to what will not violate the rights of anyone else. Since the designated aspect of each person's point of view sets this limit *by itself*, the condition is a kind of unanimity requirement.

Rights may be absolute, or it may be permissible to override them when a significant threshold is reached in the level of harm that can be prevented by doing so. But however they are defined, they must be respected in every case where they apply. They give every person a limited veto over how others may treat him.

This kind of unanimity condition is possible only for rights that limit what one person may do to another. There cannot in this sense be rights to *have* certain things – a right to medical care, or to a decent standard of living, or even a right to life. The language of rights is sometimes used in this way, to indicate the special importance of certain human goods. But I believe that the true moral basis of such claims is the priority of more urgent over less urgent individual needs, and this is essentially an egalitarian principle. To preserve distinctions I shall use the term 'right' only for a claim that gives its possessor a kind of veto power, so that if everyone has the right, that places a condition of unanimous acceptability, in this respect, on action. There can be no literal right to life in that sense, because there are situations in which any possible course of action will lead to the death of someone or other; and if everyone had a right to stay alive, nothing would be permissible in those situations.[6]

Rights of the kind I am considering escape this problem because they are agent-centered. A right not to be killed, for example, is not a right that everyone do what is required to insure that you are not killed. It is merely a right not to be killed, and it is correlated with other people's duty not to *kill* you.

Such an ethic does not enjoin that violations of rights be minimized. That would be to count them merely as particularly grave evils in the assessment of outcomes. Instead, rights limit action directly: each person is forbidden to violate directly the rights of others even if he could reduce the overall number of violations of rights indirectly by violating a few himself. It is hard to account for such agent-centered restrictions. One thing to say about them by way of interpretation is that they represent a higher degree of moral inviolability than principles requiring us to do whatever will minimize the violation of rights. For if that were the principle, then violation of the right would not always be wrong. The moral claim of a right not to be murdered even to prevent several other murders is stronger than the claim which merely counts murder as a great evil, for the former prohibits murders that the latter would permit. That is true even though the latter might enable one to prevent more murders than the former. But this does not go very far toward explaining agent-centered rights. A serious account would have to consider not only the protected interests but the relation between the agent and the person he is constrained not to treat in certain ways, even to achieve very desirable ends. The concern with what one is doing to whom, as opposed to the concern with what happens, is an important primary source of ethics that is poorly understood.

Having noted that rights yield an assessment in the first instance of actions rather than of outcomes, we can see that they also define individual moral claims more narrowly than does utilitarianism, and combine them differently. The utilitarian constructs an impersonal point of view in which those of all individuals are combined to give judgments of utility, which in turn are to guide everyone's actions. For a defender of rights, the respects in which each person is inviolable present a direct and *independent* limit to what any other person may do to him. There is no single combination of viewpoints which yields a common goal for everyone, but each of us must limit our actions to a range that is not unacceptable to anyone else in certain respects. Typically, the range of what may be done because it violates no rights is rather large.

For this reason the morality of rights tends to be a limited, even a minimal morality. It leaves a great deal of human life ungoverned by moral restrictions or requirements. That is why, if unsupplemented, it leads naturally to political theories of limited government, and, in the extreme, to the libertarian theory of the minimal state. The justification of broad government action to promote all aspects of the general welfare requires a much richer set of moral requirements.[7]

This type of limited morality also has the consequence that the numbers of people on either side of an issue do not count. In a perfectly unanimous morality the only number that counts is one. If moral acceptability is acceptability in a certain respect from each person's point of view, then even if in other respects one course of action is clearly more acceptable to most but not all of the people involved, no further moral requirement follows.[8]

The moral equality of rights, then, consists in assigning to each person the same domain of interests with respect to which he may not be directly interfered with by anyone else.

VI

Oddly enough, egalitarianism is based on a more obscure conception of moral equality than either of the less egalitarian theories. It employs a much richer version of each person's point of view than does a theory of rights. In that respect it is closer to utilitarianism. It also resembles utilitarianism formally, in being applied first to the assessment of outcomes rather than of actions. But it does not combine all points of view by a majoritarian method. Instead, it establishes an order of priority among needs and gives preference to the most urgent, regardless of numbers. In that respect it is closer to rights theory.

What conception of moral equality is at work here, i.e. what equal moral claim is being granted to everyone and how are these claims combined? Each individual's claim has a complex form: it includes more or less all his needs and interests, but in an order of relative urgency or importance. This determines both which of them are to be satisfied first and whether they are to be satisfied before or after the interests of others. Something close to unanimity is being invoked. An arrangement must be acceptable first from the point of view of everyone's most basic claims, then from the point of view of everyone's next most basic claims, etc. By contrast with a rights theory, the individual claims are not limited to specific restrictions on how one may be treated. They concern whatever may happen to a person, and in appropriate order of priority they include much more than protection from the most basic misfortunes. This means that the order of priority will not settle all conflicts, since there can be conflicts of interest even at the most basic level, and therefore unanimity cannot be achieved. Instead, one must be content to get as close to it as possible.

One problem in the development of this idea is the definition of the order of priority: whether a single, objective standard of urgency should be used in construing the claims of each person, or whether his interests should be ranked at his own estimation of their relative importance. In addition to the question of objectivity, there is a question of scale. Because moral equality is equality between persons, the individual interests to be ranked cannot be momentary preferences, desires, and experiences. They must be aspects of the individual's life taken as a whole: health, nourishment, freedom, work, education, self-respect, affection, pleasure. The determination of egalitarian social policy requires some choice among them, and the results will be very different depending on whether material advantages or individual liberty and self-realization are given priority.

But let me leave these questions aside. The essential feature of an egalitarian priority system is that it counts improvements to the welfare of the worse off as more urgent than improvements to the welfare of the better off. These other questions must be answered to decide who is worse off and who is better off, and how much, but what makes a system egalitarian is the priority it gives to the claims of those whose overall life prospects put them at the bottom, irrespective of numbers or of overall utility. Each individual with a more urgent claim has priority, in the simplest version of such a view, over each individual with a less urgent claim. The moral equality of egalitarianism consists in taking into account the interests of each person, subject to the same system of priorities of urgency, in determining what would be best overall.

VII

It is obvious that the three conceptions of moral equality with which we are dealing are extremely different. They define each person's equal moral claim differently, and they derive practical conclusions from sets of such claims in different ways. They seem to be radically opposed to one another, and it is very difficult to see how one might decide among them.

My own view is that we do not have to. A plausible social morality will show the influence of them all. This will certainly not be conceded by utilitarians or believers in the dominance of rights. But to defend liberal egalitarianism it is not necessary to show that moral equality *cannot* be interpreted in the ways that yield rights or utilitarianism. One has only to show that an egalitarian interpretation is also acceptable. The result then depends on how these disparate values combine.

Though my own view is somewhat different from that of Rawls, I shall begin by considering his arguments, in order to explain why another account seems to me necessary.[9] He gives two kinds of argument for his position. One is intuitive and belongs to the domain of ordinary moral reasoning. The other is theoretical and depends on the construction by which Rawls works out his version of the social contract and which he calls the Original Position: I shall begin with two prominent examples of the first kind of argument and then go on to a brief consideration of the theoretical construction.

One point Rawls makes repeatedly is that the natural and social contingencies that influence welfare – talent, early environment, class background – are not themselves deserved. So differences in benefit that derive from them are morally arbitrary.[10] They can be justified only if the alternative would leave the least fortunate even worse off. In that case everyone benefits from the inequalities, so the extra benefit to some is justified as a means to this. A less egalitarian principle of distribution, whether it is based on rights or on utility, allows social and natural contingencies to produce inequalities justified neither because everyone benefits nor because those who get more deserve more.

The other point is directed specifically against utilitarianism. Rawls maintains that utilitarianism applies to problems of social choice – problems in which the interests of many individuals are involved – a method of decision appropriate for one individual.[11] A single person may accept certain disadvantages in exchange for greater benefits. But no such compensation is possible when one person suffers the disadvantages and another gets the benefits.

So far as I can see, neither of these arguments is decisive. The first assumes that inequalities need justification, that there is a presumption against permitting them. Only that would imply that undeserved inequalities are morally arbitrary in an invidious sense, unless otherwise justified. If they were arbitrary only in the sense that there were no reasons for or against them, they would require no justification, and the aim of avoiding them could provide no reason to infringe on anyone's rights. In any case the utilitarian has a justification to offer for the inequalities that his system permits: that the sum of advantages is greater than it would be without the inequality. But even if an inequality were acceptable only if it benefited everyone, that would not have to imply anything as strong as the Difference Principle. More than one deviation from equality may benefit everyone to some extent, and it would require a specific egalitarian assumption to prefer the one that was most favorable to the worst off.

The second argument relies on a diagnosis of utilitarianism that has recently been challenged by Derek Parfit.[12] But even if the diagnosis is correct, it does not supply an argument for equality, for it does not say why this method of summation is not acceptable for the experiences of many individuals. It certainly cannot be justified simply by extension from the individual case, but it has enough *prima facie* appeal to require displacement by some better alternative. It merely says that more of what is good is better than less, and less of what is bad is better than more. Someone might accept this conclusion without having reached it by extending the principle of individual choice to the social case. There is no particular reason to think that the principle will be either the same or different in the two cases.

In Utilitarianism intrapersonal compensation has no special significance. It acquires significance only against the background of a refusal *in general* to accept the unrestricted summation of goods and evils – a background to which it provides the exception. This background must be independently justified. By itself, the possibility of intrapersonal compensation neither supports nor undermines egalitarian theories. It implies only that *if* an egalitarian theory is accepted, it should apply only across lives rather than within them. It is a reason for taking individual human lives, rather than individual experiences, as the units over which any distributive principle should operate. But it could serve this function for anti-egalitarian as well as for egalitarian views. This is the reverse of Rawls's argument: no special distributive principle should be applied *within* human lives because that would be to extend to the individual the principle of choice appropriate for society. Provided that condition is met, intrapersonal compensation is neutral among distributive principles.

Next let me consider briefly Rawls's contractarian argument. Though he stresses that his theory is about the morality of social institutions, its general ideas about equality can I think be applied more widely. The Original Position, his version of the social contract, is a constructed unanimity condition which attributes to each person a schematic point of view that abstracts from the differences between people, but allows for the main categories of human interest. The individual is expected to choose principles for the assessment of social institutions on the assumption that he may be anyone, but without assuming that he has an equal chance of being anyone, or that his chance of being in a certain situation is proportional to the number of people in that situation.

The resulting choice brings out the priorities that are generally shared, and combines interests ranked by these priorities without regard to the numbers of people involved. The principles unanimously chosen on the basis of such priorities grant to each person the same claim to have his most urgent needs satisfied prior to the less urgent needs of anyone else. Priority is given to individuals who, taking their lives as a whole, have more urgent needs, rather than to the needs that more individuals have.

There has been much controversy over whether the rational choice under the conditions of uncertainty and ignorance that prevail in the Original Position would be what Rawls says it is, or even whether any choice could be rational under those conditions. But there is another question that is prior. Why does what it would be rational to agree to under those conditions determine what is right?

Let us focus this question more specifically on the features of the Original Position that are responsible for the egalitarian result. There are two of them. One is that the choice must be unanimous, and therefore everyone must be deprived of all information about his conception of the good or his position in society. The other is that the parties are not allowed to choose as if they had an equal chance of being anyone in the society, because in the absence of any information about probabilities it is not, according to Rawls, rational to assign some arbitrarily, using the Principle of Insufficient Reason. The Original Position is constructed by subtracting information without adding artificial substitutes. This results directly in the maximin strategy of choice, which leads to principles that favor the worst off in general and impose even more stringent equality in the basic liberties.

Suppose Rawls is right about what it would be rational to choose under those conditions. We must then ask why a unanimous choice under conditions of ignorance, without an assumption that one has an equal chance of being anyone in the society, correctly expresses the constraints of morality. Other constructions also have a claim to counting all persons as moral equals. What makes these conditions of unanimity under ignorance the right ones? They insure that numbers do not count[13] and urgency does, but that is the issue. A more fundamental type of argument is needed to settle it.

VIII

The main question is whether a kind of unanimity should enter into the combination of different points of view when evaluative judgments are being made about outcomes. This is an issue between egalitarian and utilitarian theories, both of which concern themselves with outcomes. Rights theories are opposed to both, because although they use a kind of unanimity condition, it is a condition on the acceptability of actions rather than of outcomes. In defending an interpretation of moral equality in terms of unanimity applied in the assessment of outcomes, I am therefore denying that either utilitarianism or rights theories, or both, represent the whole truth about ethics.

As I have said, acceptance of egalitarian values need not imply total exclusion of the others. Egalitarians may allow utility independent weight, and liberal egalitarians standardly acknowledge the importance of certain rights, which limit the means that may be used in pursuing equality and other ends.[14] I believe that rights exist and that this agent-centered aspect of morality is very important. The recognition of individual rights is a way of accepting a requirement of unanimous acceptability when weighing the claims of others in respect to what one may do. But a theory based exclusively on rights leaves out too much that is morally relevant, even if the interests it includes are among the most basic. A moral view that gives no weight to the value of overall outcomes cannot be correct.[15]

So let me return to the issue of unanimity in the assessment of outcomes. The essence of such a criterion is to try in a moral assessment to include each person's point of view separately, so as to achieve a result which is in a significant sense acceptable to each person involved or affected. Where there is conflict of interests, no result can be completely acceptable to everyone. But it is possible to assess each result from each point of view to try to find the one that is least unacceptable to the person to whom it is most unacceptable. This means that any other alternative will be more unacceptable to someone than this alternative is to anyone. The preferred alternative is in that sense the least unacceptable, considered from each person's point of view separately. A radically egalitarian policy of giving absolute priority to the worst off, regardless of numbers, would result from always choosing the least unacceptable alternative, in this sense.

This ideal of individual acceptability is in fundamental opposition to the aggregative ideal, which constructs a special moral point of view by combining those of individuals into a single conglomerate viewpoint distinct from all of them. That is done in utilitarianism by adding them up. Both the separate and the conglomerate methods count everyone fully and equally. The difference between them is that the second moves beyond individual points of view to something more comprehensive than any of them, though based on them. The first stays closer to the points of view of the individuals considered.

It is this ideal of acceptability to each individual that underlies the appeal of equality. We can see how it operates even in a case involving small numbers. Suppose I have two children, one of which is normal and quite happy, and the other of which suffers from a painful handicap. Call them respectively the first child and the second child. I am about to change jobs. Suppose I must decide between moving to an expensive city where the second child can receive special medical treatment and schooling, but where the family's standard of living will be lower and the neighborhood will be unpleasant and dangerous for the first child – or else moving to a pleasant semi-rural suburb where the first child, who has a special interest in sports and nature, can have a free and agreeable life. This is a difficult choice on any view. To make it a test for the value of equality, I want to suppose that the case has the following feature: the gain to the first child of moving to the suburb is substantially greater than the gain to the second child of moving to the city. After all, the second child will also suffer from the family's reduced standard of living and the disagreeable environment. And the educational and therapeutic benefits will not make him happy but only less miserable. For the first child, on the other hand, the choice is between a happy life and a disagreeable one. Let me add as a feature of the case that there is no way to compensate either child significantly for its loss if the choice favoring the other child is made. The family's resources are stretched, and neither child has anything else to give up that could be converted into something of significant value to the other.

If one chose to move to the city, it would be an egalitarian decision. It is more urgent to benefit the second child, even though the benefit we can give him is less than the benefit we can give the first child. This urgency is not necessarily decisive. It may be outweighed by other considerations, for equality is not the only value. But it is a factor, and it depends on the worse off position of the second child. An improvement in his situation is more important than an equal or somewhat greater improvement in the situation of the first child.

Suppose a third child is added to the situation, another happy, healthy one, and I am faced with the same choice in allocation of indivisible goods. The greater urgency of benefiting the second child remains. I believe that this factor is essentially unchanged by the addition of the third child. It remains just as much more urgent to benefit the second child in this case as it was when there were only two children.[16]

The main point about a measure of urgency is that it is done by pairwise comparison of the situations of individuals. The simplest method would be to count *any* improvement in the situation of someone worse off as more urgent than any improvement in the situation of someone better off; but this is not especially plausible. It is more reasonable to accord greater urgency to large improvements somewhat higher in the scale than to very small improvements lower down. Such a modified principle could still be described as selecting the alternative that was least unacceptable from each point of view. This method can be extended to problems of social choice involving large numbers of people. So long as numbers do not count it remains a type of unanimity criterion, defined by a suitable measure of urgency. The problem of justifying equality then becomes the problem of justifying the pursuit of results that are acceptable to each person involved.

Before turning to a discussion of this problem, let me say why I think that even if it were solved, it would not provide the foundation for a correct egalitarian theory. It seems to me that no plausible theory can avoid the relevance of numbers completely. There may be some disparities of urgency so great that the priorities persist whatever numbers are involved. But if the choice is between preventing severe hardship for some who are very poor and deprived, and preventing less severe but still substantial hardship for those who are better off but still struggling for subsistence, then it is very difficult for me to believe that the numbers do not count, and that priority of urgency goes to the worse off however many more there are of the better off. It might be suggested that this is a case where equality is outweighed by utility. But if egalitarian urgency is itself sensitive to numbers in this way, it does not seem that any form of unanimity criterion could explain the foundation of the view. Nor does any alternative foundation suggest itself.

IX

For a view of the more uncompromising type, similar in structure to that of Rawls, we need an explanation of why individual pairwise comparison to find the individually least unacceptable alternative is a good way to adjudicate among competing interests. What would it take to justify this method of combining individual claims? I think the only way to answer this question is to ask another: what is the source of morality? How do the interests of others secure a hold on us in moral reasoning, and does this imply a way in which they must be considered in combination?

I have a view about the source of other-regarding moral reasons that suggests an answer to this question. The view is not very different from the one I defended in *The Possibility of Altruism*,[17] and I will only sketch it here. I believe that the general form of moral reasoning is to put yourself in other people's shoes. This leads to acceptance of an impersonal concern for them corresponding to the impersonal concern for yourself that is needed to avoid a radical incongruity between your attitudes from the personal and impersonal standpoints, i.e. from inside and outside your life. Some considerable disparity remains, because the personal concerns remain in relation to yourself and your life: they are not to be replaced or absorbed by the impersonal ones that correspond to them.[18] (One is also typically concerned in a personal way for the interests of certain others to whom one is close.) But we derive moral reasons by forming in addition a parallel impersonal concern corresponding to the interests of all other individuals. It will be as strong or as weak, as comprehensive or as restricted, as the impersonal concern we are constrained by the pressures of congruency to feel about ourselves. In a sense, the requirement is that you love your neighbor as yourself: but only as much as you love yourself when you look at yourself from outside, with fair detachment.

The process applies separately to each individual and yields a set of concerns corresponding to the individual lives. There may be disparities between a person's objective interests and his own subjectively perceived interests or wishes, but apart from this, his claims enter the impersonal domain of reasons unchanged, as those of an individual. They do not come detached from him and go into a big hopper with all the others. The impersonal concern of ethics is an impersonal concern for oneself and all others as individuals. It derives from the necessary generalization of an impersonal concern for one's own life and interests, and the generalization preserves the individualistic form of the original.

For this reason the impersonal concern that results is fragmented: it includes a separate concern for each person, and it is realized by looking at the world from each person's point of view separately and individually, rather than by looking at the world from a single comprehensive point of view. Imaginatively one must split into all the people in the world, rather than turn oneself into a conglomeration of them.

This, it seems to me, makes pairwise comparison the natural way to deal with conflicting claims. There may be cases where the policy chosen as a result will seek to maximize satisfaction rather than equalizing it, but this will only be where all individuals have an equal chance of benefiting, or at least not a conspicuously unequal chance.[19] At the most basic level, the way to choose from many separate viewpoints simultaneously is to maintain them intact and give priority to the most urgent individual claims.

As I have said, equality is only one value and this is only one method of choice. We can understand a radically egalitarian system just as we can understand a radical system of rights, but I assume neither is correct. Utility is a legitimate value, and the majoritarian or conglomerate viewpoint on which it depends is an allowable way of considering the conflicting interests of numbers of different people at once. Still, the explanation of egalitarian values in terms of separate assessment from each point of view is a step toward understanding; and if it does not imply that these values are absolute, that is not necessarily a drawback.

Notes

1 This is obviously not true of things in which interest varies greatly, like recordings of bird songs, or horror comic books.
2 John Rawls, *A Theory of Justice* (Cambridge, Mass.: Harvard University Press, 1971).
3 The argument would be that improvements in the well-being of the lowest class as a result of material productivity spurred by wage differentials are only apparent: damage to their self-respect outweighs the material gains. And even inequalities that genuinely benefit the worst off may destroy nondistributive values like community or fraternity. See Christopher Ake, 'Justice as Equality', *Philosophy & Public Affairs*, v, no. 1 (Fall, 1975), 69–89, esp. 76–7.
4 This way of looking at the problem was suggested to me by a proposal of Rawls (personal communication, 31 January 1976):

'Suppose we distinguish between the equal treatment of persons and their (equal) right to be treated as equals. (Here persons are *moral* persons.) The *latter* is more basic: Suppose the Original Position represents the latter *re* moral persons when they agree on principles and suppose they *would* agree on *some* form of equal treatment. What more is needed?'

5 T. M. Scanlon, 'Preference and Urgency', *Journal of Philosophy*, LXXII, no. 19 (6 November 1975), 659–60.

6 There may be circumstances in which nothing is permissible – true moral dilemmas in which every possible course of action is wrong. But these arise only from the clash of distinct moral principles and not from the application of one principle. See my 'War and Massacre' in *Mortal Questions* (Cambridge: Cambridge University Press, 1979).

7 The issue over the *extent* of morality is one of the deepest in ethical theory. Many have felt it an objection to utilitarianism that it makes ethics swallow up everything, leaving only one optimal choice, or a small set of equally optimal alternatives, permissible for any person at any time. Those who offer this objection differ over the size and shape of the range of choices that should be left to individual inclination after the ethical boundaries have been drawn.

8 John Taurek has recently defended essentially this position in his paper, 'Should the Numbers Count?', *Philosophy & Public Affairs*, VI, no. 4 (Summer, 1977), 293–316. He holds that given a choice between saving one life and saving five others, one is not required to save the five: one may save either the one or the five. I believe that he holds this because there is at least one point of view from which saving the five is not the better choice. Taurek does believe that some moral requirements derive from special rights and obligations, but in cases like this, where there are fundamental conflicts of interest, it is impossible to define a condition of universal acceptability, and the choice is therefore not governed by any moral requirement.

9 Some of my comments are developed in 'Rawls on Justice', *Philosophical Review*, LXXXIII (1973), 220–33.

10 Rawls, *Theory of Justice*, pp. 74, 104.

11 Rawls, *Theory of Justice*, pp. 27, 187.

12 'Later Selves and Moral Principles', in *Philosophy & Personal Relations*, ed. A. Montefiore (London: Routledge & Kegan Paul, 1973). Parfit suggests that utilitarianism could express the dissolution of temporally extended individuals into experiential sequences rather than the conflation of separate individuals into a mass person.

13 Since the Difference Principle is applied not to individuals but to social classes, conflicts of interest within the worst off or any other groups are absorbed in a set of average expectations. This means that the numbers count in a sense *within* a social class, in determining which policy benefits it most on average. But numbers do not count in determining priority among classes in the urgency of their claims. That is why the problems of this conception of social justice are similar to those of a more individually tailored egalitarianism.

14 Such a view is defended by Ronald Dworkin in *Taking Rights Seriously* (Cambridge, Mass.: Harvard University Press, 1977).

15 I have said more about this in 'Libertarianism without Foundations', *Yale Law Journal*, LXXXV (1975), a review of Robert Nozick, *Anarchy, State, and Utopia* (New York: Basic Books, 1974).

16 Note that these thoughts do not *depend* on any idea of personal identity over time, though they can *employ* such an idea. All that is needed to evoke them is a distinction between persons at a time. The impulse to distributive equality arises so long as we can distinguish between two experiences being had by two persons and their being had by one person. The criteria of personal identity over time merely determine the size of the units over which a distributive principle operates. That, briefly, is what I think is wrong with Parfit's account of the relation between distributive justice and personal identity.

17 Oxford: Clarendon Press, 1970.

18 In this respect my present view differs from the one in *The Possibility of Altruism*.

19 I leave aside the question when the equality of chances can be counted as real enough to supersede the inequality of actual outcomes. Perhaps that applies only to certain kinds of outcomes, and certain ways of determining chances.

5
Equality or Priority?[1]

Derek Parfit

In his article 'Equality', Nagel imagines that he has two children, one healthy and happy, the other suffering from a painful handicap. He could either move to a city where the second child could receive special treatment, or move to a suburb where the first child would flourish. Nagel writes:

> This is a difficult choice on any view. To make it a test for the value of equality, I want to suppose that the case has the following feature: the gain to the first child of moving to the suburb is substantially greater than the gain to the second child of moving to the city.

He then comments:

> If one chose to move to the city, it would be an egalitarian decision. It is more urgent to benefit the second child, even though the benefit we can give him is less than the benefit we can give to the first child. This urgency is not necessarily decisive. It may be outweighed by other considerations, for equality is not the only value. But it is a factor, and it depends on the worse off position of the second child.[2]

My aim, in this lecture, is to discuss this kind of egalitarian reasoning.

Nagel's decision turns on the relative importance of two facts: he could give one child a greater benefit, but the other child is worse off.

There are countless cases of this kind. In these cases, when we are choosing between two acts or policies, one relevant fact is how great the resulting benefits would be. For Utilitarians, that is all that matters. On their view, we should always aim for the greatest sum of benefits. But, for Egalitarians, it also matters how well off the beneficiaries would be. We should sometimes choose a smaller sum of benefits, for the sake of a better distribution.

How can we make a distribution better? Some say: by aiming for equality between different people. Others say: by giving priority to those who are worse off. As we shall see, these are different ideas.

Should we accept these ideas? Does equality matter? If so, when and why? What kind of priority, if any, should we give to those who are worse off?

These are difficult questions, but their subject matter is, in a way, simple. It is enough to consider different possible states of affairs, or outcomes, each involving the same set of people. We imagine that we know how well off, in these outcomes, these people would be. We then ask whether either outcome would be better, or would be the outcome that we ought to bring about. This subject we can call *the ethics of distribution*.

Some writers reject this subject. For example, Nozick claims that we should not ask what would be the best distribution, since that question wrongly assumes that there is something to be distributed. Most goods, Nozick argues, are not up for distribution, or redistribution.[3] They are goods to which particular people already have entitlements, or special claims. To decide what justice demands, we cannot look merely at the abstract pattern: at how well off, in the different outcomes, different people would be. We must know these people's histories, and how each situation came about. Others make similar claims about merit, or desert. To be just, these writers claim, we must give everyone their due, and people's dues depend entirely on the differences between them, and on what they have done. As before, it is these other facts which are morally decisive.

These objections we can here set aside. We can assume that, in the cases we are considering, there are no such differences between people. No one deserves to be better off than anyone else; nor does anyone have entitlements, or special claims. Since there are *some* cases of this kind, we have a subject. If we can reach conclusions, we can then consider how widely these apply. Like Rawls and others, I believe that, at the fundamental level, most cases are of this kind. But that can be argued later.[4]

There are many ways in which, in one of two outcomes, people can be worse off. They may be poorer, or less happy, or have fewer opportunities, or worse health, or shorter lives. Though the difference between these cases often matters, I shall be discussing some general claims, which apply to them all.

To ask my questions, we need only two assumptions. First, some people can be worse off than others, in ways that are morally relevant. Second, these differences can be matters of degree. To describe my imagined cases, I shall use figures. Nagel's choice, for example, can be shown as follows:

	The first child	The second child
Move to the city:	20	10
Move to the suburb:	25	9

Such figures misleadingly suggest precision. Even in principle, I believe, there could not be precise differences between how well off different people are. I intend these figures to show only that the choice between these outcomes makes much more difference to Nagel's first child, but that, in both outcomes, the second child would be much worse off.

One point about my figures is important. Each extra unit is a roughly equal benefit, however well off the person is who receives it. If someone rises from 99 to 100, this person benefits as much as someone else who rises from 9 to 10. Without this assumption we cannot make sense of some of our questions. We cannot ask, for example, whether some benefit would matter more if it came to someone who was worse off. Consider Nagel's claim that, in his example, it would be more urgent to benefit the handicapped child. Nagel tells us to assume that, compared with the healthy child, the handicapped child would benefit *less*. Without this assumption, as he notes, his example would not test the value of equality. Nagel's conclusion is egalitarian because he believes that it is the *lesser* benefit which *matters more*.

For each extra unit to be an equal benefit, however well off the recipient is, these units cannot be thought of as equal quantities of resources. The same increase in resources usually brings greater benefits to those who are worse off. But these benefits need not be thought of in narrowly Utilitarian terms: as involving only happiness and the relief of suffering, or the fulfilment of desire. These benefits might include improvements in health, or length of life, or education, or other substantive goods.[5]

I

What do Egalitarians believe? The obvious answer is: they believe in equality. On this definition, most of us are Egalitarians, since most of us believe in some kind of equality. We believe in political equality, or equality before the law, or we believe that everyone has equal rights, or that everyone's interests should be given equal weight.[6]

Though these kinds of equality are of great importance, they are not my subject. I am concerned with people's being *equally well off*. To count as Egalitarians, in my sense, this is the kind of equality in which we must believe.

There are two main ways in which we can believe in equality. We may believe that inequality is *bad*. On such a view, when we should aim for equality, that is because we shall thereby make the outcome better. We can then be called *Teleological* – or, for short *Telic* – Egalitarians. Our view may instead be *Deontological* or, for short, *Deontic*. We may believe we should aim for equality, not to make the outcome better, but for some other moral reason. We may believe, for example, that people have rights to equal shares. (We might of course have beliefs of both kinds. We might believe we should aim for equality both because this will make the outcome better, and for other reasons. But such a view does not need a separate discussion. It is enough to consider its components.) [7]

We can first consider Telic Egalitarians. These accept

> *The Principle of Equality*: It is in itself bad if some people are worse off than others.[8]

In a fuller statement of this principle, we would need to assess the relative badness of different patterns of inequality. But we can here ignore these complications.[9]

Suppose next that the people in some community could all be either (1) equally well off, or (2) equally badly off. The Principle of Equality does not tell us that (2) would be worse. This principle is about the badness of inequality; and, though it would be clearly worse if everyone were equally worse off, our ground for thinking this cannot be egalitarian.

To explain why (2) would be worse, we might appeal to

> *The Principle of Utility*: It is in itself better if people are better off.

When people would be on average better off, or would receive a greater net sum of benefits, we can say, for short, that there would be more *utility*. (But, as I have said, these benefits need not be thought of in narrowly utilitarian terms.)

If we cared only about equality, we would be *Pure* Egalitarians. If we cared only about utility, we would be Pure Utilitarians – or what are normally just called Utilitarians. But most of us accept a *pluralist* view: one that appeals to more than one principle or value. On what I shall call the *Pluralist Egalitarian View*, we believe that it would be better both if there was more equality, and if there was more utility. In deciding which of two outcomes would be better, we give weight to both these values.

These values may conflict. One of two outcomes may be in one way worse, because there would be more inequality, but in another way better, because there would be more utility, or a greater sum of benefits. We must then decide which of these two facts would be more important. Consider, for example, the following possible states of affairs:

(1) Everyone at 150

(2) Half at 199   Half at 200

(3) Half at 101   Half at 200

For Pure Egalitarians, (1) is the best of these three outcomes, since it contains less inequality than both (2) and (3). For Utilitarians, (1) is the worst of these outcomes, since it contains less utility than both (2) and (3). (In a move from (1) to (3), the benefits to the half who gained would be slightly greater than the losses to the half who lost.) For most Pluralist Egalitarians, (1) would be neither the best nor the worst of these outcomes. (1) would be all-things-considered worse than (2), since it would be *much* worse in terms of utility, and only *slightly* better in terms of equality. Similarly, (1) would be all-things-considered better than (3), since it would be much better in terms of equality, and only slightly worse in terms of utility.

In many cases the Pluralist View is harder to apply. Compare

(1) Everyone at 150

with

(4) Half at N Half at 200.

If we are Pluralist Egalitarians, for which values of N would we believe (1) to be worse than (4)? For some range of values – such as 120 to 150 – we may find this question hard to answer. And this case is unusually simple. Patterns of inequality can be much harder to assess.

As such cases show, if we give weight to both equality and utility, we have no principled way to assess their relative importance. To defend a particular decision, we can only claim that it seems right. (Rawls therefore calls this view *intuitionist*.)

I have said that, for Telic Egalitarians, inequality is bad. That seems to me the heart of this view. But I shall keep the familiar claim that, on this view, equality has value. It would be pedantic to claim instead that *in*equality has *dis*value.

We should next distinguish two kinds of value. If we claim that equality has value, we may only mean that it has good effects. Equality has many kinds of good effect, and inequality many kinds of bad effect. If people are unequal, for example, that can produce conflict, or envy, or put some people in the power of others. If we value equality because we are concerned with such effects, we believe that equality has *instrumental* value: we think it good as a means. But I am concerned with a different idea. For true Egalitarians, equality has *intrinsic* value. As Nagel claims, it 'is in itself good'.

This distinction, as we shall see, is theoretically important. And it makes a practical difference. If we believe that, besides having bad effects, inequality is in itself bad, we shall think it to be worse. And we shall think it bad even when it has no bad effects.

Nagel sometimes blurs this distinction. He mentions two kinds of argument 'for the intrinsic value of equality'[10]; but neither seems to deserve this description.

The first kind of argument is *individualistic*, since it appeals to what is good or bad for individuals. Nagel's example is the claim that, when there is inequality, this weakens the self-respect of those people who are worse off. But what is claimed to be bad here is not inequality itself, but only one of its effects. Nor, to judge this effect bad, need we be egalitarians. Other effects we may think bad only because our conception of well-being is in part egalitarian. Thus we may think it bad for people if they are servile or too deferential, even if this does not frustrate their desires, or affect their experienced well-being. But though such a view is, in one way, egalitarian, it too does not claim that equality has intrinsic value. As before, it claims only that inequality has bad effects.

Nagel's second type of argument is *communitarian*. According to this argument, he writes,

> equality is good for society taken as a whole. It is a condition of the right kind of relations among its members, and of the formation in them of healthy fraternal attitudes, desires, and sympathies.

For this to be a different type of argument, it must claim that such relations are not merely good for people, but have intrinsic value. This, however, would still not be the claim that *equality* has intrinsic value. What would be claimed to be good would still not be equality itself, but only some of its effects.[11]

The difference can be shown like this. Consider what I shall call the *Divided World*. The two halves of the world's population are, we can suppose, unaware of each other's existence. Perhaps the Atlantic has not yet been crossed. Consider next two possible states of affairs:

(1) Half at 100   Half at 200

(2) Everyone at 145

Of these two states, (1) is in one way better than (2), since people are on average better off. But we may believe that, all things considered, (1) is worse than (2). How could we explain this view?

If we are Telic Egalitarians, our explanation would be this. While it is good that, in (1), people are on average better off, it is bad that some people are worse off than others. The badness of this inequality morally outweighs the extra benefits.

In making such a claim, we could not appeal to inequality's effects. Since the two halves of the world's population are quite unconnected, the inequality in (1) has no bad effects on the worse-off group. Nor does the equality in (2) produce desirable fraternal relations between the two groups. If we are to claim that (1) is worse because of its inequality, we must claim that this inequality is in itself bad.

Suppose we decide that, in this example, (1) is *not* worse than (2). Would this show that, in our view, inequality is *not* in itself bad?

This would depend on our answer to another question. What should be the *scope* of an egalitarian view? Who are the people who, ideally, should be equally well off?

The simplest answer would be: everyone who ever lives. And, on the Telic View, this seems the natural answer. If it is in itself bad if some people are worse off than others, why should it matter where or when these people live? On such a view, it is in itself bad if there are or have been, even in unrelated communities, and in different centuries, people who are not equally well off. Thus it is bad if Inca peasants, or Stone Age hunter-gatherers, were worse off than we are now.

We may reject this view. We may believe that, if two groups of people are quite unrelated, it is in no way bad if they not equally well off. This might be why, in my example, we deny that (1) is worse than (2).

If that is our reaction, might we still believe that, when it holds between related groups, inequality is in itself bad? This seems un-likely. Why is it only in these cases that we object to inequality? Why would it make a difference if these groups were not aware of each other's existence? The obvious answer is that, in such cases, inequality cannot have its usual bad effects. It would be coherent to claim that inequality is in itself bad, but only when it holds between related groups. But, though coherent, this view does not seem plausible, since it would involve a strange coincidence.

We might claim, more plausibly, that inequality is in itself bad, but only when it holds within one *community*. But that would suggests that our real view is that such inequality involves social injustice. And we may then be *Deontic* Egalitarians.

II

Let us now consider this second kind of view. Deontic Egalitarians believe that, though we should sometimes aim for equality, that is *not* because we shall thereby make the outcome better, but is always for some other reason. On such a view, it is not in itself good if people are equally well off, or bad if they are not.

Such a view typically appeals to claims about justice. More ex-actly, it appeals to claims about *comparative* justice. Whether people are unjustly treated, in this comparative sense, depends on whether they are treated *differently* from other people. Thus it may be unfair if, in a distribution of resources, some people are denied their share.

Fairness may require that, if such goods are given to some, they should be given to all.

Another kind of justice is concerned with treating people as they deserve. This kind of justice is *non-comparative*. Whether people are unjustly treated, in this sense, depends only on facts about *them*. It is irrelevant whether others are treated differently. Thus, if we treated no one as they deserved, this treatment would be unjust in the non-comparative sense. But, if we treated everyone equally unjustly, there would be no comparative injustice.[12]

It is sometimes hard to distinguish these two kinds of justice, and there are difficult questions about the relation between them.[13] One point should be mentioned here. Non-comparative justice may tell us to produce equality. Perhaps, if everyone were equally deserving, we should make everyone equally well off. But such equality would be merely the effect of giving people what they deserved. Only comparative justice makes equality our aim.

When I said that, in my examples, no one deserves to be better off than others, I did not mean that everyone is equally deserving. I meant that, in these cases, we are considering benefits that no one deserves. So it is only comparative justice with which we shall be concerned.

There is another relevant distinction. In some cases, justice is *purely procedural*. It requires only that we act in a certain way. For example, when some good cannot be divided, we may be required to conduct a fair lottery, which gives everyone an equal chance to receive this good. In other cases, justice is in part *substantive*. Here too, justice may require a certain kind of procedure; but there is a separate criterion of what the outcome ought to be. One example would be the claim that people should given equal shares.

There is an intermediate case. Justice may require a certain outcome, but only because this avoids a procedural flaw. One such flaw is partiality. Suppose that we have to distribute certain publicly owned goods. If we could easily divide these goods, others might be rightly suspicious if we gave to different people unequal shares. That might involve favouritism, or wrongful discrimination.[14] We may thus believe that, to avoid these flaws, we should distribute these goods equally. The same conclusion might be reached in a slightly different way. We may think that, in such a case, equality is the *default*: that we need some moral reason if we are to justify giving to some people more than we give to others.

How does this view differ from a view that requires equality for substantive reasons? One difference is this. Suppose that we have manifestly tried to distribute equally, but our procedure has innocently failed. If we aimed for equality only to avoid the taint of partiality or discrimination, there would be no case for correcting the result.[15]

We can now redescribe my two kinds of Egalitarian. On the Telic View, inequality is bad; on the Deontic View, it is unjust.

It may be objected that, when inequality is unjust, it is, for that reason, bad. But this does not undermine this way of drawing our distinction. On the Deontic View, injustice is a special kind of badness, one that necessarily involves wrong-doing. When we claim that inequality is unjust, our objection is not really to the inequality itself. What is unjust, and therefore bad, is not strictly the state of affairs, but the way in which it was produced.

There is one kind of case which most clearly separates our two kinds of view. These are cases where some inequality cannot be avoided. For Deontic Egalitarians, if nothing can be done, there can be no injustice. In Rawls's words, if some situation 'is unalterable . . . the question of justice does not arise.'[16]

Consider, for example, the inequality in our natural endowments. Some of us are born more talented or healthier than others, or are more fortunate in other ways. If we are Deontic Egalitarians, we shall not believe that such inequality is in itself bad. We might agree that, if we *could* distribute talents, it would be unjust or unfair to distribute them unequally. But, except when there are bad effects, we shall see nothing to regret in the inequalities produced by the random shuffling of our genes.

Many Telic Egalitarians take a different view. They believe that, even when such inequality is unavoidable, it is in itself bad.[17]

III

It is worth developing here some remarks of Rawls. As I have said, Rawls assumes that injustice essentially involves wrongdoing. When he discusses the inequality of our inherited talents, he writes:

> The natural distribution is neither just nor unjust . . . These are simply natural facts. What is just and unjust is the way that institutions deal with these facts.

This may suggest a purely deontic view. But Rawls continues:

Aristocratic and caste societies are unjust because . . . the basic structure of these societies incorporates the arbitrariness found in nature. But there is no necessity for men to resign themselves to these contingencies.[18]

This use of the word *resign* seems to assume that natural inequality *is* bad. And Rawls elsewhere writes that, in a society governed by his principles, we need no longer 'view it as a *misfortune* that some are by nature better endowed than others'. These remarks suggest that Rawls is in part a Telic Egalitarian. An objection to natural inequality is, I believe, one of the foundations of his theory, and one of its driving forces. If Rawls denies that such inequality is unjust, that may only be because he wishes to preserve the analytic link between injustice and wrong-doing. And, given the substance of his theory, that may be merely a terminological decision.

Rawls's objection to natural inequality is not so much that it is bad, but that it is morally arbitrary. This objection, as Rawls suggests, can be reapplied at several points in one natural line of thought.

We can start with external goods. In some cases, we enjoy resources whose availability, or discovery, is in no sense due to us. Such resources simply appear, like manna falling from the sky. There will be inequality if such manna falls unequally on different people. Let us call these *windfall* cases.

In such cases, the inequality is entirely due to differences in the bounty of nature. Such differences are, in the clearest sense, morally arbitrary. If some people receive less than others, that is merely their bad luck. Since such inequalities have this arbitrary cause, we may conclude that they are bad. Or we may conclude that we ought to redress these inequalities, by a redistribution of resources.

Consider next cases in which we are not merely passive. We do some work, either in discovering resources, or in converting them for use. We plant seeds, prospect and mine, or fish the sea; we till the soil, and manufacture goods.

Suppose that we all work equally hard, and with equal skill. In such cases, the human input is the same. But there may still be inequality between us, which results from differences in the natural input. These might be differences in mineral wealth, or in the climate, or in the fruitfulness of the soil, or sea. Because of such variations, some of us may soon become much better off than others. These are cases of *productive luck*.[19]

Some of these cases hardly differ from pure windfalls. Perhaps we merely have to shake our trees, or stroll over to where the fruit fell. And all these cases may seem relevantly similar. Since we all work equally hard, and with equal skill, the inequality is again due to differences in the bounty of nature, which we believe to be morally arbitrary. Can the other element, the equal human input, make this fact irrelevant? Can it justify the resulting inequality? We may decide that it cannot, and that such inequality also calls for redistribution.

Now consider inequality of a third kind. In these cases, there are no differences either in external resources, or in the efforts people make. The inequality is entirely due to differences in people's native talents. These are cases of *genetic luck*.[20]

We may decide that such genetic differences are, in the relevant respect, like differences in nature's bounty. As Rawls says, they are not deserved. Our native talents are inner resources, which, like manna, merely fell upon us.

In some of these cases, people receive greater rewards simply for *having* certain natural endowments. These are like pure windfalls. But, in most of these cases, people develop and use the talents with which they were born. We must ask again whether this infusion of effort cancels out the arbitrariness of genetic luck. Can it justify the resulting inequalities?

This may be the most important question in this whole debate. Many people answer Yes. But, like Rawls and Nagel, we may answer No. We may conclude that these inequalities should also be redressed.

Consider next a fourth kind of case. The natural input is the same, and we all have equal talents. But inequality results from differences in how hard we work. These are cases of *differential effort*.

We must here note one complication. There are two uncontroversial ways in which, when people work harder, they should sometimes be paid more. They may work for a longer time, or in a more unpleasant way. In such cases, overtime or hardship pay may be mere compensation, which does not create real inequality. These are not the cases that I have in mind. I am thinking of people who enjoy working hard, and who, because they do, become much better off than others.

Of those who appeal to the arbitrariness of the natural lottery, many stop here. Differences in effort seem to them to justify such inequality. But we may press on. Such differences involve two elements: the ability to make an effort, and the decision to try. We may decide that the first is merely another native talent, which cannot justify inequality.

This leaves only inequalities that are the result of choice. To most Egalitarians, these inequalities are of no concern. That is why some writers argue for equality, not of well-being, but of *opportunity* for well-being.[21] But some of us may still press on. We may decide that it is bad if some people are worse off than others, even when this is merely because these people do not enjoy working hard, or because, for some other reason, they make choices that leave them worse off. These may seem to be merely other kinds of bad luck.

The line of thought that I have just sketched raises many questions. I shall make only three brief comments.

First, to some people this reasoning may seem a *reductio*. If these people find the last step absurd, they may be led to reject the others. But that would be too swift, since there could be grounds for stopping earlier.

Second, we should state more clearly what such reasoning might show. The reasoning appeals to the claim that certain kinds of inequality have a morally arbitrary cause. Such a claim might show that such inequality is *not* justified. But it may not show that such inequality is *un*justified, and ought to be redressed. These are quite different conclusions.

If such inequality is not justified, people have no positive claim to their advantages, or to the resources which they now control. But this conclusion only clears the decks. It means that, *if* there is a moral reason for redistribution, those who are better off can have no principled objection. It would be a further claim that there *is* such a reason, and that the aim of such redistribution should be to produce equality.[22]

The difference can be shown like this. Utilitarians would also claim that, if some distribution of resources has an arbitrary natural cause, it is not justified. Since that is so, they would claim, there can be no objection to redistribution. But, on their view, the best distribution is the one that would maximize the sum of benefits. Such a distribution would not be morally arbitrary. But it may not be an equal distribution.

Third, Rawls regards Utilitarians as his main opponents. At the level of theory, he may be right. But the questions I have been discussing are, in practice, more important. If nature gave to some of us more resources, have we a moral claim to keep these resources, and the wealth they bring? If we happen to be born with greater talents, and in consequence produce more, have we a claim to greater rewards? In practical terms, Rawls's main opponents are those who answer Yes to such questions. Egalitarians and Utilitarians both answer No. Both agree that such inequalities are *not* justified. In this disagreement, Rawls, Mill, and Sidgwick are on the same side.

IV

I have distinguished two kinds of Egalitarian view. On the Telic View, we believe that inequality is in itself bad, or unfair. On the Deontic View, our concern about equality is only a concern about what we should do.

Why does this distinction matter? It has theoretical implications. As we shall later see, these views can be defended or attacked in different ways. There are also practical implications, some of which I shall mention now.

Each view has many versions. That is especially true of the Deontic View, which is really a group of views. Telic and Deontic Views might, in practice, coincide. It might be true that, whenever the first view claims that some kind of inequality is bad, the second claims that we should prevent it, if we can. But when we look at the versions of these views that are in fact advanced, and found plausible, we find that they often conflict.

The Telic View is likely to have wider scope. As I have said, if we think it in itself bad if some people are worse off than others, we may think this bad whoever these people are. It may seem to make no difference where these people live: whether they are in the same or different communities. We may also think it irrelevant what the respects are in which some people are worse off than others: whether they have less income, or worse health, or are less fortunate in other ways. *Any* inequality, if undeserved and unchosen, we may think bad. Nor, third, will it seem to make a difference how such inequality arose. That is implied by the very notion of intrinsic badness. If some state is in itself bad, it is irrelevant how it came about.

If we are Deontic Egalitarians, our view may have none of these features.

Though there are many versions of the Deontic View, one large group are broadly contractarian. Such views often appeal to the ideas of reciprocity, or mutual benefit. On some views of this kind, when goods are cooperatively produced, and no one has special claims, all the contributors should get equal shares. There are here two restrictions. First, what is shared are only the fruits of cooperation. Nothing is said about other goods, such as those that come from nature. Second, the distribution covers only those who produce these goods. Those who cannot contribute, such as the handicapped, or children, or future generations, have no claims.[23]

Other views of this type are less restrictive. They may cover all the members of the same community, and all types of good. But they still exclude outsiders. It is irrelevant that those other people may be far worse off.

On such views, if there is inequality between people in different communities, this need not be anyone's concern. Since the greatest inequalities are on this global scale, this restriction has immense importance. (Here is one way to make this point. If Egalitarians oppose inequality only within particular communities, their view may, on a global scale, call for *less* redistribution than a Utilitarian view.)

Consider next the question of causation. The Telic View naturally applies to all cases. On this view, we always have a reason to prevent or reduce inequality, if we can.

If we are Deontic Egalitarians, we might think the same. But that is less likely. Since our view is not about the goodness of outcomes, it may cover only inequalities that result from acts, or only those that are intentionally produced. And it may tell us to be concerned only with the inequalities that we ourselves produce.

Here is one example. In a highly restricted way, Gauthier is a Deontic Egalitarian. Thus he writes that 'If there were a distributor of natural assets . . . we might reasonably suppose that in so far as possible shares should be equal.'[24] But, when assets are distributed by nature, Gauthier has no objection to inequality. He sees no ground to undo the effects of the natural lottery.

On such a view, when we are responsible for some distribution, we ought to distribute equally. But, when we are not responsible, inequality is not unjust. In such cases, there is nothing morally amiss. We have no reason to remove such inequality, by redistribution.

Is this a defensible position? Suppose we are about to distribute some resources. We agree that we ought to give people equal shares. A gust of wind snatches these resources from our hands, and distributes them unequally. Have we then no reason to redistribute?

It makes a difference here why we believe that we ought to distribute equally. Suppose, first, that our concern is with procedural justice. We believe that we should distribute equally because that is the only way to avoid partiality. Or we believe that equality is the default: what we should aim for when we cannot justify distributing unequally. When there is natural inequality, neither belief applies. Nature is not discriminatory; nor is she an agent, who must justify what she does. On such a view, *if* we distribute, we should distribute equally. But we have no ground for thinking that we *should* distribute. If the distributor is Nature, there has been no partiality. Nothing needs to be undone.

Suppose, next, that we are concerned with substantive justice. Our aim is not merely to avoid procedural flaws, since we have a separate criterion for what the result should be. On such a view, we might believe that, wherever possible, we should intervene, to produce the right result. But, as before, that belief need not be part of such a view. As in the case of procedural justice, we might believe only that, *if* we distribute, we should distribute equally. When inequality arises naturally, our view may not apply.

Things are different on the Telic View, according to which such inequality is in itself bad, or unjust. On this view, we have a reason to redistribute. The onus of the argument shifts. If people oppose redistribution, they must provide contrary reasons.

It is worth mentioning some of these reasons. Some would claim that, even if *we* should distribute equally, once there has been a natural distribution, it is wrong to intervene. Such a claim may seem to assume that what is natural is right, or that the status quo is privileged – assumptions that are now hard to defend. But there are other ways in which people might defend such claims. They might appeal to the difference between acts and omissions, or between negative and positive duties, or something of the kind.[25]

In some cases, such a view is plausible. Suppose that some natural process threatens to kill many people. We could save them if we intervened, and killed one person as a means to save the many. Many believe that, even though the deaths of many would be a worse outcome than the death of one, we ought not to intervene in such a way. We should allow this natural process to bring about the worse of these two outcomes.

Could we apply such a view to inequality? If some natural process has distributed resources in an unequal way, could it be similarly claimed that, though such inequality makes the outcome worse, we ought not to intervene? That seems less plausible. In the case of killing, our objection might appeal to the special features of this act, our relation to the person killed, her right not to be injured, or to the fact that her death is used as a means. There seem to be no such features when we correct a natural distribution. If the wind blows more manna into the laps of certain people, and we concede that, as an outcome, this is worse, there seems no ground for a constraint against redistribution. If we remove and redistribute these people's extra manna, so that everyone has equal shares, we do not injure these people, or use them as a means.

It may next be claimed that, once a natural distribution has occurred, people acquire entitlements. In pure windfall cases, such a claim seems far-fetched. The fact that the manna fell on you does not make it *yours*. But similar claims are widely made. Thus it may be said that you staked out a valid claim to the ground on which the manna fell, and that this makes it yours. Or it may be said that, once you interact with the manna – or mix your labour with it – it becomes yours.

Such claims may have some force if they are made within some existing institutional scheme, or agreement. But we are here discussing a more fundamental question. What should our institutions, or agreements, be? If such claims are not convincing, as answers to that question, we may conclude that, in pure windfall cases, we ought to redistribute. It may then be harder to defend such claims in cases of productive luck. If we reject such claims here, it may then be harder to defend them in cases of genetic luck, and so on down the series.

For those who hold a Deontic View, there is no need even to make these claims. On such a view, since natural inequality is not in itself bad, there is no argument *for* redistribution; so there need not be an argument against. This, for conservatives, is a stronger position.

V

Let us now consider two objections to the Telic View.

On the widest version of this view, any inequality is bad. It is bad, for example, that some people are sighted and others are blind. We would therefore have a reason, if we could, to take single eyes from some of the sighted and give them to the blind. That may seem a horrific conclusion.

If Egalitarians wish to avoid this conclusion, they might claim that their view applies only to inequality in resources. But, as Nozick says, such a restriction may be hard to explain. If natural inequality is in itself bad, why is that not true of the inequality between the sighted and the blind?

Should we be horrified by this conclusion? To set aside some irrelevant complications, let us purify the example. Suppose that, after some genetic change, people are henceforth born as twins, one of whom is always blind. And suppose that, as a universal policy, operations are performed after every birth, in which one eye from the sighted twin is transplanted into its blind sibling. That would be a forcible redistribution, since new-born babies cannot give consent. But I am inclined to believe that such a policy would be justified.

Some of us may disagree. We may believe that people have rights to keep the organs with which they were born. But that belief would not give us grounds to reject the Telic View. Egalitarians could agree that the State should not redistribute organs. Since they do not believe equality to be the only value, they could think that, in this example, some other principle has greater weight. Their belief is only that, if we all had one eye, that would be *in one way* better than if half of us had two eyes and the other half had none. Far from being monstrous, that belief is clearly true. If we all had one eye, that would be much better for all of the people who would otherwise be blind.[26]

A second objection is more serious. If inequality is bad, its disappearance must be in one way a change for the better, *however this change occurs*. Suppose that those who are better off suffer some misfortune, so that they become as badly off as everyone else. Since these events would remove the inequality, they must be in one way welcome, on the Telic View, even though they would be worse for some people, and better for no one. This implication seems to many to be quite absurd. I call this *the Levelling Down Objection*.[27]

Consider first those Egalitarians who regret the inequalities in our natural endowments. On their view, it would be in one way better if we removed the eyes of the sighted, not to give them to the blind, but simply to make the sighted blind. That would be in one way better even if it was in *no* way better for the blind. This we may find impossible to believe. Egalitarians would avoid this form of the objection if what they think bad is only inequality in resources. But they must admit that, on their view, it would be in one way better if, in some natural disaster those who are better off lost all of their extra resources, in a way that benefitted no one. That conclusion may seem almost as implausible.

It is worth repeating that, to criticize Egalitarians by appealing to the Levelling Down Objection, it is not enough to claim that it would be *wrong* to produce equality by levelling down. As we have seen, since they are pluralists, Telic Egalitarians could accept that claim. Our objection must be that, if we achieve equality by levelling down, there is *nothing* good about what we have done. And we must claim that, if some natural disaster makes everyone equally badly off, that is not in any way good news. These claims do contradict the Telic Egalitarian View, even in its pluralist form.

I shall return to the Levelling Down Objection. The point to notice now is that, on a Deontic view, we can avoid all forms of this objection. If we are Deontic Egalitarians, we do not believe that inequality is bad, so we are not forced to admit that, on our view, it would be in one way better if inequality were removed by levelling down. We can believe that we have a reason to remove inequality only *when*, and only *because*, our way of doing so benefits the people who are worse off. Or we might believe that, when some people are worse off than others, through no fault or choice of theirs, they have a special claim to be raised up to the level of the others, but they have no claim that others be brought down to their level.

VI

There are, then, several differences between the Telic and Deontic Views. Though these views might coincide, they are likely to have different scope, and different implications. And, as we have just seen, they can be challenged in different ways. If we are Egalitarians, it is thus important to decide which kind of view we hold.

If we are impressed by the Levelling Down Objection, we may be tempted by the Deontic View. But, if we give up the Telic View, we may find it harder to justify some of our beliefs. If inequality is not in itself bad, we may find it harder to explain, for example, why we should redistribute resources.

Some of our beliefs would also have to go. Reconsider the Divided World, in which the two possible states are these:

(1) Half at 100   Half at 200

(2) Everyone at 145

In outcome (1) there is inequality. But, since the two groups are unaware of each other's existence, this inequality was not deliberately produced, or maintained. Since this inequality does not involve wrong-doing, there is no injustice. On the Deontic View, there is nothing more to say. On this view, we cannot claim that (1) is worse than (2). If we believe that (1) is worse, and because of the inequality, we must accept the Telic form of the Egalitarian View. We must claim that the inequality in (1) is in itself bad.

We might, however, give a different explanation. Rather than believing in equality, we might be especially concerned about those people who are worse off. That could be our reason for preferring (2).

Let us now consider this alternative.

VII

In discussing his imagined case, Nagel writes:

> If one chose to move to the city, it would be an egalitarian decision. It is more urgent to benefit the second child . . . This urgency is not necessarily decisive. It may be outweighed by other consid-erations, for equality is not the only value. But it is a factor, and it depends on the worse off position of the second child. An improvement in his situation is more important than an equal or somewhat greater improvement in the situation of the first child.[28]

This passage contains the idea that equality has value. But it gives more prominence to another idea. Nagel believes it is more import-ant to benefit the child who is worse off. That idea can lead us to a quite different view.

Consider first those people who are badly off: those who are suffer-ing, or destitute, or those whose fundamental needs have not been met. It is widely claimed that we should give priority to helping such people. This would be claimed even by Utilitarians, since, if people are badly off, they are likely to be easier to help.

I am concerned with a different view. On this view, it is more urgent to help these people even if they are *harder* to help. While Utilitarians claim that we should give these people priority when, and because, we can help them *more*, this view claims that we should give them priority, even when we can help them *less*. That is what makes this a distinctive view.

Some apply this view only to the two groups of the well off and the badly off.[29] But I shall consider a more general version of this view, which can be applied to everyone. On what I shall call

> *The Priority View*: Benefiting people matters more the worse off these people are.

For Utilitarians, the moral importance of each benefit depends only on how great this benefit would be. For *Prioritarians*, it also depends on how well off the person is to whom this benefit comes. We should not give equal weight to equal benefits, whoever receives them. Benefits to the worse off should be given more weight.[30]

Like the Egalitarian Pluralist View, this view is, in Rawls's sense, intuitionist. It does not tell us how much priority we should give to those who are worse off. On this view, benefits to the worse off could be morally outweighed by sufficient benefits to the better off. To decide what would be sufficient, we must simply use our judgement.

Like the belief in equality, the Priority View can take either Telic or Deontic forms. It can be a view about which outcomes would be better, or a view that is only about what we ought to do. But, for most of my discussion, this difference does not matter.

VIII

Let us now look more closely at this view. To whom should we give priority? Here are three answers:

(1) those who are worse off in their lives as a whole,
(2) those who are worse off at the time,
(3) those who have needs that are morally more urgent.

(1) and (2) frequently diverge. One of two people may be worse off now, even though she has earlier been, and will later be, much better off.

(2) and (3), in contrast, usually coincide. If one of two people has more urgent needs, she is likely to be worse off at the time. But, on some views about the urgency of needs, that is not always true. Compare A, who is disabled, with the less fortunate but able-bodied B. A's need for a wheel-chair may be claimed to be more urgent than any of B's needs, even though A's other advantages make her, on the whole, better off.[31]

The choice between (1) and (2) is the choice of what Nagel calls *units* for distributive principles: the items to which we apply these principles.[32] Nagel takes these units to be 'individual persons, individual human lives'. And he writes, 'what makes a system egalitarian is the priority it gives to the claims of those whose overall life prospects put them at the bottom.' Rawls and many others take the same view.

If lives are the relevant units, this increases the difference between giving priority to those who are worse off, and giving priority to meeting more urgent needs.

Nagel sometimes favours the second of these. Thus he claims that an egalitarian view 'establishes an order of priority among needs and gives preference to the most urgent'. And he writes:

> An arrangement must be acceptable first from the point of view of everyone's most basic claims, then from the point of view of everyone's next most basic claims, etc . . . [T]he principles grant to each person the same claim to have his most urgent needs satisfied prior to the less urgent needs of anyone else.[33]

This implies that we should give priority to needs rather than persons. The more urgent needs of someone who, on the whole, is better off, take priority over the less urgent needs of someone who is worse off.

Nagel seems to have overlooked this implication. Thus he also writes, 'Priority is given to individuals who, *taking their lives as a whole, have more urgent needs*'.[34] This claim conflates the distinction I have drawn. X's needs may *now* be more urgent than Y's, even though, in most of her life, X has been, and will later be, much better off than Y. If we should give priority to more urgent needs, we should help X. If we should give priority to those who are worse off in their lives as a whole, we should help Y.

Which answer should we give? Suppose that we could support one of two programs. The first would provide treatment for a painful illness that occasionally afflicts the rich. The second would benefit an equal number of the poor, by subsidizing sports grounds, or seaside holidays. Which of these should have priority?

For this case to be relevant, it must be true that, even without the treatment, the rich would on the whole be better off. And it must be true that our decision would make *less difference* to them: that it would give them lesser benefits. We can thus suppose that the treatment in question would not bring much relief to this painful illness. Since the benefits to both groups would be hedonistic, they can be roughly estimated by an appeal to people's preferences. Let us suppose that everyone involved would prefer a seaside holiday, or a new sports ground, to the relief of this amount of suffering.

Suppose we believe that, even in such a case, the relief of suffering should take priority. And suppose we take a similar view about other urgent needs, such as those produced by disability. We then have a view which is not, in any way, egalitarian. We think it more important to give *lesser* benefits to people who, in the relevant sense, are *better off.*

Such a view is not, I think, absurd. But, because it is so different, I shall ignore it here. I shall assume that, on the Priority View, we should give priority, not to meeting special needs, but to benefiting those people who are worse off. And I shall assume that, in my examples, there is no difference between those who would be worse off at the time, and those who would be worse off in their lives as a whole.

IX

What is the relation between the Priority View and Egalitarianism?

On the Priority View, it is morally more important to benefit the people who are worse off. But this claim, by itself, does not define a different view, since it would be made by all Egalitarians. If we believe that we should aim for equality, we shall think it more important to benefit those who are worse off. Such benefits reduce inequality. If that is why we give such benefits priority, we do not hold the Priority View. On this view, as I define it here, we do *not* believe in equality. We give priority to the worse off, not because this will reduce inequality, but for other reasons. That is what makes this a distinctive view.

As before, we may hold a mixed view. We may give priority to the worse off, partly because this will reduce inequality, and partly for other reasons. But such a view does not need a separate discussion. It is enough to consider the pure version of the Priority View.

How does this view differ from an Egalitarian view?

One difference is purely structural. As we have seen, equality cannot plausibly be our only value. If we are Egalitarians, we must hold some more complicated view. Thus, on the Telic form of the Pluralist View, the belief that inequality is bad is combined with the belief that benefits are good. The Priority View, in contrast, can be held as a complete moral view. This view contains the idea that benefits are good. It merely adds that benefits matter more the worse off the people are who receive them. Unlike the Principle of Equality, which might be combined with the Principle of Utility, the Priority View can replace that principle. It can be regarded as the only principle we need.

The chief difference can be introduced like this. I have said that, on the Priority View, we do not believe in equality. We do not think it in itself bad, or unjust, that some people are worse off than others. This claim can be misunderstood. We do of course think it bad that some people are worse off. But what is bad is not that these people are worse off than *others*. It is rather that they are worse off than *they* might have been.

Consider next the central claim of the Priority View: benefits to the worse off matter more. The same ambiguity can lead one astray. On this view, if I am worse off than you, benefits to me are more important. Is this *because* I am worse off than you? In one sense, yes. But this has nothing to do with my relation to you.

It may help to use this analogy. People at higher altitudes find it harder to breathe. Is this because they are higher up than other people? In one sense, yes. But they would find it just as hard to breathe even if there were no other people who were lower down. In the same way, on the Priority View, benefits to the worse off matter more, but that is only because these people are at a lower *absolute* level. It is irrelevant that these people are worse off *than others*. Benefits to them would matter just as much even if there *were* no others who were better off.

The chief difference is, then, this. Egalitarians are concerned with *relativities*: with how each person's level compares with the level of other people. On the Priority View, we are concerned only with people's absolute levels.[35]

This is a fundamental structural difference. Because of this difference, there are several ways in which these views have different implications.

One example concerns scope. Telic Egalitarians may, I have said, give their view wide scope. They may believe that inequality is bad even when it holds between people who have no connections with each other. But this can seem a dubious view. Why is it bad if, in some far off land, and quite unknown to me, there are other people who are better off than me?

On the Priority View, there is no ground for such doubts. This view naturally has universal scope. And that is true of both its telic and deontic forms. If it is more important to benefit one of two people, because this person is worse off, it is irrelevant whether these people are in the same community, or are aware of each other's existence. The greater urgency of benefiting this person does not depend on her *relation* to the other person. It depends only on her lower absolute level.

There are other ways in which, given the structural difference between these views, they are likely to have different implications. I cannot discuss these here. But I have described the kind of case in which these views most deeply disagree. These are the cases which raise the Levelling Down Objection. Egalitarians face this objection because they believe that inequality is in itself bad. If we accept the Priority View, we avoid this objection. We are more concerned for people the worse off these people are. But, as we have just seen, it makes no difference to our concern whether there are other people who are better off. On this view, when inequality is not bad for people, it simply does not matter. If the better off suffer some misfortune, so that they become as badly off as anyone else, we do not think this in any way a change for the better.

X

I have explained the sense in which, on the Priority View, we do not believe in equality. Though we give priority to benefiting those who are worse off, that is not because such benefits reduce inequality.

It may be objected that, on the Priority View, we shall often aim for equality. But that is not enough to make us Egalitarians. In the same way, Utilitarians often aim for equality, because inequality has bad effects. But Utilitarians are not Egalitarians, since they regard equality as a mere means.

It is worth pursuing this analogy. There is an important Utilitarian reason to aim for equality, not of well-being, but of resources. This reason appeals to *diminishing marginal utility*, or the claim that, if resources go to people who are better off, they will benefit these people less. Utilitarians therefore argue that, whenever we transfer resources to those who are worse off, we shall produce greater benefits, and shall thereby make the outcome better.

On the telic version of the Priority View, we appeal to a similar claim. We believe that, if benefits go to people who are better off, these benefits matter less. Just as *resources* have diminishing marginal *utility*, so *utility* has diminishing marginal *moral importance*.

Given the similarity between these claims, there is a second similar argument in favour of equality: this time, not of resources, but of well-being. On this argument, whenever we transfer resources to people who are worse off, the resulting benefits will not merely be, in themselves, greater. They will also, on the moral scale, matter more. There are thus *two* ways in which the outcome will be better.

The Utilitarian argument in favour of equality of resources is, as Nagel says, a 'non-egalitarian instrumental argument'. It treats such equality as good, not in itself, but only because it increases the size of the resulting benefits. A similar claim applies to the Priority View. Here too, equality is good only because it increases the moral value of these benefits.[36]

There are, however, two differences. First, diminishing marginal utility is not a universal law. In some cases, if resources went to the people who were better off, they would give these people *greater* benefits.[37] Utilitarians would then believe that we should transfer resources to these people. That would increase inequality.

The law of diminishing moral goodness is, in contrast, quite secure. As a moral claim, it always holds. On the Priority View, benefits to the worse off always matter more. This argument for equality is thus more securely grounded. But this does not make it different in kind. Like the Utilitarian argument, it still treats equality as a mere means.

A second difference goes deeper. Since diminishing marginal utility is an empirical generalization, the Utilitarian argument for equality is, in a way, coincidental. It merely happens to be true that, if people are better off, resources give them smaller benefits.

On the Priority View, there is no coincidence. It does not merely happen to be true that, if people are worse off, benefits to them matter more. On this view, these benefits matter more *because* these people are worse off. This is a fact, not about the size of these benefits, but about their distribution. And, in telling us to give priority to such benefits, this view has what Nagel calls 'a built-in bias towards equality'.

On the definition with which I began, the Priority View is not Egalitarian. On this view, though we ought to give priority to the worse off, that is not because we shall be reducing inequality. We do not believe that inequality is, in itself, either bad or unjust. But, since this view has a built-in bias towards equality, it could be called Egalitarian in a second, looser sense. We might say that, if we take this view, we are *Non-Relational Egalitarians*.

XI

Though equality and priority are different ideas, the distinction is often overlooked, with unfortunate results.

It is worth suggesting why this distinction has been overlooked. First, especially in earlier centuries, Egalitarians were often fighting battles in which this distinction did not arise. They were demanding legal or political equality, or attacking arbitrary privileges, or differences in status. These are not the kinds of good to which our distinction applies. And it is here that the demand for equality is most plausible.

Second, when Egalitarians considered other kinds of good, they often assumed that, if equality were achieved, this would either increase the sum of these goods, or would at least not reduce this sum. If they thought of benefits in utilitarian terms, they may have assumed that the redistribution of resources would increase the resulting benefits. If instead they were concerned only with resources, they may have regarded these as a fixed sum, which would not be altered by redistribution. In either of these cases, equality and priority cannot conflict.

Third, even when a move to equality might reduce the total sum of benefits, Egalitarians often assumed that such a move would at least bring *some* benefits to the people who were worse off. In such cases, equality and priority could not deeply conflict. Egalitarians overlooked the cases where equality could not be achieved except by levelling down.

I shall now mention certain recent statements of Egalitarian views. In the case of some views, though they are presented as being about equality, that fact is superficial. These views could be restated as views about priority, and they would then become more plausible. But other views are essentially about equality, and cannot be restated in this way.

We can start by asking which kind of view Nagel holds. In his review of Nozick's book, Nagel seemed to conflate equality and priority. He wrote:

> To defend equality as a good in itself, one would have to argue that improvements in the lot of people lower on the scale of well-being took priority over greater improvements to those higher on the scale.[38]

In his article 'Equality', Nagel does argue this. And, after claiming that it is more urgent to benefit the child who is worse off, he writes:

> This urgency is not necessarily decisive. It may be outweighed by other considerations, for equality is not the only value.[39]

This suggests that, to the question 'Why is it more urgent to benefit this child?', Nagel would answer, 'Because this would reduce the inequality between these two children.' But I doubt that this is really Nagel's view. Would it be just as urgent to benefit the handicapped child, even if he had no sibling who was better off? I suspect that, on Nagel's view, it would. Nagel is thus one writer who sometimes uses the language of equality, when he is really appealing to the Priority View.[40]

Consider next a remark of Dworkin's:

> It is perhaps the final evil of a genuinely unequal distribution of resources that some people have reason for regret just in the fact that they have been cheated of the chances others have had to make something valuable of their lives.[41]

Why does Dworkin write 'the chances *others* have had'? That suggests that there would be no evil if *no one* had such chances. That seems wrong. The real evil seems to be that these people were cheated of the chances that *they* could have had. The argument for an equal distribution is not to give people *equal* chances to make something valuable of their lives. That could be achieved by levelling down. The argument is rather that, while an unequal distribution gives good chances only to some people, the same resources, if shared out, would give them to everyone.[42]

We can now turn to the idea of distribution according to need. Several writers argue that, when we are moved by this idea, our aim is to achieve equality. Thus Raphael writes:

> If the man with greater needs is given more than the man with lesser needs, the intended result is that each of them should have (or at least approach) the same level of satisfaction; the inequality of nature is corrected.[43]

Others make similar claims. Thus, when discussing the giving of extra resources to meet the needs of the ill, or the handicapped,

Norman writes, 'the underlying idea is one of equality. The aim is that everybody should, as far as possible, have an equally worthwhile life.'[44] As before, if this is the aim, it could be as well achieved by levelling down. This cannot be what Norman means. He could avoid this implication by omitting the word 'equally'. He could simply say, 'the aim is that everybody should, as far as possible, have a worthwhile life.' With this revision, Norman could no longer claim that equality is the underlying idea. But that, I believe, would strengthen his argument. Distribution according to need is more naturally interpreted as a form of the Priority View.[45]

Some ideas, however, cannot be reinterpreted in this way. For example, Cohen suggests that 'the right reading of egalitarianism' is that 'its purpose is to eliminate involuntary disadvantage'.[46] He means by this comparative disadvantage: being worse off than others. That is an essentially relational idea. Only equality could eliminate such disadvantage. Cohen's view could not be re-expressed in the language of priority. Remember next the view that it is in itself bad, or unfair, that some people are born abler or healthier than others, or that through the differences in the natural distribution of resources, some people are worse off than others. That view is essentially about inequality. There are many other cases. For example, Ake writes:

> Justice in a society as a whole ought to be understood as a complete equality of the overall level of benefits and burdens of each member of that society.

The various maxims of distributive justice, Ake claims, can all be interpreted as having as their aim 'to restore a situation of complete equality to the greatest degree possible'.[47]

It is sometimes claimed that, though Egalitarians may seem committed to the intrinsic value of equality, that is not really so, and that no Egalitarian would believe that there was any case for levelling down.[48] But, while that is true of some Egalitarians, it is not true of all. For example, Ake writes:

> What about the case of someone who suddenly comes into good fortune, perhaps entirely by his or her own efforts? Should additional burdens ... be imposed on that person in order to restore equality and safeguard justice? ... Why wouldn't it be just to impose any kind of additional burden whatsoever on him in

order to restore the equality? The answer is that, strictly speaking, it would be . . .[49]

Ake concedes that, on his view, it would be just to level down, by imposing burdens on this person. He merely believes that the claim of justice would here be overridden, just as the claims of efficiency, or happiness, can be overridden. Levelling down would be in one way good, or be something that we would have a moral reason to do. Similarly, Temkin writes:

> I, for one, believe that inequality is bad. But do I *really* think that there is some respect in which a world where only some are blind is worse than one where all are? Yes. Does this mean I think it would be better if we blinded everybody? No. Equality is not all that matters.[50]

Several other writers make such claims.[51]

XII

Since some writers are unmoved by the Levelling Down Objection, let us now reconsider what that objection claims. The objection appeals to cases where, if some inequality were removed, that would be worse for some people and better for no one. As I have said, these are the cases which raise the deepest disagreement between our two kinds of view.

On the Priority View, we do not object to inequality except when it is bad for people. We shall see nothing good in the removal of inequality, when this would benefit no one. Telic Egalitarians disagree. On their view, inequality is *in itself* bad. This implies that inequality is bad *whether or not it is bad for people*.

My last claim assumes that inequality is not in itself bad for people. Is this assumption justified? If we are worse off than other people, is that in itself bad for us?

Inequality may, of course, have bad effects. For example, if I am worse off than other people, this may put me in their power, or make me envious, or undermine my self-respect. But such effects are irrelevant here. We are concerned with the mere fact that I am worse off than other people. To isolate this fact, we can suppose that I am not aware of these people, and that their existence has no other effect on me. In such a case, though the inequality has no effects, it remains true that I am worse off than these other people. Is that bad for me?

This question is easily misunderstood. It is, of course, in one sense bad for me that I am worse off than these people. It would be better for me if I was not worse-off than them, *because I was as well-off as they actually are.* If that were true, I would be better off. But this is not the relevant comparison. Clearly, it is bad for me that *I am not* that well off. But is it bad for me that *they are*?

It may help to rephrase our question. We should not ask, 'Is it bad for me that I am worse off than other people?' This suggests that the relevant alternative is my being better off. Rather we should ask, 'Is it bad for me that, unknown to me, there are other people who are better off than me? Would it be better for me if there were no such people? Would it be better for me if these people had never existed, or were as badly off as me?'

The answer depends on our view about what is in or against people's interests, and there are several theories here. But I shall simply claim that, on all the plausible versions of these theories, the answer is No. The mere fact of inequality is not, in itself, bad for the people who are worse off. Such inequalities may be naturally unfair. And it would of course be better for these people if they themselves were better off. But it would not be better for them if, without any effects on them, the other people were just as badly off.[52]

We can now return to my earlier claim. For Telic Egalitarians, inequality is in itself bad. If that is so, it must be bad even when it is not bad for people. For these Egalitarians, inequality is bad *even when it is bad for no one.*

That may seem enough reason to reject this view. We may think that nothing can be bad if it is bad for no one. But, before we assess this objection, we must distinguish two versions of this view. Consider these alternatives:

(1) Everyone at some level

(2) Some at this level   Others better off

In outcome (1) everyone is equally well off. In outcome (2), some people are better off. In (2) there is inequality, but this outcome is worse for no one. For Telic Egalitarians, the inequality in (2) is bad. Could this make (2), all things considered, a worse outcome than (1)?

Some Egalitarians answer Yes. These people do not believe that inequality would always make outcomes, all things considered, worse. On their view, the loss of equality could be morally outweighed by a sufficient increase in the sum of benefits. But inequality is a great evil. It *can* make an outcome worse, even when this outcome would be better for everyone. Those who hold this view I shall call *Strong Egalitarians*.

Others hold a different view. Since they believe that inequality is bad, they agree that outcome (2) is in one way worse. But they do not think it worse on balance, or all things considered. In a move from (1) to (2), some people would become better off. For these Egalitarians, the loss of equality would be morally outweighed by the benefits to these people. On their view, (2) would be, on balance, better than (1). Those who hold this view I shall call *Moderates*.

This version of Egalitarianism is often overlooked, or dismissed. People typically produce the standard objection to Strong Egalitarianism: the appeal to cases where a move to inequality would be bad for no one. They then either ignore the Moderate view, or treat it as not worth considering. They assume that, if we claim that the badness of the inequality would always be outweighed by the extra benefits, our view must be trivial.[53]

This, I believe, is a mistake. Our view would indeed be trivial if we held that any loss of equality, however great, could be outweighed by any gain in utility, however small. But that is not what Moderates claim. They claim only that, in *this* kind of case, those in which greater inequality would be worse for no one, the badness of the inequality would in fact be outweighed by the extra benefits. This claim can be subdivided into a pair of claims. One is a view about the relative importance of equality and utility. The other, which has been overlooked, is a claim about the structure of these cases. If there is greater inequality, in a way that is worse for no one, the inequality must come from benefits to certain people. And there cannot be a *great* loss of equality unless these benefits are also great. These gains and losses would roughly march in step.

In the simplest cases, this is obvious. Consider these alternatives:

(1) All at 100

(2) Half at 100   Half at 101

(3) Half at 100   Half at 110

(4) Half at 100   Half at 200

In a move from (1) to (2), there would be a small gain in utility but only a small loss in equality. In a move from (1) to (3) the loss in equality would be greater, but so would be the gain in utility. As we move lower down the list, both gains and losses would steadily grow. In more complicated cases, the point still holds. If one of two outcomes involves more inequality, but is worse for no one, the better-off must gain. There can be much more inequality only if the better-off gain a great deal. But there would then be much more utility.[54]

Since these gains and losses roughly march in step, there is room for Moderates to hold a significant position. Moderates claim that, in all such cases, the gain in utility would outweigh the loss in equality. That is consistent with the claim that, in other kinds of case, that may not be so. Moderates can claim that *some* gains in utility, even if *great*, would *not* outweigh some losses in equality. Consider, for example, these alternatives:

(1) All at 100

(4) Half at 100   Half at 200

(5) Half at 70   Half at 200.

Moderates believe that, compared with (1), (4) is better. But they might claim that (5) is worse. This would not be a trivial claim. In a move from (1) to (5), the worse-off would lose, but the better-off would gain more than three times as much. Compared with (1), (5) would involve a great gain in utility. But, for these Moderates, this gain would be too small to outweigh the loss of equality. They would here choose a smaller sum of benefits, for the sake of a more equal distribution. That is why, though Moderate, they are true Egalitarians.

Return now to the Levelling Down Objection. Strong Egalitarians believe that, in some cases, a move towards inequality, even though it would be worse for no one, would make the outcome worse. This may seem incredible. We may claim that one of two outcomes *cannot* be worse if it would be worse for no one. To challenge Strong Egalitarians, it would be enough to defend this claim.

To challenge Moderates, this claim may not be enough. Moderates believe that, if the outcome with greater inequality would be worse for no one, it would *not* be a worse outcome. But their claim is only that it would not be worse on balance, or all-things-considered.

They must agree that, on their view, this outcome would be *in one way* worse. On their view, inequality is *bad*, even when it is bad for no one. To reject their view, we must claim that even this cannot be true.

In the space remaining, I can make only a few remarks about this disagreement. It is widely assumed that, if an outcome is worse for no one, it cannot be in any way worse. This we can call the *Person-affecting Claim*.

This claim might be defended by an appeal to some view about the nature of morality, or moral reasoning. Some, for example, argue as follows. It is not hard to see how an outcome can be worse for particular people. But it can seem puzzling how an outcome can be simply worse – worse, period. What is meant by this impersonal use of 'worse'? Some suggest that this use of 'worse' can be explained, or constructed, out of the concept 'worse for'. There are other lines of thought which may lead to the Person-affecting Claim, such as a contractualist view about moral reasoning.[55]

Egalitarians might respond by defending a different meta-ethical view. Or they might argue that this claim has unacceptable implications, since it conflicts too sharply with some of our beliefs.

Temkin responds in the second way. The Person-affecting Claim, he argues, is incompatible with many of our ideals.[56]

Temkin's best example seems to me his appeal to what he calls 'proportional justice'. Would it not be bad, he asks, if 'the evilest mass murderers fare better than the most benign saints?' But this might not be bad for any of these people.

It may be bad that the saints fare worse than the murderers. But this comparative element is too close to the question at issue: whether inequality is bad. So we should forget the saints. Is it bad that the murderers fare as well as they do? Would it be better if they fared worse?

We might think this better if it would give the murderers the punishment that they deserve. Note that, in thinking this, we are not merely claiming that they ought to be punished. We may think that, if they are not punished, perhaps because they cannot be caught, this would be bad. The badness here may not involve any further wrongdoing. And we may think this bad even if their punishment would do no one any good – perhaps because, as in Kant's example, our community is about to dissolve.

If we accept this retributive view, we must reject the Person-affecting Claim. We believe that, if people are not punished as they deserve, this would be bad, even if it would be bad for no one. And, if that is true, the same could be true of the badness of inequality.

Even if we reject the retributive view, as I do, this analogy may still be useful. Consider the claim that it would have been better if Hitler, unknown to others, had suffered for what he did. If we reject this claim, what would our reason be? Would it be enough to say, 'How could this have been better? It would not have been better for him.' This remark may seem to us inadequate. We may reject retribution, not because it is good for no one, but because we do not believe in the kind of free will that it seems to require. Perhaps we believe that, to deserve to suffer for what we do, we would have to be responsible for our own characters, in a way that seems to us to make no sense.

If that is why we reject retribution, this analogy may still, in a somewhat curious way, tell against the Person-affecting Claim. We believe that, in one sense, retribution could have been good, even when it is good for no one. Or rather, what makes this impossible is not the truth of the Person-affecting Claim, but the incoherence of the required kind of free will. We might imagine coming to believe that this kind of freedom is not incoherent. We may agree that, in that case, we could not reject retribution *merely* by claiming that it is good for no one. If that objection would not be sufficient, why should it be sufficient as an objection to Egalitarianism?

Fully to assess the Person-affecting Claim, we would need to discuss meta-ethics, or the nature of morality and moral reasoning. Since I cannot do that here, I shall merely express an opinion.[57] The Person-affecting Claim has, I think, less force than, and cannot be used to strengthen, the Levelling Down Objection.

XIII

I shall now summarize what I have claimed.

I began by discussing the view that it is in itself bad, or unfair, if some people are worse off than others through no fault or choice of theirs. This, the Telic Egalitarian view, can seem very plausible. But it faces the Levelling Down Objection. This objection seems to me to have great force, but is not, I think, decisive.

Suppose we began by being Telic Egalitarians, but are convinced by this objection. Suppose that we cannot believe that, if inequality were removed in a way that is bad for some people, and better for no one, that change would be in any way good. If we are to salvage something of our view, we then have two alternatives.

We might become Deontic Egalitarians. We might believe that, though we should sometimes aim for equality, that is not because we would thereby make the outcome better. We must then explain our view in some other way. And the resulting view may have a narrower scope. For example, it may apply only to goods of certain kinds, such as those that are co-operatively produced, and it may apply only to inequality between certain people, such as members of the same community.

We may also have to abandon some of our beliefs. Reconsider the Divided World:

(1) Half at 100   Half at 200

(2) Everyone at 145

On the Deontic View, we cannot claim that it would be better if the situation changed from (1) to (2). Our view is only about what people ought to do, and makes no comparisons between states of affairs.

Our alternative is to move to the Priority View. We could then keep our view about the Divided World. It is true that, in a change from (1) to (2), the better off would lose more than the worse off would gain. That is why, in utilitarian terms, (2) is worse than (1). But, on the Priority View, though the better off would lose more, the gain to the worse off counts for more. Benefits to the worse off do more to make the outcome better. We could claim that this is why (1) is worse than (2).

The Priority View often coincides with the belief in equality. But, as I have suggested, they are quite different kinds of view. They can be attacked or defended in different ways. The same is true of Telic and Deontic views. So, in trying to decide what we believe, the first step is to draw these distinctions. Taxonomy, though unexciting, needs to be done. Until we have a clearer view of the alternatives, we cannot hope to decide which view is true, or is the best view.

Appendix: Rawls's view

How do the distinctions I have drawn apply to Rawls's theory?

Rawls's Difference Principle seems to be an extreme version of the Priority View: one which gives *absolute* priority to benefiting those who are worse off. There are, however, three qualifications. We should apply the Difference Principle (1) only to the basic structure of society, (2) only in conjunction with Rawls's other principles, which require equal liberty and equality of opportunity, and (3) we do not apply this principle to individuals, but only to the representative member of the worst-off group.

Instead of claiming that the worst-off group should be as well off as possible, Rawls states his view in a less direct way. He makes claims about when inequality is unjust. On his view, whether some pattern of inequality is unjust depends on its effects upon the worst-off group. What these effects are depends on what alternatives were possible. Let us say that inequality *harms* the worst-off group when it is true that, without this inequality, this group could have been better off. Inequality *benefits* this group when it is true that, in every possible alternative without this inequality, they would have been even worse off.

Rawls often claims

(A) Inequality is not unjust if it benefits the worst-off group.

Egalitarians might accept this claim. They might say, 'Even in such cases, inequality is bad. But it is not unjust. Such inequality is, all things considered, justified by the fact that it benefits the worst off.' They might add that this inequality is, in a way, naturally unfair. It would then be a case of what Barry calls justified unfairness.

Rawls's arguments do not suggest that such inequality is, in itself, bad. He seems to accept claim (A) in the spirit of the Priority View. On his Difference Principle, since we should give absolute priority to the worst-off group, if inequality benefits this group, it is straightforwardly morally required. There is no moral balancing to be done – no intrinsic badness needing to be outweighed.

Rawls just as often claims

(B) Inequality is unjust if it harms the worst-off group.

Egalitarians might make this claim. But, here again, it could be fully explained on the absolute version of the Priority View. On this view, if the worst-off group could have been made better off, this is what should have been done. What is unjust is that the required priority has not been given to these people.

I have suggested that Rawls's view could be regarded as one version of the Priority View. What would show that it *cannot* be so regarded?

That might be shown by Rawls's answer to a further question. On his view, inequality is *not* unjust if it benefits the worst-off group, and it *is* unjust if it harms this group. What if inequality neither benefits nor harms this group? Would it then be unjust?

Suppose that, in some case, the only possible alternatives are these:

(1) Everyone at some level

(2) Some at this level   Others better off

If we choose (2), there would be inequality, and this would not benefit those who are worst-off. But there is no way in which the gains to the better off could be shared by both groups. The benefits to the better off are, for some reason, not transferable. Since that is so, though the inequality in (2) would not benefit the worst-off group, it would not be worse for them.

In such cases, on the Priority View, we *must* favour (2). The benefits to the better off are unequivocally good. The fact that they increase inequality is, for us, of no concern. But, if we are Egalitarians, we might oppose (2). We might claim that the inequality in (2) is bad, or unjust.

Would Rawls agree? If he would, this *would* show that he does not hold a version of the Priority View.

It is clear that, on Rawls's view, inequality is not unjust *if* it benefits the worst-off group. Does he mean 'if and only if'? Is inequality unjust if it does *not* benefit this group?

The answer may seem to be Yes. Rawls's Second Principle merely reads 'Social and economic inequalities are to be arranged so that they are . . . to the greatest benefit of the least advantaged'. This is compatible with either answer. But his General Conception reads, 'All social primary goods . . . are to be distributed equally unless an unequal distribution . . . is to the advantage of the least favored.' Similarly, Rawls writes, 'Injustice, then, is simply inequalities that are not to the benefit of all.' And he often makes such claims.[58] This suggests that he accepts

(C) Inequality is unjust, unless it benefits the worst-off group.

But Rawls may not intend (C). When he makes these claims, he may be assuming that the levels of the different groups are what he calls *close-knit*. This is true when any change in the level of one group would change the levels of the other groups.[59] When levels are close-knit, if inequality does *not* benefit the worst-off group, it must *harm* that group. In such cases, (C) coincides with

(D) Inequality is unjust only if it harms the worst-off group.

In the passages to which I have referred, this may be all that Rawls means.

In one section of his book, Rawls directly addresses my question. He considers a case in which the alternatives are these:

(1) Two people are both at some level

(2) One is at this level   The other is better off

On Rawls's Difference Principle, which of these outcomes should we choose?

Rawls gives three answers. The Difference Principle, he writes, 'is a strongly egalitarian conception in the sense that unless there is a distribution that makes both persons better off ... an equal distribution is to be preferred'. (76) On this first answer, outcome (2) is *worse* than outcome (1). This remark *does* commit Rawls to a version of claim (C). It tells us to avoid inequality unless it benefits those who are worst-off.

Rawls's second answer is implied by the indifference map with which he illustrates this case (Figure 5.1):[60]

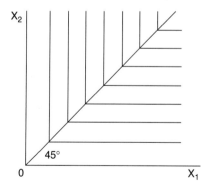

Figure 5.1

This shows (2) to be *as good as* (1). On this map, (1) would be some point on the 45-degree diagonal, and (2) would be on the horizontal line passing through this point. Since this is an *indifference* map, all points on this line are equally good. As Rawls writes, 'No matter how much either person's situation is improved, there is no gain from the standpoint of the difference principle unless the other gains also'. No *gain* from the standpoint of this principle; but also, as the indifference map implies, no *loss*. Later in this section, however, Rawls writes, 'the difference principle is compatible with the principle of efficiency'. (79) This implies that (2) is *better* than (1). Compared with (1), (2) is better for someone, and worse for no one.

Given the further assumptions that Rawls makes, and the use to which he puts his principles, this inconsistency is not in practice damaging. But, for the purposes of theory, it is worth asking which of these three answers is Rawls's true view. If he accepts the first or second answer, he cannot hold a version of the Priority View. And this would affect the arguments that could be given for or against his view.

I believe that the third answer, though less often supported in his text, is Rawls's true view. He would accept, not (C), but (D). On his view, inequality is unjust only if it worsens the position of those who are worse off. That is what is implied by the Lexical version of his Difference Principle. On that principle, if we cannot make other groups better off, we should, if we can, make the *best*-off group even better off. We should, that is, *increase* inequality, in a way that does not benefit any of the people who are worse off.

More important, this is the view to which we are led by Rawls's main arguments. From the standpoint of the Original Position, we would clearly favour giving benefits to the better off, when this would not worsen the position of those who are worse off. For all we know, we might *be* the people who are better off. On Rawls's assumptions, we would not limit the gains to ourselves if we *were* in this position for the sake of limiting other people's gains if we were not. Describing the motivation of his parties, Rawls writes: 'Nor do they try to gain relative to one another . . . They strive for as high an absolute score as possible. They do not wish a high or a low score for their opponents, nor do they seek to maximize or minimize the difference between their successes and those of others.' (144)

As these last remarks suggest, Rawls's view is not merely compatible with the Priority View. Given his main argument, it *must* be, in its content, a version of this view, since it must be concerned with absolute not relative levels. On the Difference Principle, we should make the worst-off group as well off as possible. It is quite irrelevant whether, in so doing, we reduce or increase inequality. This means that, on my definition, Rawls is at most a Non-Relational Egalitarian.

Rawls's view is not, however, *merely* a version of the Priority View. If it were, it would be implausibly extreme. If we are not egalitarians, and are not concerned with whether some people are worse off *than others*, it is hard to see why we should give *absolute* priority to benefiting people who are worse off. And that view seems too extreme even when, as in Rawls's case, it applies only to the basic structure of society, and only to the representative member of the worst-off group. If we are not concerned with relative levels, why should the smallest benefit to the representative worst-off person count for infinitely more than much greater benefits to other representative people?

To explain this feature of Rawls's view, we should, I believe, reintroduce the moral importance of equality. An objection to natural inequality is, I have suggested, one of the foundations of Rawls's theory. And Rawls himself claims that, in an account of justice, equal division is the natural first step, and provides the benchmark by reference to which we can defend our final principles.

As Barry notes, this suggests a different way to defend Rawls's Difference Principle.[61] First we argue for equality, by appealing to the arbitrariness of the natural lottery. Then we allow departures from equality provided that these are not worse for those who are worst off. This explains why, in Rawls's phrase, the worst-off have the *veto*, so that benefits to them should have absolute priority.

Notes

1 This article owes much to the ideas of Brian Barry, David Brink, Jerry Cohen, Ronald Dworkin, James Griffin, Shelly Kagan, Dennis McKerlie, David Miller, Thomas Nagel, Richard Norman, Robert Nozick, Ingmar Persson, Janet Radcliffe Richards, Joseph Raz, Thomas Scanlon, and Larry Temkin.

2 Thomas Nagel, *Mortal Questions* (Cambridge: Cambridge University Press, 1979), pp. 123–4 [pp. 75–6 in this volume]. See also Nagel's *Equality and Partiality* (New York: Oxford University Press, 1991).

3 Robert Nozick, *Anarchy, State, and Utopia* (New York: Basic Books, 1974), pp. 149–50.

4 Since acts may differ morally from omissions, we can also assume that each of the possible outcomes would result from the same kind of act. And, since it may make a difference whether any outcome would be a continuation of the status quo, we should assume that this would not be so.

5 For two such broader accounts of well-being, see Amartya Sen, 'Capability and Well-Being', and Thomas Scanlon, 'Value, Desire, and the Quality of Life', both in *The Quality of Life*, edited by Martha Nussbaum and Amartya Sen (Oxford, Oxford University Press, 1993), and Amartya Sen, *Inequality Reexamined* (Oxford: Oxford University Press, 1992), ch. 3.

6 See Sen, *Inequality Reexamined*, ch. 1.

7 On these definitions, we are Egalitarians if, in any area, we believe we should aim for equality. If we had that belief in only some small area, we would not naturally be called 'Egalitarians'. In that respect my definitions are misleading.

8 We might add, 'through no fault or choice of theirs'.

9 They are well discussed in Larry Temkin's *Inequality* (New York: Oxford University Press, 1993).

10 *Mortal Questions*, op. cit., p. 10. Cf. David Miller, 'Arguments for Equality', *Midwest Studies in Philosophy*, vol. VII (Minneapolis: University of Minnesota Press, 1982).

11 There are other some other possibilities. As Kagan and Brink suggest, equality might be intrinsically good, neither by itself, nor because of its effects, but because it was an essential part of some larger good. Cf. Miller, 'Arguments for Equality', op. cit.

12 Cf. Joel Feinberg, 'Noncomparative Justice', *Philosophical Review*, vol. 83 (July 1974).

13 Cf. Philip Montague, 'Comparative and Non-comparative Justice', *Philosophical Quarterly*, vol. 30 (April 1980).

14 See Robert Goodin, 'Egalitarianism, Fetishistic and Otherwise', *Ethics*, vol. 98 (October 1987), and 'Epiphenomenal Egalitarianism', *Social Research*, vol. 52 (Spring 1985).

15 Cf. the distinctions drawn in Lawrence Sager and Lewis Kornhauser, 'Just Lotteries', *Social Science Information* (Sage, London, Newbury Park and New Delhi, vol. 27, 1988).

16 John Rawls, *A Theory of Justice* (Cambridge, Mass.: Harvard University Press, 1971), p. 291.

17 There is now a complication. Those who take this second view do not merely think that such inequality is bad. They often speak of natural injustice. On their view, it is unjust or unfair that some people are born less able, or less healthy, than others. Similarly, it is unfair if nature bestows on some richer resources. Talk of unfairness here is sometimes claimed to make no sense. I believe that it does make sense. But, even on this view, our distinction stands. For Telic Egalitarians, it is the state of affairs which is bad, or unjust; but Deontic Egalitarians are concerned only with what we ought to do.

18 *A Theory of Justice*, op. cit., p. 102.

19 They include environmental or circumstantial luck. Cf. Brian Barry, *Theories of Justice* (London: Harvester, 1989), p. 239.

Equality or Priority? 123

20 Some object that it cannot be luck that we have the genes we do, since we could not have had other genes. But this use of 'luck' does not imply that things could have been otherwise. Something is 'luck', in this sense, if it is not something for which we ourselves are responsible. (Cf. Thomas Nagel, 'Moral Luck', *Mortal Questions* (Cambridge: Cambridge University Press, 1979).

21 Cf. G. A. Cohen, 'On the Currency of Egalitarian Justice', *Ethics*, vol. 99, 1989, and R. Arneson, 'Equality and Equality of Opportunity for Welfare', *Philosophical Studies*, vol. 56, 1989.

22 Cf. Nozick, *Anarchy, State, and Utopia*, op. cit., p. 216, and Nagel, *Mortal Questions*, op. cit., p. 119 [p. 71 in this volume].

23 See, for example, David Gauthier, *Morals by Agreement* (Oxford: Oxford University Press, 1980), pp. 18 and 268.

24 Gauthier, op. cit., p. 220.

25 Cf. Nagel, *Equality and Partiality*, op. cit., pp. 99–102, and Thomas Pogge's discussion of Nozick, in his *Realizing Rawls* (Ithaca: Cornell University Press, 1989), ch. 1.

26 Cf. Nozick, *Anarchy, State, and Utopia*, op. cit., p. 206 (though Nozick's target here is not the Principle of Equality but Rawls's Difference Principle).

27 Such an objection is suggested, for example, in Joseph Raz, *The Morality of Freedom* (Oxford: Oxford University Press, 1986), ch. 9, and Larry Temkin, *Inequality*, op. cit., pp. 247–8.

28 Nagel, *Mortal Questions*, op. cit., p. 124 [pp. 75–6 in this volume].

29 Cf. H. Frankfurt, *The Importance of What We Care About* (Cambridge: Cambridge University Press, 1988), ch. 11, and Joseph Raz, *The Morality of Freedom*, op. cit., ch. 9.

30 Several other writers have suggested such a view. See, for example, Thomas Scanlon, 'Nozick on Rights, Liberty, and Property', *Philosophy & Public Affairs*, vol. 6, no. 1, Fall 1976, pp. 6–10, Joseph Raz, *The Morality of Freedom*, op. cit., Harry Frankfurt, 'Equality as a Moral Ideal', in *The Importance of What We Care About*, op. cit., David Wiggins, 'Claims of Need', in his *Needs, Values, Truth* (Oxford: Blackwell, 1987), Dennis McKerlie, 'Egalitarianism', *Dialogue*, vol. 23 (1984), and 'Equality and Priority', *Utilitas*, vol. 6 (1994).

31 Cf. Frankfurt, The Importance of What We Care About, op. cit., p. 149.

32 Nagel, *Mortal Questions*, op. cit., p. 111 [p. 64 in this volume]. I have claimed elsewhere that, on what I take to be the truth about personal identity, there is an argument for taking these units to be people at particular times, and that, on that view, our distributive principles move us towards Negative Utilitarianism. (*Reasons and Persons*, Oxford: Oxford University Press, 1984, Section 117; and 'Comments', *Ethics*, July 1986, pp. 869–72.)

33 *Mortal Questions*, op. cit., pp. 117 and 121 [pp. 69 and 73 in this volume].

34 Ibid., p. 121 [p. 73 in this volume].

35 Raz puts the difference well. He writes:

what makes us care about various inequalities is not the inequality but the concern identified by the underlying principle. It is the hunger of the hungry, the need of the needy, the suffering of the ill, and so on. The fact that they are worse off in the relevant respect than their neighours is relevant. But it is relevant not as an independent evil of inequality. Its relevance is in showing that their hunger is greater, their need more pressing, their suffering more hurtful, and therefore our concern for the hungry, the needy, the suffering, and not our concern for equality, makes us give them priority. (*The Morality of Freedom*, op. cit., p. 240.)

When we are comparing benefits to different people, it is easy to confuse concern with relative and absolute levels. On the Priority View, if one of two people is worse off, benefits to this person matter more. They matter more, as I have said, because this person is at a lower absolute level. But in calling this a *lower* level, I cannot help describing the *relation* between these levels. (This is why I sometimes say: benefits to people matter more the worse off *these people* are.)

36 We might go even further. In some Utilitarian arguments, equality plays an essential causal role. It really is a means, because it has various good effects. But, in the argument that appeals to diminishing marginal utility, this may not be so. Suppose that, as Utilitarians, we set out to redistribute resources whenever this would increase the sum of benefits. We might not even notice that, if we carry this process to its limit, equality of resources will be the result. And, even when we do notice this, we may regard equality, not as a means, but as a by-product. If we decide to aim for equality, this may be like aiming at a target merely to ensure that our arrow passes through some point en route.

37 See, for example, Amartya Sen, *On Economic Inequality* (Oxford: Oxford University Press, 1973), pp. 15–23. Sen has argued that this may be true of those who are crippled. While this would seldom be true of those with physical disabilities, it seems plausible for those who have certain kinds of mental illness, or impairment. If such people gain less from each unit of resources, utilitarians must claim that they should get *fewer* resources. On Sen's proposed *Weak Equity Axiom*, they should either get more, or at least no fewer.

38 *Reading Nozick*, edited by Jeffrey Paul (Blackwell, 1981), p. 203.

39 *Mortal Questions*, op. cit., p. 124 [p. 75 in this volume].

40 Similar remarks apply to section 117 of my *Reasons and Persons* (Oxford: Oxford University Press, 1984). Nagel returns to the choices between these views in his later *Equality and Partiality*, op. cit., chs 7 and 8.

41 'What is Equality? Part 1: Equality of Welfare', *Philosophy & Public Affairs*, vol. 10, no. 3, Summer 1981, p. 219.

42 Cf. Frankfurt, op. cit., pp. 147–8. It may of course be unfair if these people were cheated of such chances, while others had them. I am not claiming that Dworkin's claim can be fully phrased in terms of priority. But equality is not the only issue, or, it seems, the most important.

43 D. D. Raphael, *Justice and Liberty* (London: Athlone Press, 1980), p. 10. Cf. p. 49.

44 Richard Norman, *Free and Equal* (Oxford: Oxford University Press), p. 80.

45 See, however, the excellent discussion in David Miller, 'Social Justice and the Principle of Need', in *The Frontiers of Political Theory*, ed. Michael

Freeman and David Robertson (Brighton: Harvester Press, 1980).
46 Cohen, 'On the Currency of Egalitarian Justice', op. cit., p. 916.
47 Christopher Ake, 'Justice as Equality', *Philosophy & Public Affairs*, Fall 1975, pp. 71 and 77.
48 See, for example, Robert Young, 'Envy and Inequality', *Journal of Philosophy*, November 1992. (But Young may only be claiming that, in the terms I introduce below, there are no Strong Egalitarians.)
49 Ake, 'Justice as Equality', op. cit., p. 73.
50 *Inequality*, p. 282.
51 See for example Amartya Sen, *Inequality Reexamined*, op. cit., pp. 92–3.
52 For a contrary view, which would need a further discussion, see John Broome, *Weighing Goods* (Oxford: Blackwell, 1991), ch. 9.
53 See, for example, Antony Flew, *The Politics of Procrustes* (Buffalo, NY: Prometheus, 1981), p. 26; McKerlie, 'Egalitarianism', op. cit., p. 232, See also Nozick, op. cit., p. 211.
54 Shelly Kagan has suggested a possible counter-example: one in which a very few people became much better off than everyone else. The gain in utility would here be very small, and, on certain views, the loss of equality would be great. On Temkin's account, that would be true of views which take the badness of inequality to depend on how much worse off people are than the best-off person. On other views, however, which I find more plausible, the loss of equality would not be great. That would be true of views which appeal to how much worse off people are than the average person, or than everyone who is better off than them.
55 Such as the view advanced in Thomas Scanlon's 'Contractualism and Utilitarianism', in ed. Amartya Sen and Bernard Williams, *Utilitarianism and Beyond* (Cambridge: Cambridge University Press, 1982).
56 Temkin, *Inequality*, op. cit., ch. 9.
57 Another objection to the Person-affecting View comes from what I have called the *Non-Identity Problem* (in my *Reasons and Persons*, op. cit.), ch. 16.
58 Cf. 'The inequality in expectation is permissible only if lowering it would make the working class even . . . worse off.' (78) 'No one is to benefit from these contingencies except in ways that redound to the well-being of others.' (100) 'Those who have been favoured by nature . . . may gain from their good fortune only on terms that improve the situation of those who have lost out.' (101) 'the more fortunate are to benefit only in ways that help those who have lost out.' (179) 'Inequalities are permissible when they maximize, or at least contribute to, the long-term expectations of the least fortunate group in society.' (151)
59 As Rawls writes: 'it is impossible to raise or lower the expectation of any representative man without raising or lowering the expectation of every other representative man'. (80) Though he knows that this is not always true, and he claims that his principles apply even when it is not true, he writes, at one point, 'close-knitness is assumed in order to simplify the statement of the Difference Principle.' Perhaps it was assumed in all of the passages quoted above.
60 *Rawls, A Theory of Justice*, Figure 5 on p. 76.
61 See Barry, *Theories of Justice*, op. cit., ch. VI.

6
Equality, Priority, and the Levelling Down Objection*

Larry Temkin

I. Introduction

This essay aims to clarify a number of issues regarding egalitarianism. These include the relation between equality and priority, and whether one should be a *non-instrumental* egalitarian or 'merely' an *instrumental* egalitarian. However, this essay's principal aim is to address the *Levelling Down Objection* or, more accurately, the key premise or view that I believe underlies the Levelling Down Objection.

The Levelling Down Objection is, perhaps, the most prevalent and powerful anti-egalitarian argument, and it underlies the thinking of most non-egalitarians as well as many who think of themselves as egalitarians. I claim that at the heart of the Levelling Down Objection is a person-affecting view that I call the *Slogan*. The Slogan has enormous appeal, but I argue that there is reason to doubt the Slogan and the arguments invoking it. Thus, both the Slogan

* This essay combines, summarizes, and revises material contained in chapter nine of *Inequality* (Oxford University Press, 1993), 'Harmful Goods, Harmless Bads' (in *Value, Welfare and Morality*, edited by R. G. Frey and Christopher Morris, Cambridge University Press, 1993, pp. 290–324), and section three of 'Weighing Goods: Some Questions and Comments' (*Philosophy & Public Affairs* 23, 1994, pp. 350–80). Over the years, many people have given me useful comments regarding this topic. My memory is too poor to properly acknowledge them all, but they include Tyler Cowen, Jonathan Dancy, James Griffin, Shelly Kagan, F. M. Kamm, Thomas Scanlon, Seana Shiffrin, and Andrew Williams. Special thanks are due to John Broome, Roger Crisp, Ingmar Persson, and, most of all, Derek Parfit. Finally, let me thank Thomas Nagel, whose comments on other work of mine, many years ago, first prompted my thinking about this topic.

and the Levelling Down Objection can be resisted. If I am right, the Levelling Down Objection is not the devastating objection many have thought it to be. Correspondingly, one need not reject or seriously revise egalitarianism because of the Levelling Down Objection.

The essay is divided into thirteen sections. In section II, I present and discuss a view, *prioritarianism*, that is often conflated with egalitarianism. I argue that prioritarianism is not concerned with equality *per se*, and hence that it is not plausible as a version of non-instrumental egalitarianism — though it is plausible as a version of instrumental egalitarianism. In section III, I present the Levelling Down Objection as a powerful objection to non-instrumental egalitarianism. I suggest that some may be attracted to prioritarianism as the most defensible kind of egalitarian position, since it avoids the Levelling Down Objection. Most importantly, I suggest that much of the Levelling Down Objection's force is derived from a person-affecting view I call the Slogan. In sections IV–X, I present and assess the Slogan. I begin by showing that the Slogan has widespread appeal, and illustrate many cases where it is implicitly invoked. I next note how the Slogan must be interpreted to support the strong conclusions for which it is used. I then show how the Slogan is challenged by Derek Parfit's Non-Identity Problem, and even more so by a principle of proportional justice. More generally, I point out that *any* impersonal moral principle – of which the principle of proportional justice is but one particularly appealing example – will conflict with a person-affecting position like the Slogan. Finally, I note that the Slogan asserts a connection between one's theory of the good regarding self-interest and one's theory of the good regarding outcomes, and consider whether any plausible theories of the good support such a connection. Canvassing the Mental State Theory, the Desire-Fulfillment Theory, and the Objective List Theory, I suggest that no plausible theory of the good supports the arguments and conclusions for which the Slogan has been invoked. In section XI, I respond to objections John Broome raises to my central example of proportional justice. In section XII, I present an argument of Ingmar Persson's, suggesting that prioritarianism and non-instrumental egalitarianism both express impersonal views, and hence that both have a common enemy in the person-affecting spirit of the Levelling Down Objection. If this is right, then one ought not to forsake non-instrumental egalitarianism in favor of prioritarianism because of the Levelling Down Objection. Finally, in section XIII, I consider whether I am really willing to reject the

Levelling Down Objection, and accept the implications of non-instrumental egalitarianism. I am. Though none of this essay's arguments depends on this answer.

II. Prioritarianism, instrumental egalitarianism, and non-instrumental egalitarianism

Many who think of themselves as egalitarians hold a view like the following one. They want each person to fare as well as she possibly can, but they are especially concerned with the worse-off.[1] This view tends to favor redistribution between the better- and worse-off, even if a loss in utility accompanies such redistribution. Naturally, how much loss in utility to the better-off would be compensated by lesser gains to the worse-off would depend upon how much greater weight, or priority, was attached to one's concern for the worse-off. In any event, on this view the worse off someone was the greater priority they would receive in our moral deliberations. This is only a rough statement of the view in question, but it is sufficient for my purposes. The key point to note is that, while on this view one has a special concern for the worse-off, one's ultimate goal is for each to fare as well as possible.

Since humanitarians are people who want to improve the lot of the worse-off (their principal concern being to relieve suffering), I once called such a view 'extended humanitarianism.' Derek Parfit has called such a view *The Priority View*, expressing the fact that the view's focus is on giving priority to the worse-off.[2] For simplicity, I shall refer to the view, inelegantly, as *prioritarianism*.

As a version of egalitarianism, prioritarianism faces many problems. For example, it is unable to account for the widely held view that lowering the best-off group to the level of the next best-off would clearly and unequivocally improve a situation's equality. Nor can it account for the widely held view that proportional increases in a population's levels would worsen inequality not improve it. So, for example, although many believe that a situation where some were at level 2000 and others at level 1000, would be better, *all things considered*, than one where some were at level 20 and others at level 10, it is hard to deny that from an egalitarian perspective the inequality is worse in the former situation – where there is a gap of 1000 between the better- and worse-off – than in the latter situation – where there is only a gap of 10. Additionally, prioritarianism cannot plausibly account for why some egalitarians

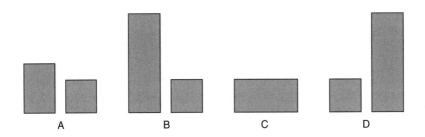

Diagram 1

feel guilt or shame about how they fare relative to others. After all, on prioritarianism, one would have reason to regret that the worse-off fare badly, and that neither he nor society is doing enough about their lot, but one's only regret about how *he* fares, should be that he is not even *better-off*, not that he fares well, while others fare worse.

Finally, consider Diagram 1, where the column heights represent how well off people are, and the widths represent the number of people in each group.

According to prioritarianism, there would be *no* reason for one to prefer A to B. In fact, there wouldn't even be reason – *any* reason – to prefer C to D.

As an egalitarian position, the problem with prioritarianism is clear. *It is not concerned with equality.* Equality describes a relation obtaining between people that is *essentially comparative*. People are more or less equal *relative to one another*. Prioritarianism is concerned with how people fare, but *not* with how they fare relative to each other.

Since many prioritarians think of themselves as egalitarians, it may be useful to distinguish between *instrumental* and *non-instrumental* egalitarianism. On instrumental egalitarianism, equality is extrinsically valuable – that is, valuable when it promotes some other valuable ideal. On non-instrumental egalitarianism, equality is intrinsically valuable – that is, valuable in itself, over and above the extent to which it promotes other ideals.

Non-instrumental egalitarians care about *equality*. More specifically, on my view, they care about *undeserved, nonvoluntary,* inequalities, which they regard as bad, or objectionable, because unfair. Thus, the non-instrumental egalitarian thinks it is bad, or objectionable, to *some* extent – because unfair – for some to be worse off than others through no fault or choice of their own. Importantly, non-instrumental egalitarians need not believe that equality is *all* that matters, or even the ideal that matters most. But they believe that equality is one ideal, among others, that has independent moral value.

To sum up. Prioritarianism is often conflated with egalitarianism. This is unfortunate. As we have seen, prioritarianism expresses a special concern, or priority, for the worse-off, but it is *not* concerned with how the worse-off fare *relative to others*. Thus, prioritarianism licenses vast *increases* in inequality, if necessary for improving – however slightly – the worse-off. Indeed, as seen, prioritarianism approves vast increases in the levels of the very best-off, as long as those increases don't come at the expense of the worse-off in terms of the extra priority their situation warrants. Of course, giving priority to the worse-off will generally promote equality, by favoring many transfers from better- to worse-off, as well as giving benefits to the worse-off rather than similar benefits to the better-off. Hence, prioritarianism *is* fairly plausible as an *instrumental* egalitarian position. However, in this respect prioritarianism is not unlike utilitarianism, which also frequently favors transfers from better- to worse-off, or benefiting the worse-off rather than the better-off, as a way of increasing utility. Still, neither prioritarianism nor utilitarianism is plausible as a non-instrumental egalitarian position. Neither values equality, *per se*.

III. Prioritarianism, the levelling down objection, and the Slogan

As a version of non-instrumental egalitarianism, prioritarianism is a non-starter. Nevertheless, I think I understand why many who think of themselves as egalitarians are drawn to it. People are drawn to prioritarianism not necessarily as a position expressing what the egalitarian *does* care about, but rather as a position expressing what one *should* care about. Besides giving direct expression to a powerful concern for those worse-off, it may seem the reflective egalitarian is forced to prioritarianism, i.e. that it is the closest thing to an egalitarian position one can plausibly adopt. The gist of this view is *not* that prioritarianism is a plausible version of non-instrumental egalitarianism, but rather that non-instrumental egalitarianism is implausible. Hence, if one generally favors transfers from better- to

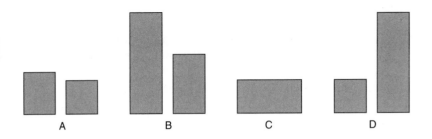

Diagram 2

worse-off – as people who think of themselves as egalitarians do – one should be a prioritarian *instead* of a non-instrumental egalitarian.

Many are attracted to the foregoing by the *Levelling Down Objection.* Diagram 2 helps illustrate this objection.

Suppose we could transform A into B. Many find it hard to believe there could be *any* reason not to do this. In B, *everybody* is better off than they were in A. In fact, B's worse-off have even better lives than A's better-off. True, there is greater inequality in B than A. But so what? Doesn't that just show we shouldn't attach weight to equality *per se*? After all, one might wonder, how *could* B's inequality be bad, *when there is no one for whom it is worse*?

Or consider C and D, and imagine that D is a world where half are blind, C a world where all are. One *could* always transform D into C by putting out the eyes of the sighted. However, many find the view that this would improve the situation in even one respect *more* than incomprehensible, they find it abominable. That C is more equal than D gives one *no reason at all*, they think, to transform D into C; and only a hardened misanthrope, or someone motivated by the basest form of envy, could think otherwise. After all, they ask, how *could* C's greater equality make it better in *any* respect, if there is *no one* for whom it *is* better?[3, 4]

It is clear why considerations such as the preceding have been dubbed 'the Levelling Down Objection.' Non-instrumental egalitarianism attaches value to equality *itself*. So non-instrumental egalitarianism would support transforming B into A, and D into C, by 'levelling down' the relevant groups. But such moves benefit *no one*, not even the worse-off. Indeed, the move from B to A would significantly *harm* the worse-off. In such cases, many think, surely there is *nothing* to be said in favor of promoting greater equality.

Greater equality is only desirable when it *benefits* the worse-off, not when it results from levelling down the better-off! Hence, the Levelling Down Objection concludes, equality is only extrinsically valuable, not intrinsically valuable. Non-instrumental egalitarianism should be rejected.

Such considerations have tremendous force, and I believe they underlie the thinking of most non-egalitarians. Correspondingly, one can see how the Levelling Down Objection might drive someone who cares about the worse-off, and who favors redistribution where it (sufficiently) benefits the worse-off, from non-instrumental egalitarianism towards prioritarianism.[5]

I believe that prioritarianism is a plausible position in its own right. Hence I believe there is reason to be a prioritarian. I also believe the preceding considerations are extremely plausible. But they are not, in the end, compelling. They do not force the non-instrumental egalitarian to abandon her view in favor of prioritarianism. If one decides to adopt prioritarianism and abandon non-instrumental egalitarianism, it should be for reasons other than those presented above.

At the heart of the Levelling Down Objection is a position I refer to as

> *The Slogan*: One situation *cannot* be worse (or better) than another if there is *no one* for whom it *is* worse (or better).

Derek Parfit refers to such a position as the *Person-affecting Claim*.[6] The Person-affecting Claim expresses the view that outcomes should be assessed solely in terms of the way the sentient beings in those outcomes are *affected* for better or worse. A change makes an outcome better insofar as sentient beings are affected positively (benefited), worse insofar as sentient beings are affected negatively (harmed). Referring to the position in question as 'the Slogan' has several advantages, and I shall continue to do so in this essay. However, as we will see later, it is important to both recognize, and emphasize, the person-affecting spirit of the position.

I believe it is the Slogan that gives the Levelling Down Objection much of its powerful rhetorical force. Indeed, if one rejects the Slogan, there seems to be little principled basis for rejecting the non-instrumental egalitarian's (modest?) claim that undeserved inequality is unfair, that unfairness is bad, and hence that there is at least *one* respect in which outcomes like B and D, in Diagram 2, are worse than A and C. But the Slogan can, and should, be challenged. In the next seven sections, I shall mount such a challenge. In doing this it will be useful, and illuminating, to interpret and criticize the Slogan in its own terms. In particular, I want to assess the Slogan and its implications in a much wider context than simply its role in challenging non-instrumental egalitarianism. This will allow us to see the Slogan's shortcomings more clearly, and enable us to evade the charge of attacking the Slogan, or begging the question against it, simply in order to preserve non-instrumental egalitarianism. Of course, in this essay, my primary interest in the Slogan concerns its implications for prioritarianism, non-instrumental egalitarianism, and the Levelling Down Objection. But as we shall see, I think the Slogan has far-reaching implications which should be questioned whatever one's views about non-instrumental egalitarianism.

Let me turn now to a direct consideration of the Slogan itself.

IV. Cases implicitly invoking the Slogan

Like certain other slogans – for example, each person is deserving of equal consideration and respect – the Slogan enjoys widespread acceptance. It underlies many arguments in philosophy and economics, and those appealing to it span a wide range of theoretical positions. In addition, most believe the Slogan expresses a deep and important truth. So, like a powerful modern-day Ockham's razor, often the Slogan is wielded to carve out, shape, or whittle down the domain of moral value.

Unfortunately, the Slogan is almost always invoked both implicitly and rhetorically. Perhaps it has been thought an ultimate moral principle – providing justification for *other* claims, but not *itself* needing, or capable of, justification. More likely, the Slogan has been thought too obvious to need explicit acknowledgment or defense. 'After all,' one might rhetorically ask, 'how *could* one situation be worse than another if there is *no one* for whom it *is* worse?'

I believe the Slogan should be rejected, and that in any event the Slogan does not support most of the particular positions it has been thought to support. I also believe that careful reflection about the Slogan requires us to get much clearer than we previously have about different theories of the good. Before defending these claims, let me begin by offering a sample of the many cases, besides the Levelling Down Objection, where the Slogan is seemingly invoked.

(1) A situation is *Pareto optimal* if no one's lot could be improved without worsening the lot of someone else. Economists think non-Pareto optimal situations are inefficient. Many, in fact, think that whenever we could improve the lot of some, without worsening the lot of anyone else, it would be irrational, and wrong, not to do so. This position derives much of its force from the Slogan. After all, if a non-Pareto optimal situation *could* be better than a (more) Pareto optimal one, though there was no one for whom it was better, it need not be either irrational or wrong to fail to transform the former into the latter.

(2) The Slogan also explains why some find Rawls's Difference Principle (DP) more plausible than egalitarianism, and others find it too egalitarian to be plausible. When DP allows vast gains for the better-off to promote tiny gains for the worse-off, it is often defended by invoking the Slogan. Likewise, DP is criticized via the Slogan for failing to permit gains to the better-off that are not accompanied by gains to the worse-off.[7]

(3) Though the point of Nozick's Wilt Chamberlain example is that liberty upsets patterns, much of its force seems derived from the Slogan. Thus, Nozick writes:

> Each of these persons *chose* to give twenty-five cents of their money to Chamberlain. They could have spent it on going to the movies, or candy bars.... Can anyone else complain on grounds of justice?.... After someone transfers something to Wilt Chamberlain, third parties *still* have their legitimate shares; *their* shares have not changed.[8]

Again, the implication seems to be that if no one is worsened by the exchange, it cannot be bad.[9]

(4) Locke's theory of acquisition holds that people have a property right to any unowned thing they mix their labor with 'at least where there is enough and as good left in common for others'.[10] Nozick writes of this position that 'the crucial point is whether appropriation of an unowned object worsens the situation of others'.[11] It seems the implication is that as long as there is no one for whom acquiring the property is worse, it cannot be bad.

(5) Consider Diagram 3.

In discussing such a diagram, Derek Parfit wrote:

> Let us compare A with A+. The only difference is that A+ contains an extra group, who have lives worth living, and who affect

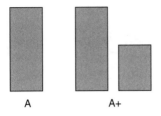

A   A+

Diagram 3

no one else... it seems [hard]... to believe that A+ is *worse* than A. This implies that it would have been better if the extra group had never existed. If their lives are worth living, and they affect no one else, why is it bad that these people are alive?[12]

Here, too, the Slogan seems to support Parfit's position, for the question is, 'how could A+ be worse than A when there is no one for whom it is worse?'[13]

(6) In 'Rights, Goals, and Fairness' Thomas Scanlon observes: 'rights... need to be justified somehow, and how other than by appeal to the human interests their recognition promotes and protects? This seems to be the uncontrovertible insight of the classical utilitarians.'[14] Many extend Scanlon's view to argue against the intrinsic value of respecting rights. Thus, it is contended that since the whole point of a system of rights is (must be?) to promote and protect human, or sentient, interests, there is no reason to respect apparent rights in those cases where doing so fails to promote or protect anyone's interests. Analogously, many claim there is nothing intrinsically bad about violating apparent rights when this benefits some and harms no one. These claims derive much of their force from the Slogan, according to which a situation where rights are violated (or respected) *cannot* be worse (or better) than one where they are not, if there is *no one* for whom it *is* worse (or better).

(7) Finally, we may note that standard objections to rule-utilitarianism, virtue-based, and deontological theories often parallel those noted against equality and rights-based theories. That is, they involve constructing cases where no one benefits and some are harmed, or where some benefit and no one is harmed, if only one does or doesn't (a) follow the rule, (b) act virtuously, or (c) do

one's duty in these theories' terms.[15] Once more, much of the force of these objections seems to rest on the Slogan's appeal.

These are merely some of the positions, besides the Levelling Down Objection, implicitly involving the Slogan. The list is by no means exhaustive. As we shall see, one should be wary of any appeals to the Slogan. Hence, one must seek other justifications for the positions one finds plausible.

V. Interpreting the Slogan

The Slogan is ambiguous. In this essay, I shall interpret the Slogan as shorthand for the following claim:

> One situation *cannot* be worse (or better) than another *in any respect* if there is *no one* for whom it *is* worse (or better) *in any respect*.

This interpretation makes plain the Slogan's full force. It isn't merely that one situation *is* never worse than another if there is no one for whom it is worse – as if this might be true in some respects, but not 'all things considered'. Rather, it is that one situation *cannot* be worse than another if there is no one for whom it is worse – as if there is *no* respect in which this might be so, and hence no *question* that in some cases the positive features might outweigh the negative ones.

It is this strong position that explains people's confident rhetorical uses of the Slogan. Moreover, while weaker interpretations of the Slogan are possible, they are less interesting and would not license many conclusions for which the Slogan has been invoked. In particular, the non-egalitarian who insists that, in a world where half are sighted and half are blind, there is *no reason at all* to put out the eyes of the sighted implicitly relies on a position like the foregoing to rule out non-instrumental egalitarianism. The claim is not merely that the all-blind world is worse than the half-blind world, *all things considered*, as if the value of equality in the all-blind world is outweighed by the greater disvalue of blinding the sighted. Rather, the claim is that since there is no respect in which blinding the sighted is better for anyone – by hypothesis it isn't better for either the sighted or the blind – there is *no* respect in which the situation is better. *A fortiori*, the greater equality in the all-blind situation does not make that situation in *any* way *better*.

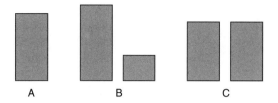

A   B   C

Diagram 4

Hence, equality has *no* intrinsic value, and non-instrumental egalitarianism must be rejected.

VI. Challenging the Slogan, Part One: the Non-Identity Problem

The Slogan has great force and appeal. Nevertheless, it must be rejected or limited in scope. To see this, consider a variation of Derek Parfit's *Non-Identity Problem*, illustrated with the aid of Diagram 4.[16]

Let A represent a generation contemplating two policies. On the *live for today* policy they have children immediately and deplete natural resources for current use. B would result; *they* would be better off, but their children would fare less well. On the *take care of tomorrow* policy they postpone having children a few years and conserve resources. C would result; *they* would fare slightly less well than they do now, but the children they have would fare as well as they.

Most believe the 'take care of tomorrow' policy should be adopted. But this judgment cannot be accounted for given the Slogan. This follows from two plausible positions defended by Parfit: (*P*) the children born in C would be *different people* than the children born in B (being conceived later, they would come from different sperm and ova, or, as some might think relevant, be raised by older and wiser parents, and so on), and (*Q*) one cannot harm or act against the interests of someone who will never exist and, more particularly, one does not harm someone by failing to conceive her. Given P and Q, there is *no one* the 'live for today' policy affects for the worse: not the parents, who fare better in B than in either A or C; not the children in B, because *they* wouldn't exist if the 'take care of tomorrow' policy was adopted; and not the children in C, because they don't exist and never will exist if the 'live for today'

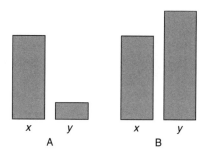

Diagram 5

policy is adopted. On the other hand, if the 'take care of tomorrow' policy is adopted there *will* be someone adversely affected, namely the parents. According to the Slogan, then, the 'live for today' policy *cannot* be worse than the 'take care of tomorrow' policy, since there is *no one* for whom it is worse. But this is surely wrong. The 'live for today' policy *is* worse than the 'take care of tomorrow' policy.[17] Thus, the Slogan must be rejected or limited in scope.

Many find the Non-Identity Problem puzzling. Most, at least initially, try to undermine it. Some question assumption *P*, others *Q*. I shall not discuss such views. They are surely mistaken.

More plausibly, some believe Parfit's argument does not substantially undermine the Slogan. They claim that what we learn from Parfit is that there is a limited and peculiar range of cases where the Slogan does not apply – in particular, it does not apply in the narrow range of cases where our choices determine who comes to be. Interestingly, Parfit himself may have contributed to this view – first, by placing his discussion of the Non-Identity Problem in a chapter on future generations, and second, by emphasizing that 'this problem arises because the identities of people in the further future can be very easily affected' and thus 'because, in the different outcomes, different people would be born'.[18]

VII. Challenging the Slogan, Part Two: saints, sinners, and proportional justice

Is the Slogan acceptable in all cases besides those where our decisions determine who comes to be? I think not. Consider Diagram 5, and the conception of *proportional justice* according to which there ought to be a proportion between doing well and faring well.

Let A and B represent alternative afterlives, with the x columns representing the saints' quality of lives, and the y columns the sinners'. Furthermore, assume A accurately reflects how the two groups 'should' fare according to proportional justice and their earthly lives. Clearly, in accordance with proportional justice, A would be better than B.

Is this implausible? Many, including Aristotle, Kant, and Ross, have thought not. Yet, according to the Slogan, not only would B be better than A, there would be *no* respect in which it was worse.

Most would find this hard to accept. They believe there would be *something* morally bad about the evillest mass murderers faring better than the most benign saints, even if there was *no one* for whom it was worse.[19]

These considerations suggest that unless one is willing to reject proportional justice entirely, and abandon the view that there is *some* respect in which B is worse than A, one must reject the Slogan. To the question 'how *could* one situation be worse than another if there is *no one* for whom it *is* worse?' one might respond, 'it could be worse if it were worse regarding proportional justice.' This would express the view that an outcome's being better or worse for people is *not* all that matters, proportional justice does too.

At this point one has several alternatives. First, one might retain the Slogan by simply rejecting the ideal of proportional justice. Second, one might accept that proportional justice has intrinsic, or objective, value, beyond the extent to which it is good or bad *for* people, and reject the Slogan. Third, one might further restrict the Slogan, claiming that it applies in all cases except where our decisions determine who comes to be or where proportional justice is involved. Or fourth, one might retain the Slogan by continuing to insist that injustice is always bad for someone independently of any other respects in which people are better or worse off.

I favor the second alternative. The principle of proportional justice is most naturally, and plausibly, interpreted as an *impersonal* principle. It assesses outcomes in terms of what people *deserve*, and not merely in terms of whether people are *affected* for better or worse (regardless of desert). Therefore, it is not surprising that the principle of proportional justice conflicts with a person-affecting position like the Slogan. More generally, as soon as one grants that some things are intrinsically, or objectively, valuable – or, alternatively, that some things have 'non-derivative' or 'ultimate' value –

beyond the way they affect beings for better or worse, one has carved out a role for impersonal principles in the assessment of outcomes. And, importantly, to accept the moral significance of impersonal principles is to reject the hegemonic person-affecting view of the Slogan.

Before going on, let me add that if one moves in the direction of the third or fourth alternatives noted above, one can no longer rhetorically appeal to the Slogan to undermine any particular ideals. If the third alternative is to avoid the charge of being *ad hoc* it requires defense. It needs to be *shown* that ideals that conflict with the Slogan are not further exceptions to it, and obviously one cannot appeal to the Slogan in doing this without simply begging the question against the ideals whose moral significance is at issue. Similarly, the fourth alternative saves the Slogan only by robbing it of its teeth. In particular, it is always open to the proponent of an ideal against which the Slogan has been invoked to insist that the ideal is objectively good for people. So, for example, the egalitarian might simply insist that, like injustice, inequality is always bad for someone independently of any other respects in which people are better or worse off.[20] Moreover, even when the Slogan's defender could plausibly argue against such claims, this still would not license rhetorical appeals to the Slogan against any particular ideal. As noted, such appeals beg the question in favor of the Slogan, as it remains possible that the Slogan should be rejected or further limited in scope.

VIII. Challenging the Slogan, Part Three: the Mental State Theory

The Slogan is most naturally interpreted as making a claim about what is relevant to a situation's being good. Correspondingly, to fully assess the Slogan and the arguments invoking it, it is necessary to consider whether any plausible theories of the good support them. I have attempted this task elsewhere,[21] and shall not repeat my efforts here. But let me note some of my results regarding three candidates that have been offered as theories of the good: the *Mental State Theory*, the *Desire-Fulfillment Theory*, and the *Objective List Theory*.

I begin with the Mental State Theory (MST) of the classical utilitarians. According to this theory, only conscious states have intrinsic value or disvalue, and everything else has value or disvalue only to the extent that it promotes positive or negative conscious states.

I believe MST represents a significant insight of the classical utilitarians. Indeed, it is arguable that *most* things only have value or disvalue in virtue of their effects on conscious states. Nevertheless, MST goes too far in claiming that *only* conscious states are intrinsically valuable. Such a position would undermine virtually *every* ideal. Specifically, on such a view there would be nothing intrinsically valuable about justice, equality, freedom, autonomy, virtue, duty, rights, and so on. Such factors would be valuable *only* to the extent that they promoted positive conscious states, to the extent they promoted negative conscious states they would be disvaluable.

Most agree that MST has serious shortcomings as a full theory of the good. But many would disagree on exactly where MST goes wrong. Though easily ignored, the source of this disagreement is important. To illustrate it, let us distinguish between theories of the good regarding self-interest and theories of the good regarding outcomes, where the former tell us what is good or bad *for* someone, the latter what makes an *outcome* good or bad. Unfortunately, the precise relationship between these is not evident, and failure to carefully distinguish them has been the source of much confusion, as well as, perhaps, the Slogan's appeal.

Some rejecting MST object to it as a theory about outcomes, though not as a theory about self-interest. They think it plausible that something can only be good or bad *for* someone insofar as it affects her conscious states, but deny that only conscious states are intrinsically good or bad. For example, advocates of proportional justice could agree that sinners faring better than saints needn't be worse *for* anyone, yet insist that such a situation might still be bad, because proportional justice has value beyond its being good *for* people. On the other hand, some rejecting MST object to it as a theory about outcomes *because* they think it inadequate as a theory about self-interest. For example, some believe that freedom is good *for* people beyond its influence on conscious states. So, they might regard a world with higher conscious states but less freedom as worse than one with lower conscious states but more freedom, precisely *because* they believe people are better off in the latter than the former. Naturally, one might reject MST for both reasons.

MST was first offered as a full theory of the good. Believing that only the quality of conscious states was relevant to the good for both individuals *and* outcomes, the classical utilitarians saw no need for different theories of the good. Regrettably, many have unwittingly followed their path, assuming the same theory would suffice for self-interest, outcomes, and the full theory of the good. Thus, convinced of MST's implausibility as a full theory of the good, many dismissed it without pursuing the source of its shortcomings. This is unfortunate, for I think that on reflection some would believe that while MST is *not* an adequate theory about outcomes, it *is* an adequate theory about self-interest. That is, it is arguable that one of the great insights of the classical utilitarians was not only that *most* things are only good insofar as they promote positive mental states, but the further point that *nothing* is good *for* someone, i.e. in her self-interest, except insofar as it positively affects the quality of her conscious states.

The foregoing is not only of general importance, it directly bears on our central issue. According to the Slogan, one situation *cannot* be worse than another in even one respect, if there is *no one* for whom it *is* worse in even one respect. This implies that one's theory of outcomes must be a direct function of (perhaps, in a sense, supervenient on) one's theory of self-interest. Clearly, however, to accept MST as a theory about self-interest, while rejecting it as a theory about outcomes, is to deny the relation in question. More specifically, it is to insist that some factors can be relevant to the goodness of outcomes other than those relevant to what is good *for* people. Thus, on the view in question, one must reject the Slogan and the arguments invoking it.

Interestingly, once one distinguishes between theories about self-interest and theories about outcomes, one may wonder why the Slogan seemed plausible in the first place. After all, while the quality of people's lives will certainly play a major role – perhaps the major role – in the goodness of outcomes, why should the correct theory about outcomes be dependent on the correct theory about self-interest in the way the Slogan would have us believe?

Still, if one thinks MST fails as a theory about self-interest, one may yet believe that the correct theory about outcomes will involve an alternative to MST which does support the Slogan. Let us next consider if a Desire-Fulfillment Theory yields this result.

IX. Challenging the Slogan, Part Four: the Desire-Fulfillment Theory

The Desire-Fulfillment Theory (DFT) holds that something will be good or bad for someone insofar, and only insofar, as it promotes or contravenes the fulfillment of her desires; where, roughly, the value of fulfilling an agent's desires is ultimately derivable from her desires themselves. So, on this view, the agent is, within certain limits, the ultimate arbiter of her own good. What she desires is good for her and, importantly, it is her desiring it which makes it so.

One question about which there is much dispute is whether DFT should be *Restricted* – only attaching weight to the fulfillment of an agent's self-regarding desires, her desires about how *she* fares and how *her* life progresses – or *Unrestricted* – also attaching weight to an agent's other-regarding desires, her desires about how *others* fare and how *their* lives progress, as well as any desires she may have about the world *per se*. Now, in general, any desire intimately connected with one's deepest projects and commitments will count as self-regarding in the relevant sense. Still, whether a particular desire is self-regarding is not simply a matter of the desire's strength. People can have strong desires about others – for example, that the President be virtuous, or weak desires about themselves, for example, that their meal be tasty.

The dispute between Restricted and Unrestricted DFTs is important for two reasons. First, its root may partly lie in a failure to distinguish between a theory's plausibility as a theory about self-interest or outcomes, and its plausibility as a full theory of the good. Second, reflection on the dispute suggests that DFT does not support the Slogan.

Consider two cases. Case I is put by Parfit. He writes:

> Suppose that I meet a stranger who has what is believed to be a fatal disease. My sympathy is aroused, and I strongly want this stranger to be cured. Much later, when I have forgotten our meeting, the stranger is cured. On the Unrestricted Desire-Fulfillment Theory, this event is good for me and makes my life go better. This is not plausible. We should reject this theory.[22]

Case II may be put as follows.

> Suppose Jean has a strong other-regarding desire that certain graves be well-tended. And suppose Liz could, with equal ease, fulfill either this strong desire or Jean's much weaker self-regarding desire for some sun-tan oil. Assuming Liz had no duty to do the latter, most would agree that, other things equal, *if* she were going to fulfill one of the desires, it would be better to fulfill the strong one.

Reflecting on Case I, many are drawn to the conclusion that a Restricted DFT is more plausible than an Unrestricted one. Reflecting on Case II, many are drawn to the opposite conclusion. There is an element of truth to both positions, but its exact nature is easily, and too often, overlooked.

Case I illustrates that an Unrestricted DFT is implausible *as a theory about self-interest*. Case II illustrates that a Restricted DFT is implausible *as a theory about outcomes*. Together, then, Cases I and II suggest that neither a Restricted nor an Unrestricted DFT is plausible *as a full theory of the good*. But this does *not* show that each should be rejected out of hand. It remains possible that a Restricted DFT is plausible as a theory about self-interest, an Unrestricted DFT is plausible as a theory about outcomes, and neither is more plausible than the other *simpliciter*.

An Unrestricted DFT will count certain things as good or bad which we do not think are good or bad *for* anyone. This shows we must either reject the Unrestricted DFT, even as a theory about outcomes, or reject the Slogan. Similarly, a Restricted DFT fails to count as good for people certain factors we regard as good. This shows we must either reject the Restricted DFT, even as a theory about self-interest, or reject the Slogan. Thus, once one gets clear about the strengths and weaknesses of the two views, one sees that neither a Restricted nor Unrestricted DFT will plausibly support the Slogan.

I have claimed that neither a Restricted nor an Unrestricted DFT will support the Slogan. Let me next suggest that even if some version of DFT were both to ultimately prove true, and to support the Slogan, it would *not* support the numerous arguments that invoke the Slogan.

On any plausible version of DFT one will want to count as good *for* someone the satisfaction of those desires intimately connected with her deepest projects and commitments. It follows that on DFT there would be good reason to strive for freedom, justice, equality, autonomy, and so on. After all, those count among (some) people's deepest desires.

Consider again Nozick's Wilt Chamberlain example, from section IV. While on DFT it might be true that Chamberlain's receiving a million dollars could not be bad *if* there was no one for whom it was worse, the 'if' clause would not be fulfilled. As long as there are people for whom the advance of equality is among their deepest projects and commitments, there *will be* someone for whom the situation in question is worse in terms of the contravening of their relevant desires. Hence, on DFT, the Slogan would not support the kind of position Nozick put forward. Similar remarks would apply to each of the positions noted in section IV. One must look elsewhere for a position supporting both the Slogan and the arguments invoking it.

X. Challenging the Slogan, Part Five: the Objective List Theory

Let me next comment on the Objective List Theory (OLT). As a theory about self-interest, OLT would hold that some things are good or bad *for* people independently of the quality of their conscious states or the fulfillment of their desires. Similarly, as a theory about outcomes, OLT would hold that some things are intrinsically good or bad – that is, make an outcome good or bad – independently of the quality of people's conscious states or the fulfillment of people's desires.

Let me begin by discussing OLT as a theory about outcomes. Specifically, let me suggest that once one moves to OLT as a theory about outcomes, there seems to be little reason to be wedded to the Slogan.

Once we recognize that some things are intrinsically valuable independently of people's desires or conscious states it seems an open question what the full range of objective values would involve regarding their nature, content, or relation to sentient beings. Though presumably there will be some essential connection between our nature and the boundaries of moral value, why must it be one of *benefit*, for either us or others? Why *can't* the boundaries of the objectively good extend beyond what is good *for* someone – perhaps focusing on our capacity *to lead a morally* good life, as well as on our capacity *to have* a *prudentially* good life?

To be sure, an Objective List for outcomes would include many factors regarded as good on our theory about self-interest. Still, there seems to be plenty of room for our Objective List about outcomes to include some factors, like certain moral ideals, whose attainment is not necessarily good *for* anyone.

Importantly, one might preserve the Slogan by adopting an Objective List Theory about self-interest and including on it those moral ideals to which people are committed. Specifically, with a broad enough Objective List Theory, any case in which one outcome is better or worse than another in any respect will also be a case in which there is someone for whom that outcome is better or worse in some respect. But, as suggested in section VII, such a move will save the Slogan only by robbing it of its teeth. In particular, if it is an open question what factors or ideals will appear on the correct Objective List about self-interest – as it surely must be given the present state of argument about such issues – one cannot appeal to the Slogan to undermine any particular positions. After all, to do so would simply beg the question against whether the positions in question belong on the correct Objective List Theory about self-interest. Thus, even if the Slogan could be defended given a sufficiently broad Objective List Theory about self-interest, it would not yet serve any of the particular conclusions for which it has been invoked.

One might simply insist that the Slogan *must* be right, so that any ideals that are not intrinsically good *for* anyone must be rejected. But to do so would probably be wrong and certainly be unwarranted. Such an assertion begs the questions that most need addressing. Instead of advancing the level of moral argument it cuts off debate where it needs to begin. In sum, until significant reasoning about the nature and foundation of the correct Objective Lists establishes otherwise, arguments based on rhetorical appeal to the Slogan should be rejected.

I have discussed a Mental State Theory, a Desire-Fulfillment Theory, and an Objective List Theory. Our considerations suggest that once one distinguishes between theories about self-interest and theories about outcomes there is reason to doubt the Slogan and the arguments invoking it. Correspondingly, there is reason to resist the Levelling Down Objection, insofar as it purports to establish that non-instrumental egalitarianism is an absurd view that must be rejected.

XI. Broome's objection and a response

In his interesting and important book, *Weighing Goods*, John Broome presents and defends the following position.

> *The principle of personal good.* (a) Two alternatives are equally good if they are equally good for each person. And (b) if one alternative is at least as good as another for everyone and definitely better for someone, it is better.[23]

The principle of personal good is similar to the Slogan, and Broome rightly recognizes that my arguments against the Slogan also challenge the principle of personal good. Not surprisingly, then, Broome considers and rejects my key argument against the Slogan. Let us consider the adequacy of Broome's response.

Broome's target is my saints and sinners example, presented in section VII. Broome redescribes this example as one where the 'saints are initially better off than the sinners, but then the condition of the sinners improves whilst the condition of the saints remains the same'.[24] He then writes: 'Suppose the sinners end up better off than the saints. Temkin suggests *this* change may be bad, even though it is bad for no one. I agree the change may be bad. But if it is, I think that is because it is bad for the saints. The saints deserve better than the sinners, so if they fare worse they are suffering an injustice. To suffer an injustice is bad for you. So, although at first the saints may have seemed no worse off, they are actually worse off in this less obvious way. The harm of injustice done them may make the change worse on balance.'[25]

I find this response unconvincing. Let me note several reasons for this. First, suppose the saints are blissfully unaware of the sinners' existence. They are in one heaven, the sinners, in another, even better, one. Or suppose the saints don't mind the sinners' situation. They might even be relieved and happy for the sinners, without the *slightest* tinge of jealousy, self-pity, or remorse. They are, after all, saints! In such circumstances, I seriously doubt that the saints are *suffering* an injustice, or are *harmed* by the injustice, or that in any other contentful way their lives are actually *worse off* due to their world's injustice. But this does not lessen the significance of their world's injustice, or the extent to which B is worse than A regarding justice.

To assume that if injustice is bad there *must* be someone *for whom* it is bad, is to conflate one's theory of the good about *outcomes* – which tells what makes an outcome good or bad – with one's theory of the good about *self-interest* – which tells what is good or bad *for* individuals. Like the Slogan, Broome's principle of personal good serves as a Procrustean bed, fitting the goodness of outcomes to what is good for individuals. So, insofar as a factor contributes to an outcome's goodness, there 'must' first be individuals for whom that factor is, to the same extent, good. But I see no reason to believe this. Even if one believes, as I do, that '*societies* aren't the proper objects of moral concern, individuals *in* societies are',[26] one must recognize that outcomes, or societies, are not individuals. In addition, concerns about individuals extend beyond concerns about how well they fare, or what is better or worse *for* them. Correspondingly, the relevant factors for judging whether an outcome is better or worse, differ from those for judging whether an individual is better- or worse-off.

So, I deny Broome's claim that if B's injustice is bad, there must be someone for whom it is bad and, in particular, that it is bad for the saints. However, suppose we grant that injustice is bad for the saints. Would this be enough to support our judgment about the relative merits of A and B?

In describing my example, Broome assumed that in moving from A to B the sinners' conditions improved while the saints' remained constant. Suppose we don't make that assumption. Specifically, assume that as the sinners' conditions improve, so do the saints', so that in fact the saints would be better off in B than in A, were it not for the injustice they suffer due to the sinners' *disproportionate* gains. So, imagine that B *accurately* represents the saints' and sinners' levels, taking full account of both the improvement in the sinners' and saints' conditions in moving from A to B, *and* the worsening of the saints' conditions due to the injustice they suffer from the sinners' disproportionate gains.

Now what should we say about A and B? On the principle of personal good, we must now conclude that B is better than A, since, by hypothesis, B is now as least as good as A for the saints, and definitely better for the sinners. Should we accept this conclusion? Broome might. He might insist that having already taken account of the adverse effects of injustice on the saints, our judgments about A and B should be guided by the principle of personal good. Moreover, he might claim, with some plausibility, that any temptation to favor A over B on grounds of justice, must involve an illicit double counting of B's injustice. Nevertheless, it is hard reconciling these claims with the view that B's saints genuinely *suffer* injustice, so that as a result of the *harm* done them they are now actually *worse off* than the sinners. If, in B, the saints genuinely *are* worse off than the sinners, then it seems advocates of proportional justice can, and should, stick to their original contention that B is worse than A. Sinners should not fare better than saints.

So, I don't think Broome's response removes my example's sting. Whether or not injustice is bad for those who 'suffer' the injustice, the principle of proportional justice seems to support judgments incompatible with the principle of personal good. Of course, Broome might urge that we revise or dispense with proportional justice.

But I, for one, find it easier to reject the principle of personal good, than the principle of proportional justice. Even if B is better for some and worse for no one, it is not better than A. An outcome where mass murderers fare better than saints is not better than an outcome where saints and sinners all get what they deserve.[27]

Next, consider a variation of the saints and sinners case, where there are no saints, only sinners.[28] In New A, the sinners get what they deserve. In New B, the sinners fare even better than they would have deserved to, had they been saints. Many would agree that in one respect – regarding justice – New B is worse than New A. Since there isn't anyone besides sinners, if there must be someone for whom New B's injustice is bad, it must be bad for the sinners themselves. This is implausible. I think New B's injustice is bad, but not because it is bad *for the sinners* to spend eternity at a saintly level, rather than at their vastly lower deserved level.[29]

Broome agrees that New B is not worse for the sinners than New A. But he denies that this tells against the principle of personal good. This is because, according to Broome, 'in the example without saints, no one suffers an injustice'.[30] For Broome, the key issue here is 'how retributive justice works. If it determines *absolutely* how a person ought to fare on grounds of desert, then Temkin would be right. But I think it determines how a person ought to fare *relative* to other people. . . . Sinners should be worse off than saints, but retributive justice does not determine how well off each group should be absolutely'.[31] To Broome, a world of saints who fare poorly due to natural conditions may not be 'a very good one' but it is not unjust. 'Similarly,' Broome writes, 'in a world containing only sinners, I see no injustice if the sinners fare well'.[32]

Broome is right that if retributive justice matters, then the principle of personal good requires that it be understood relatively *rather than* absolutely. But I deny that we should choose between a relativistic conception and an absolute one. To the contrary, I believe retributive justice includes both a relative *and* an absolute component. Let me defend this position, beginning with an example that supports a relative component. Consider Diagram 6.

In A, the saints receive what they 'deserve', the sinners much more than they deserve. In B, both the saints and the sinners receive more than they deserve, but the saints receive more than the sinners in proportion to how much better they lived their lives. If all we cared about was absolute justice, then we should prefer A to B. But although some *strict* retributivists might rank A better than

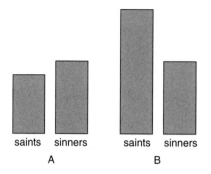

saints   sinners   saints   sinners
     A   B

Diagram 6

B, most would not. As noted previously, surely most retributivists would judge that, all things considered, B, a world where saints fare proportionally better than sinners, is more just than A, a world where mass murderers fare better than saints.

Such considerations support Broome's claim that retributive justice is concerned with 'how a person ought to fare *relative* to other people. . . . Sinners should be worse off than saints'.[33] However, such considerations do not show retributive justice is *only* concerned with relative well-being, *rather than* absolute well-being.

To see the centrality of retributive justice's absolute component, consider its role in views about the justice of punishment. Kant, for example, believes that 'the right of retaliation (*jus talionis*) . . . is the only principle which . . . can definitely assign both the quantity and quality of a just penalty'.[34] This principle is just the old biblical injunction to return like for like, 'an eye for an eye, and a tooth for a tooth,' and Kant claims it determines both 'the mode and measure of punishment'.[35] For Kant, punishing the innocent is *always* unjust. Moreover, it is not merely that murderers should be punished more than thieves, who should be punished more than slanderers, rather it is that 'if you slander another, you slander yourself; if you steal from another, you steal from yourself; . . . if you kill another, you kill yourself'.[36] Thus, for Kant, punishment is to fit the crime, and the fit is to be absolute, not relative.

H. J. McCloskey also believes that punishing the innocent is unjust, and insists that 'the key to the morality of punishment is to be found in a retributive theory, namely the theory that evil should be distributed according to desert, and that the vicious deserve to suffer'.[37]

In addition, for McCloskey, justice requires that 'punishment must not be excessive. . . . the person punished . . . [must have] deserved to be punished as he was punished'.[38] Similarly, W. D. Ross contends 'that we feel certain that it is unjust that very severe penalties should be affixed to very slight offenses . . . [in fact] the injury to be inflicted on the offender should be not much greater than that which he has inflicted on another. Ideally, . . . it should be no greater.'[39]

The firm views that the guilty should be punished, that the innocent should not, and that punishment should not be excessive, all reflect an *absolute* component of retributive justice. On Broome's view, as long as decent citizens are *proportionately* better off than vicious thugs, we should be completely indifferent, regarding justice, between whether everybody leads great lives, everybody leads wretched lives, or decent citizens lead good lives while thugs lead poor lives. I claim we are not indifferent between these alternatives, nor should we be. *Regarding justice*, the first two alternatives are both worse than the third. Insofar as we care about retributive justice, decent citizens should fare well, and thugs poorly.[40]

I conclude that retributive justice contains an important absolute component.[41] Thus, we must choose between retributive justice and the principle of personal good. Broome finds 'the intuitive appeal of the principle [of personal good] greater than the intuitive appeal of the [counter] examples [to it].'[42] My intuitions go the other way. Justice is relevant to assessing outcomes in ways that are not fully reducible to what is good or bad *for* individuals. The same may be true of other ideals, such as equality.

XII. Prioritarianism, egalitarianism, and a common enemy

As indicated previously, many who favor transfers from better- to worse-off are attracted to prioritarianism as a way of avoiding the Levelling Down Objection. However, Ingmar Persson has argued that while, strictly speaking, prioritarianism avoids the Levelling Down Objection, it runs afoul of the person-affecting spirit naturally associated with the Levelling Down Objection.[43] Although I am not completely sure what to make of Persson's argument, it is interesting and has important implications. It may be reformulated and summarized as follows.

As seen, non-instrumental egalitarianism conflicts with the Slogan, which holds that one situation *cannot* be worse (or better)

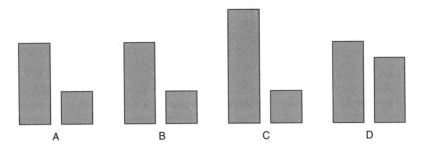

Diagram 7

than another if there is *no one* for whom it *is* worse (or better). A corollary of the Slogan is

> *Slogan**: if one situation *is* worse (or better) than another, there must be *someone* for whom it *is* worse (or better).

Both the Slogan and Slogan* express *person-affecting* views, according to which the goodness of outcomes is assessed in terms of the extent to which the people in those outcomes are *affected* for better or worse. Correspondingly, the spirit of the Slogan and Slogan* also supports the following position.

> *Improvement*: the extent to which a change improves a situation will be a direct function of the extent to which individuals in that situation are (collectively) *benefitted* by the change (where harms count as negative benefits for the purposes of aggregation); so, for one situation to be improved more by change than another situation, the members of the first situation must, collectively, benefit *more* from its change, than the members of the second situation benefit, collectively, from its change.

Intuitively, Improvement expresses a person-affecting view that changes improve an outcome *only* to the extent that they *benefit* people in that outcome – the better the changes are *for* people, the greater the improvement in the outcome.

The preceding *suggests* that those who are attracted to the Slogan should also be attracted to Slogan* and Improvement, and vice versa. Similarly, those who reject the Slogan should also reject Slogan* and Improvement, and vice versa.

Importantly, most prioritarians will reject Improvement. Given the choice between benefitting a worse-off person or benefitting a better-off person *to the exact same extent*, they favor benefitting the worse-off person. Moreover, most prioritarians believe, rightly I think, that the outcome where the worse-off person is benefitted is a *better* outcome than the outcome where the better-off person is similarly benefitted. So, consider Diagram 7.

Suppose one could transform A into C, by benefitting A's better-off a certain amount, or B into D, by benefitting B's worse-off the exact same amount. Prioritarians are committed to the view that they should bring about D, rather than C. Furthermore, most prioritarians would hold that D is a better outcome than C.[44] But, by hypothesis, B's worse-off do *not* benefit more in the change to D, than A's better-off would in the change to C. Each group would be benefitted to the *exact* same extent. Thus, according to Improvement, there would be *no* reason to favor D over C.

As indicated, most prioritarians would reject Improvement. They share, along with proponents of proportional justice and non-instrumental egalitarianism, a commitment to an *impersonal* principle which evaluates outcomes in ways that are not fully reducible to what is good or bad *for* individuals. Thus, prioritarians reject the kind of person-affecting reasoning that underlies Improvement, Slogan*, and the Slogan. Correspondingly, it is a mistake to think prioritarianism is much preferable to non-instrumental egalitarianism because it avoids the Levelling Down Objection. Although prioritarianism *does* avoid the Levelling Down Objection, and may be plausible in its own right, most prioritarians reject the person-affecting spirit naturally associated with the Levelling Down Objection. In so doing, they open up the possibility that one situation *could* be worse (or better) than another in *some* respect, even if there is no one for whom it is worse (or better). One respect in which it *might* be worse is in terms of equality.

The preceding considerations do not directly support non-instrumental egalitarianism. But they suggest that insofar as person-affecting intuitions are at issue, non-instrumental egalitarianism and prioritarianism have a similar status. Consequently, they suggest, though do not prove, that whatever reasons one might have for endorsing prioritarianism or non-instrumental egalitarianism, it would be a mistake to favor the former over the latter because of the person-affecting spirit naturally associated with the Levelling Down Objection.

XIII. Summary and conclusion

Many who think of themselves as egalitarians are in fact prioritarians. I argued that it is a mistake to conflate prioritarianism with egalitarianism. While prioritarianism is plausible as a version of instrumental egalitarianism, it is not plausible as a version of non-instrumental egalitarianism. Prioritarianism expresses a special concern for the worse-off that will often support transfers from better- to worse-off, but it is not concerned with equality *per se*.

Many believe that only instrumental egalitarianism is plausible. In particular, many think that the Levelling Down Objection provides a convincing refutation of non-instrumental egalitarianism. This essay challenged that belief. The Levelling Down Objection has great appeal, but it is hardly the crushing, conclusive, objection it is widely assumed to be. I claimed that the Levelling Down Objection derives much of its powerful rhetorical force from the Slogan. But while the Slogan expresses a person-affecting view that initially seems plausible, it should be rejected. The Slogan conflicts with our views about the Non-Identity Problem, is incompatible with the principle of proportional justice and, more generally, rules out giving weight to *any* impersonal moral principles in assessing outcomes. The Slogan asserts a relation between the goodness of individuals and the goodness of outcomes that is not supported by any standard theories of the good. Specifically, the Slogan and the conclusions for which it has been invoked are not supported by a Mental State Theory, a Desire-Fulfillment Theory, or an Objective List Theory of the good.

Finally, I noted that most prioritarians accept an impersonal view that conflicts with the Slogan's person-affecting spirit. Correspondingly, if I am right that the Levelling Down Objection derives much of its force from the Slogan, prioritarians, as well as non-instrumental egalitarians, should find the Levelling Down Objection less forceful than it is commonly taken to be.

Some people accept my claims about the Slogan, but still find the Levelling Down Objection crushing against non-instrumental egalitarianism. I don't understand this position. If one situation *couldn't* be worse than another in *any* respect, if there was no one for whom it was worse in any respect, then the Levelling Down Objection would be compelling. But if one situation *could* be worse than another in *one* respect, even if there was no one for whom it was worse in any respect, then the Levelling Down Objection does little more than point out an implication of non-instrumental egalitarianism that one may or may not find unpalatable. The non-instrumental egalitarian claims equality is valuable in itself, even if there is no one for whom it is good. The Levelling Down Objection's proponent insistently denies this. But, however heartfelt, an insistent denial hardly constitutes an argument, much less a crushing one.

Isn't it unfair for some to be worse off than others through no fault of their own? Isn't it unfair for some to be blind, while others are not? And isn't unfairness bad? These questions, posed rhetorically, express the fundamental claims of the non-instrumental egalitarian. Once one rejects the Slogan, as I have argued one should, there is little reason to forsake such claims in the face of the Levelling Down Objection.

But, the anti-egalitarian will incredulously ask, do I *really* think there is some respect in which a world where only some are blind is worse than one where all are? Yes. Does this mean I think it would be better if we blinded everyone? No. Equality is not all that matters. But it matters some.

Advocates of the Levelling Down Objection are mesmerized by 'pure' equality's terrible implications. But equality is not the only ideal that would, if exclusively pursued, have implausible or even terrible implications. The same is true of justice, utility, freedom, and probably every other ideal. Recall Kant's view that 'justice be done though the heavens should fall'. Do we really think, with Kant, that it would be wrong to falsely imprison an innocent man for even five minutes, if that were necessary to save a million innocent lives? Or consider the principle of utility, which would require us to torture an innocent person if only *enough* people had their lives improved by the tiniest of amounts because of our action. Or finally, consider the implications of unfettered freedom to act as one wants without government interference, as long one doesn't interfere with the rights or liberties of others. Such a principle might allow *complete* neglect of the least fortunate, even regarding basic necessities such as food, clothing, shelter, and healthcare. Such considerations do *not* show that justice, utility, and freedom should be rejected moral ideals, only that morality is complex.

The main lesson of the Levelling Down Objection is that we should be pluralists about morality. Egalitarians have long recognized, and accepted, this lesson. Unfortunately, the same cannot be said for their opponents.

Notes

1 This approach is suggested by Thomas Nagel who refers to 'a very strong
   egalitarian principle ... [which] is constructed by adding to the general value of improvement a condition of priority to the worst off' (*Mortal
   Questions*, Cambridge University Press, 1979, p. 110) [p. 63 in this volume].
   See, also, Nagel's discussion of egalitarianism in ch. 7 of *Equality and Partiality*
   (Oxford University Press, 1991), especially, pp. 65–6.
2 See Derek Parfit's 'Equality or Priority', The Lindley Lecture, University
   of Kansas, 1991, p. 19 [p. 101 in this volume]. To my knowledge, Parfit
   first introduced this terminology in his unpublished manuscript 'On
   Giving Priority to the Worse-off' (1989).
3 Note, one could imagine scenarios where blinding the sighted *would* be
   better for the blind. However, the Levelling Down Objection assumes,
   for its purposes, that the blind do not gain *at all*, the sighted merely
   lose, and are 'levelled down' to the situation of the blind. As noted in
   section V, this is the case that represents the most powerful objection
   to non-instrumental egalitarianism.
4 This rhetorically laden example is fraught with complexity, and prompts
   many possible responses. I shall confront the example head-on, but
   other moves are available to the egalitarian, including granting the specific
   claim that there is *nothing* to be said for putting out the eyes of the
   sighted, but denying that this undermines non-instrumental egalitarianism.
        One move open to egalitarians is to lean heavily on the distinction
   between the right and the good, and contend that in some cases questions about good or bad, or better and worse, are irrelevant to questions
   about right and wrong, and what we have reason to do. On this view,
   where certain strict duties or prohibitions are involved we may have *no*
   reason to do what is *wrong*, even if it would improve the outcome. A
   variation of the Pauline principle, that one must not do evil that good
   may come of it, the contention would be that putting out the eyes of
   the sighted is *wrong*, and hence that there cannot be reason to do it,
   even if some good, such as promoting equality, would result. On this
   view the rhetorical force of the levelling down objection derives from
   the wrongness of inflicting harm on the innocent, but leaves the central contention of non-instrumental egalitarianism untouched. Equality
   remains an ideal with independent value, and a situation in which all
   are blind is in one respect *better* than a situation in which half are
   blind, even if this fact provides no reason to put out the eyes of the
   sighted.
        A second move open to egalitarians is to grant the particular conclu-
   sion that a situation where all are blind is in no respect better than
   one where only half are, but deny that this supports the general conclusion that non-instrumental egalitarianism must be rejected. One might
   contend that equality is non-instrumentally valuable in the sense that
   it *sometimes* improves a situation over and above the extent to which
   it promotes other valuable ideals, without believing that equality is
   always a desirable feature. This kind of position is discussed, and defended, in Shelly Kagan's 'The Additive Fallacy' (*Ethics* 99, 1988, pp.

5–31), and in F. M. Kamm's *Morality, Mortality* vol. II (Oxford University Press, 1996), see Part I, ch. 2. Kamm refers to the 'general fact that a property's role, and most importantly, its effect may differ with its context . . . . as the *Principle of Contextual Interaction* (p. 51),' and there is reason to believe that a property can have genuine significance in some settings even if it lacks significance in other settings. Thus, there is room for the egalitarian to contend that *even if* equality is lacking value in situations where all are blind – perhaps because in such situations everyone's blindness somehow *cancels out*, and not merely *outweighs* the (prima facie) value of equality – there may still be other situations where equality has value over and above the extent to which it promotes other ideals. Andrew Williams suggested the term *conditional non-instrumental egalitarianism* for such a position, to distinguish it from *unconditional non-instrumental egalitarianism*, the view that equality *always* has *some* value, no matter what the circumstances. In sum, one might hold that the levelling down objection threatens unconditional non-instrumental egalitarianism, but leaves a 'suitably revised' conditional non-instrumental egalitarianism untouched.

I mention the foregoing positions, but shall not pursue them further. Although they represent important positions in their own right, I think the levelling down objection can and should be rejected more directly.

5 Alternatively, such considerations might drive one towards person-affecting or deontological versions of egalitarianism. For a discussion of such views, see Parfit's 'Equality or Priority?' and my *Inequality* (Oxford University Press, 1993).

6 Parfit puts the view as follows: 'if an outcome is worse for no one, it cannot be in any way worse' ('Equality or Priority?' p. 32) [p. 114 in this volume]. This kind of view receives extensive treatment in Part Four of *Reasons and Persons* (Oxford University Press, 1984). Jan Narveson advocates this kind of a view in his pioneering article, 'Utilitarianism and New Generations,' *Mind* 76, 1967, pp. 62–72, and also in 'Moral Problems of Population,' *Monist* 57, 1973, pp. 62–86.

7 Actually, Rawls's *lexical* version of the difference principle allows some gains of the sort in question, but at various places in the text Rawls seems to rule out any inequalities which do not 'maximize, or at least contribute to, the long-term expectations of the least fortunate group in society' (*A Theory of Justice*, Cambridge, Mass.: Harvard University Press, 1971, p. 151; see also pp. 64–5, 78–9, 83, and 150). My point here is not about Rawls's considered view regarding the permissibility of gains to the better-off that are not accompanied by gains to the worse-off, but to illustrate another example where the Slogan has been appealed to; namely to criticize the suggestion that gains to the better-off might only be permissible if they also benefit the worse-off.

8 *Anarchy, State, and Utopia* (Oxford: Basil Blackwell, 1974), p. 161.

9 Note, I am not claiming that the Slogan actually supports Nozick's example. Nor am I claiming that Nozick was relying on, or intending to appeal to, the Slogan in presenting his example. My claim is simply that much of its *force* is derived from the Slogan. By stressing the fact

that third parties '*still* have their legitimate shares; *their* shares have not changed,' Nozick – whether wittingly or not – naturally leads his readers to assume that third parties are not worse off as a result of the exchanges between Chamberlain and his fans. Hence, his example draws force from the Slogan's appeal. Consider how our view about Nozick's example might change if we added a few details. Suppose we found out that as a result of market forces and Chamberlain's wealth, the price of housing, food, and medical care had risen such that third parties (including elderly and children!) were now *much* worse off than before. Presumably, Nozick would still contend that the voluntary exchanges between Chamberlain and his fans were morally permissible and that no one else could 'complain on grounds of justice'. But I suspect many would no longer share his firm convictions. Certainly, it would no longer seem so 'obvious' or 'uncontroversial' that there was nothing wrong with many people choosing 'to give twenty-five cents of their money to Chamberlain'.

In sum, I think much of the power of Nozick's Chamberlain example is derived from the Slogan. Take away the implicit assumption that there is no one for whom the voluntary exchanges are worse, and Nozick's example is far less compelling. (Similar remarks apply to several of the cases noted below.)

10 See Locke's *Second Treatise on Civil Government*, sections 26–33 (the passage in quotes comes from section 26).

11 *Anarchy, State, and Utopia*, p. 175.

12 'Future Generations: Further Problems', *Philosophy & Public Affairs* 11, 1982, pp. 158–9.

13 I vividly recall the first time I heard the Mere Addition Paradox, from which this example is taken. I was auditing a Princeton graduate seminar where Parfit drew A and A+ on the board and asked us how they compared. Several students suggested that A+ was worse than A, since it involved inequality. Parfit immediately offered the following response. How could A+ be worse than A, when it involves the *mere addition* of an extra group of people all of whom have lives worth living and who affect no one else; everyone in A exists in A+ *and is just as well off*, it is just that *in addition* there is the extra group of people whose lives are well worth living; thus, by hypothesis, A+ *isn't* worse for the A group, they are just as well off in A+ as A, and it *isn't* worse for the extra group, since their lives are worth living and *they* wouldn't exist in A, so how could A+ be worse than A, when there is *no one* for whom it is worse? I recall that at the time I, and most of my colleagues, found this response crushing. I now think this is because we were caught in the Slogan's grip.

Interestingly, Parfit himself claims he was not appealing to the Slogan when he asked us how A+ could be worse than A if there was *no one* for whom it was worse, and there is textual evidence to support his claim. Still, whatever Parfit's own view of his example, I am convinced that many who accepted Parfit's claims about how A and A+ compare were being influenced by the Slogan. (I know I was originally, as were many others with whom I have discussed this issue.)

14 In *Public and Private Morality*, edited by Stuart Hampshire (Cambridge University Press, 1978), p. 93.

15 One might think that the Slogan couldn't be used against deontological theories, since deontological theories make claims about what we ought to *do*, and deny that these claims presuppose any views about the relevant goodness of outcomes. But this is not quite right. Deontologists insist that duty is not the same as promoting the best possible outcome, but most deontologists would admit that acting wrongly is bad, and that *other things equal* an outcome where one has acted wrongly will be worse than an outcome where one has acted rightly. Thus, if someone can construct a case where breaking one's promise or lying will be worse for *no one*, they can use the Slogan to conclude that in such a case there is *no* respect in which the outcome would be worse if one broke one's promise or lied. Hence, on the assumption noted above, breaking one's promise or lying must not be wrong in such a case. Thus, the Slogan might be invoked to undermine the claim that breaking one's promise or lying is intrinsically wrong, i.e. that there is always something wrong about such actions independently of their consequences. I have heard such arguments invoked against deontologists. In response, deontologists must either deny that right or wrong actions themselves contribute to the goodness or badness of outcomes, insist that in such cases there really *must* be someone for whom the promise breaking or lying will be worse (perhaps the moral agent doing the action), or reject the Slogan. Note, on the last alternative deontologists claim it is not only wrong if I lie, it is bad – it makes the outcome in one respect worse – and they claim this is true even if there is *no one* for whom my lie is worse. It is a testimony to the Slogan's appeal that many find this position nonsensical.

16 The Non-Identity Problem is discussed in chapter 16 of *Reasons and Persons*.

17 This is a stronger conclusion than one needs to undermine the Slogan. All one needs is that the 'live for today' would be in at least *one* respect worse than the 'take care of tomorrow' policy, and *surely* this is so. Note, however, that for the argument to tell against the Slogan the example must suppose that there is *no* respect in which the 'live for today' policy would be worse for the parents. In the real world this would be unlikely, but one could imagine a case where this would hold, and that is all the argument requires.

18 Parfit, *Reasons and Persons* (Oxford University Press, 1984), pp. 363, 359 and 378.

19 B isn't worse for the saints; by hypothesis, they fare as well in B as in A. And it certainly isn't worse for the sinners! Hence there is no one for whom it is worse. (We may suppose, if we want, that the saints are blissfully unaware of how the sinners are faring, though if they are truly saints this supposition may be unnecessary. I leave God and His feelings out of this discussion (perhaps He doesn't exist); but notice, on the view being called into question, what reason could He have for preferring A to B, when there is no one for whom B is worse?)

20 John Broome advocates such a position in *Weighing Goods* (Oxford: Basil

Blackwell, 1991). See his discussion of *individualistic egalitarianism* in ch. 9.

21 In chapter 9 of *Inequality*, op. cit., and also in 'Harmful Goods, Harmless Bads'.

22 *Reasons and Persons*, op. cit., p. 494.

23 *Weighing Goods*, p. 165.

24 Ibid., p. 168.

25 Ibid.

26 *Inequality*, p. 304.

27 If one denies these claims, but accepts the view that there is at least one morally relevant respect in which B is worse than A, then one is committed to rejecting the Slogan even if one accepts the Principle of Personal Good. This illustrates one respect in which the Principle of Personal Good is weaker, and therefore more defensible, than the Slogan.

28 Derek Parfit presents this variation of my example in 'On Giving Priority to the Worse-off'.

29 Hegel disagrees. He believes punishment honors the criminal as a rational being, and that the guilty have a *right* to be punished. For Hegel, punishment is good for the wicked. (See, for example, section 100 of *The Philosophy of Right*.) Contrary to Hegel, I believe the right to be punished is one which clear thinking, rational, criminals could forgo without reservations. Obviously, I do not share Hegel's view of rational beings.

30 *Weighing Goods*, p. 168.

31 Ibid., p. 169.

32 Ibid.

33 Ibid.

34 See *The Philosophy of Law*, Part II, trans. W. Hastie (Edinburgh: T. T. Clark, 1887), pp. 194–8. Reproduced in Gertrude Ezorsky's *Punishment* (State University of New York Press, 1972), pp. 103–6. The quotation appears on p. 104.

35 Ibid.

36 Ibid.

37 'A Non-Utilitarian Approach to Punishment', *Inquiry* 8, 1965, pp. 239–55. Reprinted in *Punishment*, pp. 119–34. See p. 120.

38 Ibid., p. 121 of *Punishment*.

39 *Punishment*, p. 151. Excerpted from *The Right and the Good* (Oxford: Clarendon Press, 1965), pp. 56–64.

40 Of course, we may think the first alternative, where everyone fares well, is better than the third, *all things considered*. But this wouldn't show that retributive justice lacks an absolute component; only that retributive justice is not all that matters. Sometimes other concerns outweigh our concern for retributive justice.

41 I have been discussing the notion of retributive justice in its classic form, and I do believe that it is powerfully appealing, has an absolute component, and undermines both the Slogan and the principle of personal good. However, many humane people may be leery of endorsing my discussion, even if they accept my view about the Slogan and the principle of personal good. In particular, many humane people may

balk at the suggestion that the guilty deserve to *suffer* greatly, or in ways comparable to their victims. I have much sympathy with this view, and even more with the view that no finite earthly acts could warrant an eternity in Hell (which is why I talked about the sinners being at the level they deserved given their earthly lives, leaving it open the level this would involve). However, even if one believes that no one deserves to *suffer* immensely, or perhaps even at all, it is sufficient for my view that one believes that crime should not pay, and in particular that evil people should not lead *blissful* lives or be better off than saints. Even humane people might accept some such 'mildly retributivist' position, and that is enough to generate counter-examples to the Slogan and the principle of personal good. (I am grateful to Andrew Williams for this suggestion.)

42 Ibid., p. 168.
43 Persson makes this point in two important unpublished papers, 'Telic Egalitarianism vs. the Priority View' and 'Levelling Down and the Distinction between Equality and Priority'.
44 Strict *deontic* prioritarians could deny this claim. On their view, we have a *duty* to benefit the worse-off more than the better-off, but our doing so does not make the outcome better. More generally, deontic prioritarians may deny that any outcomes can be meaningfully judged as better or worse than others. Although some may hold such a position, prioritarianism is generally introduced as an alternative to egalitarianism that is at least relevant to assessing outcomes.

7
The Pareto Argument for Inequality

G. A. Cohen

I. Introduction

Some ways of defending inequality against the charge that it is unjust require premises that egalitarians find it easy to dismiss, statements, for example, about the contrasting deserts and/or entitlements of unequally placed people. But a defence of inequality suggested by John Rawls and elaborated by Brian Barry[1] (who themselves reject the premises that egalitarians[2] dismiss) has often proved irresistible even to people of egalitarian outlook. The persuasive power of this defence of inequality has helped to drive authentic egalitarianism, of an old-fashioned, uncompromising, kind, out of contemporary political philosophy. The present essay is part of an attempt to bring it back in.

In his recent *Theories of Justice*, Barry devotes some fifteen pages to sympathetic reconstruction of the Rawlsian argument that I have in mind. He resolves it into two stages. In the first stage, which Barry calls 'From Equal Opportunity to Equality', 'Rawls establishes equality as the only *prima facie* just basis of distribution'. In the second stage ('From Equality to the Difference Principle') there is an 'argument for a move from an equal distribution to a[n unequal] distribution governed by the difference principle',[3] to, that is, a Pareto-superior[4] unequal distribution in which the people at the bottom and, therefore, all the people, are better off than they were in the initial state of equality. The difference principle is (at least) logically compatible with an equal distribution of goods, for it says that inequality is justified *if* (and only if) it renders the worst off better off than they would otherwise be: the principle itself does not say when, if ever, that condition on the justifiability

162

of inequality is satisfied, as a matter of social fact. But Rawls believes that it generally is satisfied, that 'deep inequalities' in initial life prospects are 'inevitable' in any modern society, and that the difference principle tells us *which* inequalities of that deep type are justifiable.[5] In the present exercise, I challenge neither the difference principle nor the Pareto principle, that Pareto-superior distributions are always to be preferred. My object is to show that the two-stage argument does not establish the justice of the inequalities that Rawls thinks are just.

Now, as Barry recognizes, the two-stage argument, which I shall call the *Pareto argument*, is not Rawls's official argument for difference principle inequality, because this argument dispenses with the device of the original position. And Barry has interesting things to say about the relationship between this argument and the official, contractual one, which he thinks less good.[6] Because, moreover, the Pareto argument is avowedly a product of Barry's reconstruction, one may doubt whether Rawls would endorse all of its details, as Barry sets them out. But whatever role the argument is supposed to play, or does play, in Rawls's writings, it manifestly serves to advance the Rawlsian purpose, which is, here, to reconcile certain inequalities with justice, and many, like Barry, have found the argument convincing. So it is worth scrutinizing.

Before looking at the argument in detail, I shall summarize its course, as we find it in Barry, and outline my reasons for rejecting it.

The starting point of the argument is the ideal of equality of opportunity, and there are, essentially, two thoughts in the argument's first stage. The first thought is that true equality of opportunity is achieved only when all morally arbitrary causes of inequality are eliminated, where, so I take it, a cause of inequality is 'morally arbitrary' if it does not justify that inequality because of the kind of cause of inequality that it is. (To get what I mean by that, reflect that non-Rawlsians think that causes of inequality which are appropriately associated with desert or entitlement do justify the inequality that they cause). And the second thought in the argument's first stage is that there exist no causes of inequality that are not arbitrary in the specified sense. Accordingly, so Barry claims, true equality of opportunity 'amounts to equality of outcome',[7] which is therefore designated as *'prima facie* just'.[8]

But full equality of opportunity, or, equivalently, equality of outcome, is only *prima facie* just, since although no *cause* of inequality can make it just, it might yet be true that inequality can be just in virtue of its consequences. And that brings us to the second stage of the argument, which pleads that inequality is indeed just when and because it has the particular consequence that it causes everyone to be better off, including, of course, those who end up least better off, the worst off in the new dispensation, who are so placed that, if anyone has the right to complain about inequality, they do. The two thoughts in the second stage of the argument are, first, that it is irrational to insist on equality when it is a Pareto-inferior state of affairs (why would anyone, and, in particular, the worst off, prefer equality to an inequality in which everyone is better off?); and, second, that sometimes, and indeed typically, equality *is* Pareto-inferior.

The essence of my objection to the argument is that consistent adherence to the rationale of its first move puts its second move in question: I shall argue that anyone who believes that, because the possible sources of inequality are morally arbitrary, an initial equality is *prima facie* just, has no reason to believe that the recommended Pareto improvement preserves justice, even if that improvement should be accepted on other grounds.[9] The set of possible social worlds will, moreover, usually contain a Pareto-optimal equal distribution that is also Pareto-superior to the initial equality, and which must be preferred to the recommended unequal distribution, on pain of abandoning the rationale of the initial equality. As Rawls says, 'it is obvious . . . that there are indefinitely many ways in which all may be advantaged when the initial arrangement of equality is taken as a benchmark.'[10] I claim that the particular type of Pareto improvement picked by Rawls contradicts the rationale of the original move from equality of opportunity to equality.

Although I am in sympathy with the first part of the Pareto argument, and hostile to the second, I do not have to endorse or reject either part to prosecute the present critique. For my critical contention is that the two parts of the argument are inconsistent with one another, that those who, like Rawls and Barry, make the second move after making the first, have failed to see how far-reachingly egalitarian the argument's first move is. Someone who agrees with my criticism could respond by rejecting the argument for an initial equality, rather than, as I would, by rejecting (at least) the argument for abandoning it.[11]

There exists an argument for inequality which is simpler than the one I shall criticize, and which I do not address here. This simpler argument is easy to confuse with the one I shall focus on. It runs as follows: the distribution of goods must be either equal or unequal. But the best feasible equal distribution is Pareto-inferior to some feasible unequal distribution. An unequal distribution is, therefore, always to be preferred. In this different argument, equality and inequality are symmetrically placed. Equality is not a privileged starting point dictated by justice from which we are asked to pass on to inequality. Accordingly, the simpler argument provides no reason for starting with equality that a critic could press as a reason for not departing from it. But Rawls says that

> *since* the parties regard themselves as [free and equal moral] persons, – the obvious starting point is for them to suppose that all social primary goods, including income and wealth, should be equal: everyone should have an equal share.[12]

Rawls lays out a rationale for starting with equality, and its detailed development, expounded below, impugns, so I shall argue, the subsequent case for abandoning equality. (The simpler argument could not be Rawls's, for it does not mandate difference-principle inequality in particular, as what I call the Pareto argument does. It is, indeed, the considerations that motivate the difference principle which tell against replacing the initial equality by an unequal distribution.)

The two-stage argument stakes out a middle ground between *laissez-faire* libertarianism and radical egalitarianism. Such ground may be tenable, but not, if I am right, in the way that it is staked out here. One theme in my 1991 Tanner lectures,[13] which I continue to pursue here, is that the sort of inequality that Rawls tolerates, and indeed encourages, requires for its defence the very notions of desert and entitlement that he wants to reject. Accordingly, if I am right, there should be more polarization in political philosophy between left and right positions. If there is to be a middle position, it cannot be defended in Rawls's way.

II. The argument expounded

The first part of the Pareto argument takes its departure from equality of opportunity as that conception is understood by *laissez-faire* libertarians: opportunity is, for them, equal when there is no legal bar, such as exists under slavery or serfdom, to anyone's economic or social self-advancement. In this conception, the unequalizing effect on opportunity of 'natural and social contingencies'[14] (of birth, upbringing, and so forth) is tolerated, and the conception is consequently untrue to the ideal of equal opportunity that it purports to advance: its 'most obvious injustice . . . is that it permits distributive shares to be improperly influenced by these factors [that is, 'natural and social contingencies'] so arbitrary from a moral point of view'.[15]

A few remarks on the character, and the limits, of this rejection of *laissez-faire*. To be convicted of infidelity to his own principle of equality of opportunity, the proponent of *laissez-faire* must reject feudal and other status barriers for a particular reason, to wit, just *because* they defeat equality of opportunity, and not, for example, because a society without status barriers is optimific in a utilitarian sense (although he may, of course, believe that as well). If he were against feudalism for utilitarian reasons, and in favour of equal opportunity for those reasons alone, he would not be vulnerable to the charge that the opportunity he favours is not truly equal, since he would not have to claim that it is; and he could also not be accused of trafficking in the morally arbitrary.[16] And he would also be immune to the present argument if he affirmed *laissez-faire* because he considered it to be the social structure answering to the principle of self-ownership: that is the position of most contemporary philosophical libertarians. The target libertarian, who cannot be a very clear thinker, and who is statistically rare,[17] must say that he supports *laissez-faire because* he believes in equality of opportunity, and that he believes in the latter because he thinks it unfair for people's progress to be differentially impeded and promoted by restrictions and advantages for which they are in no way responsible. Then, and only then, is he exposed to the indicated immanent criticism.

Having rejected *laissez-faire*, Rawls and Barry move on to a conception of equality of opportunity that seeks to remove social barriers to advancement: it says for example, that children from deprived backgrounds should not have less good education than what privileged children get. In this sub-stage 'equal opportunity' is identified 'with the elimination of all [unequalizing] factors except that of genetic endowment'.[18] But Rawls maintains that the 'natural distribution of abilities' is quite as 'arbitrary from a moral perspective'[19] as is that distribution modified by unequal social prospects. Accordingly, we pass on to, and come to rest with, a truly complete equality of opportunity, in which neither natural nor social advantages contribute to distinguishing anyone's well-being from that of others.[20]

Barry says that this radical interpretation of equal opportunity, as 'nothing other than equal prospects of success for all', 'amounts to equality of outcome'.[21] Now, that might be thought a strange identification, so let me explain what I take Barry to mean. To put his point in the form of a familiar image, he means that, in a perfectly handicapped race, everyone crosses the finishing line at the same time: equality of outcome is the test of equality of opportunity.

That conveys Barry's meaning well enough for the special case where one good is at stake, and all are assumed to want it equally. To express his point more generally, we can say that, in the dispensation under discussion, such differences in outcome as may obtain are due not to differences in opportunity or ability but to differences of taste or choice, and for that reason, and in that sense, no such difference in outcome counts as an inequality. If you can reach only the oranges, and I can reach both them and the apples, and I get two oranges and two apples, and you get only two oranges, then you are on the down side of an inequality between us. But if we can each reach both, and I end up with oranges and you with apples, or even if I end up with more of each than you do (because you care less than I do for fruit), then no relevant inequality of distribution holds (unless, what I here assume to be false, the menu was rigged to suit my tastes). It does not matter whether the outcome, in which there is no inequality that reflects unequal opportunity, can or should be called *equality*, *tout court*, as opposed to *justified* (on egalitarian grounds) *inequality*. What matters is that the outcome is a distribution that egalitarians would endorse,[22] and which here functions, whatever its name should be, as the initial stage in the Rawls/Barry argument construction. Following Barry, I shall call it 'equality' here.[23]

So much, then, on how we arrive at the initial equality. Let me now display some texts in which Rawls defends the second movement, from equality to inequality. I shall then (in section III below) ask some disambiguating questions about the character of the first, equality, stage.

Rawls frequently remarks that inequality of primary[24] goods is justified when and because it represents a Pareto-superior alternative to an equal share-out. For example:

> ... the parties start with a principle establishing equal liberty
> for all, including equality of opportunity, as well as an equal
> distribution of income and wealth. But there is no reason why
> this acknowledgement should be final. If there are inequalities
> in the basic structure that work to make everyone better off in
> comparison with the benchmark of initial equality, then why
> not permit them? The immediate gain[25] which a greater equality
> might allow can be regarded as intelligently invested in view of
> its future return.[26]

Again, and more compendiously:

> an equal division of all primary goods is irrational in view of
> the possibility of bettering everyone's circumstances by accept-
> ing certain inequalities.[27]

And then, in a passage which, more explicitly than others, separates the two stages in fictional time:

> Imagine ... a hypothetical initial arrangement in which all the
> social primary goods are equally distributed: everyone has simi-
> lar rights and duties, and income and wealth are evenly shared.
> This state of affairs provides a benchmark for judging improve-
> ments. If certain inequalities of wealth and organizational powers
> would make everyone better off than in this hypothetical start-
> ing situation, then they accord with the general conception,

according to which,

> all social values – liberty and opportunity, income and wealth,
> and the bases of self-respect – are to be distributed equally un-
> less an unequal distribution of any, or all, of these values is to
> everyone's advantage.[28]

It is clear, from other passages, that, in the inequality recommended
in those exhibited above, the people who do better than others are
those with more productive talent. They get more primary goods
than do their less gifted fellow citizens. And, as I have indicated,
Rawls invites (even) egalitarians to endorse that result, on pain of
displaying irrationality.

Now, as we have seen, Rawls emphasizes that greater talent is good fortune, which means both that it is a good for those who have it and that it is sheer luck that they have it. And the fact that their possession of talent is mere good luck is treated as a reason why they should not have further advantages except on terms that also benefit those who lack their initial advantages: because they are *already* better off, they should not have more primary goods than others do unless, as a result, the less fortunate have more primary goods than they would otherwise have had. 'Those who have been favored by nature . . . may gain from their good fortune only on terms that improve the situation of those who have lost out.'[29]

Consider the following characteristic passage:

> the better endowed (who have a place in the distribution of na-
> tive endowments they do not morally deserve) are encouraged
> to acquire still further benefits – they are already benefited by
> their fortunate place in that distribution – on condition that
> they train their native endowments and use them in ways that
> contribute to the good of the less endowed.[30]

Now, what, exactly, does Rawls mean by '*still* further benefits'? It appears that what the well endowed already have counts as *benefit* in virtue of a comparison of their endowment with that of others: it is a matter of 'their fortunate *place* in [the] distribution' of en-dowment. One may then infer that the 'further benefits' they 'are encouraged to acquire' means still further *differential* advantage, that is, larger additions to their stock of primary goods than the ill endowed get. The phrase can hardly mean primary goods as such (conceived as a benefit beyond that of having talent), for they al-ready have *some* primary goods (and if they did not, then, on the suggested interpretation, and given the rest of what is said, '*still* further benefits' would imply that the talented should starve to death unless the terms on which they survive benefit the untal-ented!) Someone might question my confidence that the meaning I discern in them can be wrung out of this particular trio of words ('still further benefits'). But no one can doubt that, in the recom-mended Pareto-superior inequality, the talented have, typically, more primary goods than the untalented. Rawls makes it abundantly clear that the inequality of reward serves as an encouragement to the talented in particular.

III. The argument challenged

So we start with equality in social primary goods and inequality in the (non-social primary) good of talent, a state of affairs that I shall label 'D1'; and we move to a Pareto-superior alternative state, D2, in which the talented enjoy not only their original advantage but the further one of a larger social primary goods bundle. Notice, then, that in the movement away from D1, inequality of talent is reinforced (and not, for example, counterbalanced) by an inequality in social primary goods. We might find it surprising that the talented in particular should end up with more, since a principal insistence of the first part of the argument, which took us to D1, was that the circumstance of their greater talent justifies no distributive effect. And egalitarians might regret this 'giving [more] to those who have'[31] than to those who have not.

With such thoughts in mind, I now begin to scrutinize Rawls's irrationality thesis (the thesis that it is irrational not to replace D1 by an unequal state of affairs).

The first thing to notice is that the baseline situation, D1, is significantly underdescribed. We lack information about D1 which we require for a comprehensive assessment of the recommendation that it should give way to D2, and, so I believe, the underdescription, the lack of information, makes the glide from D1 to D2 more frictionless than it otherwise would be. D1, the 'initial equality', 'provides a benchmark for judging improvements'. We cannot say whether, and how, D2 improves on D1 until we know more than Rawls tells about what D1 *is*.

In D1 'all the social primary goods are equally distributed: everyone has similar rights and duties, and income and wealth are evenly shared'.[32] But the baseline is thereby underdescribed in the following respects, among others. First, since we know only about social primary goods, we do not know what labour inputs talented and untalented people supply in D1.[33] We know neither how much time they spend working nor how toilsome that time is.[34] And we also do not know what the initial equality of primary goods is, precisely, in one crucial dimension, an equality of. Consider the goods of income and wealth. We can suppose that wealth-holdings are intended to be strictly equal in economic value (that is, therefore, that *each* of income and wealth is equal: it is not (merely) the value of some function of the two that is equal). Unearned incomes are, consequently, equal in a straightforward sense. But equality

of earned income (henceforth, for simplicity: income) is more problematic. Is it, here, an equality of wage-rate (that is, of income per
period of time worked), with, consequently, possibly different weekly
or annual incomes; or an equality of weekly or annual income,
with possibly different wage-rates; or something else again? Finally,
and more globally, at what level is the equality of income and
wealth in D1 pitched, and why is it not postulated to be higher, or
lower, than whatever that level is?

I have no view about what Barry (or Rawls) intended by way of
answers to those surely relevant questions. But what matters is not
what was intended but whether the questions admit of natural answers
that preserve the initial persuasiveness of the recommendation that
D1 be abandoned in favour of an unequal distribution of goods.

Now setting aside the questions about the toilsomeness of labour
and about the level of income and wealth in D1 – to both of which
I shall return – let us suppose, so that we have something sufficiently determinate to think about, that the D1 income equality is
of wage per hour (call the D1 wage-rate 'W'); that talented and
untalented people work the same number of hours and apply themselves with the same degree of effort: this is a plausible partial reading
of the stipulation that their 'duties' are 'similar'[35]; and that, being
more talented, and putting in the same effort, the talented consequently produce more than the untalented do, although (*ex hypothesi*)
they gain no more as a result. Many would regard that as unfair,
but the greater output of the more able is here to be regarded as
due to the morally arbitrary circumstance of their lucky talent endowment, which is among the factors whose effects are to be
discounted in the argument for an initial equality.

Now, on the foregoing assumptions about D1, we can infer that
at D2 both talented and untalented enjoy wage-rates higher than
W, here labelled, respectively, as Wt and Wu. We also know that Wt
is greater than Wu; that it is the extra productivity (over what they
supply at W) supplied by the talented when they receive Wt that
enables the untalented to be paid Wu; and that the difference between
Wu and W is thought by Rawls to be necessary to justify the difference
between Wt and Wu. Let us also suppose, for simplicity, and to
improve the case for the inequality that will here be opposed, that
the untalented produce no more in D2 than they do in D1.

Of course, that is just one way of filling in some of the spaces
left blank by Rawls and Barry. But it is quite a natural way, and I
am in any case confident that the result of reflecting on the issue

when the baseline is thus specified will be robust, that other acceptable specifications would generate similar conclusions.

Consider, now, a logically possible distribution, D3, which may or may not be practically feasible, in which the same amount is produced as in D2, but which differs from D2 in that in D3 wages are equal, at a rate labelled We, where We exceeds W and Wu but is less than Wt (so: $Wt > We > Wu > W$). D3 is Pareto-superior to D1, but, unlike D2 (with which it is Pareto-incomparable[36]), D3 preserves equality, and the untalented are better off in D3 than they are in D2, while the talented are less well off in D3 than in D2, and both are better off in D3 than they are in D1[37]. *If* D3 is feasible, *and* talented people are *willing* to produce at We what they do at Wt, then Rawls's claim about the irrationality of insisting on equality in the face of the possibility of a Pareto-superior inequality would lose its force, since a Pareto-improving *equality-preserving* move, in which no one is as badly off as some are in D2, would now also be available. We can suppose that, if D3 is indeed feasible, then the additional product, vis-à-vis D1, is, once again, wholly due to the greater productivity of talented people. But, wage-rates being equal in D3, the talented do not in D3 gain differentially from the increase in product, as they do in D2.

IV. The argument rejected

Let us now ask: what might explain and/or justify replacing D1 by D2, rather than by D3?

The first answer to be considered is that, by contrast with D2, D3 would be unfair to talented people, who, in D3, produce more than others do and yet get no more than others do by way of reward. But that was already true of, but, because of Rawls's egalitarian argument, no objection to D1, so it cannot, in all consistency, be pressed against D3.

A second answer is that D3 is objectively unfeasible, where 'objectively' means that the unfeasibility is not a matter of human will. This answer says that D3 is unfeasible because, with all the will in the world, the talented *could* not produce at We as much as they do at Wt. But that is hardly likely, for realistic assignments of Wt and We.[38] It might be true under special circumstances, in which case the Pareto argument for inequality works, but only (on this showing) in special circumstances. In normal circumstances, nothing but the unwillingness (be it justified or not) of the talented to share, equally, the greater product produced in D2 could make D3 impossible when D2 is possible.

Next there is the answer that D3, although objectively feasible, is indeed ruled out by the attitude of talented people: they are not willing to work at *We* as long and/or as hard as they do at *Wt*. There are three pertinently different subvariants of this case, each of which calls for separate comment, and which I shall label the bad case, the good case, and the standard case, so naming the last of the three because I believe it to be the most likely one.

The bad case: if their wage-rate were *fated* to be *We*, then the talented would happily produce at *We* precisely what they do at *Wt*,[39] but they refuse for strategic reasons to produce that much when offered *We*, since their refusal induces an offer of *Wt*. But this answer sullies the recommendation of D2. It is not irrational, here, in the sense Rawls intended, even if it is quixotic, in the face of the power of the talented, to express a preference for the equality-preserving D3.

By contrast with what holds for the bad case, in both the good and the standard cases talented people prefer, and are resolved, to produce less at *We* than at *Wt*, and that is why D3 is unfeasible (though it is not objectively so). In the good variant of that, the work of the talented in D2 is more arduous than that of the untalented, sufficiently more so to justify the difference between *Wt* and *Wu*. (Notice that, to acknowledge this possibility, I need not say how such judgements of arduousness, and of what would compensate for it, are to be reached.) In that case, paying everybody *We* would be unfair, *from an egalitarian point of view*: in the good case the talented carry a special burden that any reasonable egalitarian must think should be compensated. Thus, suppose, to take a different sort of example from the one that confronts us here, that although people are of equal talent, circumstantial constraints mean that some work more hours than others, that all other things (including people's utility functions) are equal, and that utility is a decreasing function of labour time. Then no clear-headed egalitarian would approve of equal total weekly payment, whether or not – this would depend on further features of the case – he should insist on (precisely) equal payment per hour.

The egalitarian principle that greater burden justifies greater compensating reward, operates, in our context, in favour of D2 and against D3 in the good case. Where work is specially arduous, or stressful, higher remuneration is a counterbalancing equalizer, on a sensible view of how to judge whether or not things are equal. Accordingly, and because we are examining a supposed justification of inequality, the good or special burden case poses no problem for us, for what we get when special burden is invoked is not a justification of an inequality, all things considered, but a denial that there is an inequality, all things considered.

Now, in what I call (because it seems to me to be) the standard case, the work of talented people is not distinctively burdensome, but, on the contrary, characteristically more congenial than the work of others is.[40] It is untrue, in the standard case, that high pay compensates the talented for specially arduous toil. Suppose, then, that we are in the standard case, in which Wt in particular is not required to compensate the talented for a special burden, and that there is, more generally, no special burden case against paying everyone We. Then although talented people may, as in the bad case, successfully hold out for Wt as a condition of producing more than what they do in D1, and thereby make D3 impossible, it is hard to see why an egalitarian should be expected to regard what they then do as acceptable, even if nothing can be done about it. In explaining his refusal to endorse the justice of D2, the egalitarian can draw on the notions used by Rawls to pass from equality of opportunity to D1. He can say that, in knocking D3 out of the feasible set, talented people are violating

> a conception of justice that nullifies the accidents of natural endowment and the contingencies of social circumstance as counters in the quest for . . . economic advantage.[41]

Instead, they are operating within the terms of a conception of justice which, in significant degree (albeit, to be sure, not in the same degree as *laissez-faire* does)

> weight[s] men's share in the benefits and burdens of social cooperation according to their social fortune or their luck in the natural lottery.[42]

At one point Rawls says that the Pareto-improving inequalities might work by 'set[ting] up various incentives which succeed in eliciting more productive efforts', and another passage suggests that this is the principal form of Pareto-improving inequality that he contemplates.[43] This means that talented people require an unequalizing incentive to produce more than they do at D1: it is their demand for more than what the untalented could then have that knocks out D3. Now, it is entirely reasonable for the talented to get more than the *W* they get in D1 when they produce more, as they indeed do in D2, but they do get more than *W* when they get *We* in D3. What is startling is that Rawls recommends a rate of pay, *Wt*, which is higher than that of others, a rate they secure by virtue of the bargaining power associated with their superior talent, when that superior talent was originally, in the construction of D1, said to justify no superior reward. If the talented had objected to the equality of D1, on the ground that they produce more than others do in D1, they would have been told that they were seeking to exploit morally arbitrary advantages. They can be told the same thing when they reject D3 in favour of D2. We can ask: why was the original equality not pitched at D3, instead of at D1, when D3 is Pareto-superior to D1 (at least on the present assumption, to wit, that the labour of the talented is not specially burdensome)? Had we begun with D3, D2 would have been seen for what it is: an unjustifiable (on the assumptions that lead to D1) falling away from an objectively feasible equal condition.

Let us now set aside, because they would only complicate things unprofitably, cases in which the talented carry a special labour burden for which *We* fails to compensate but for which *Wt* overcompensates. We can then state the following dilemma for the Pareto argument. Either the talented carry, in D2, a special burden compensated for by the difference between *Wt* and *Wu*, in which case *it is myopic to represent movement from D1 to D2 as issuing in an inequality*;[44] or *Wt* is not required to compensate for any burden, in which case *there is no reason for an egalitarian to regard D2 as acceptable, and every reason for him to recommend D3*. In other words: either the extra money that the talented get in D2 makes them no better off, all things (including labour burden) considered, or it does make them better off, all things considered. In the first alternative there is no justified *inequality*, all things considered, because there is no inequality, all things considered; in the second, there is no *justified* inequality, or at any rate the inequality that obtains still awaits its justification, *and it is difficult to see how it could be justified by anyone who approves of the first Rawlsian move, from equality of opportunity to equality*. Only when the issue of labour burden is obscured can it be made to seem that a justified (all things considered) inequality has emerged. [. . .]

V. Conclusion

I have contended that the two parts of the Pareto argument are inconsistent with one another. The grounds given in its first part for choosing equality as a just starting point contradict the grounds given in its second part for endorsing a departure from equality as just. For departure from equality is necessary only if and because talented people do not adjust their behaviour to the demands of the conception of justice required by the grounds given for starting with equality. The final recommendation of the Pareto argument accedes to injustice in its account of what justice is.

The Pareto argument proposes a dilemma: you cannot have both (1) equality and (2) Pareto-optimality. I have argued that, strictly speaking, the Pareto principle does not require inequality; and that, unstrictly speaking – taking the behaviour of the talented as given – the inequality it requires is unjust.[45]

Notes

1   See John Rawls, *A Theory of Justice* (Cambridge, Mass.: Harvard University Press, 1971), sections 10–17; and Brian Barry, *Theories of Justice* (London: Harvester Wheatsheaf, 1989), pp. 213–34.
2   Whether they should themselves be styled 'egalitarians' is not a matter that needs to be addressed in this essay.
3   Barry, *Theories of Justice*, p. 217.
4   Definitions: State A is *strongly Pareto-superior* to state B if everyone is better off in A than in B, and *weakly Pareto-superior* if at least one person is better off and no one is worse off. If state A is Pareto-superior to state B, then state B is *Pareto-inferior* to state A. State A is *Pareto-inferior* (*tout court*) if some state is Pareto-superior to A. State A is *Pareto-optimal* if no state is Pareto-superior to A: it is *strongly* Pareto-optimal if no state is weakly Pareto-superior to it and *weakly* Pareto-optimal if no state is strongly Pareto-superior to it. States A and B are *Pareto-incomparable* if neither is (even weakly) Pareto-superior to the other. A change is a *weak Pareto-improvement* if it benefits some and harms none, and a *strong Pareto-improvement* if it benefits everyone. The *Pareto principle* mandates a Pareto-improvement whenever one is feasible: the strong one mandates (even) weak Pareto improvements, and the weak one only strong Pareto improvements.
5   Rawls, *A Theory of Justice*, p. 7. Cf. John Rawls, *Political Liberalism* (New York: Columbia University Press, 1993), p. 80.
6   See Barry, *Theories of Justice* pp. 213–15, and see Rawls, *A Theory of Justice*, p. 104.
7   Barry, *Theories of Justice*, p. 224. That may seem to be a strange thing to say. On p. 167 below I try to make it seem less strange.

8   Ibid., p. 226.
9   The claim that the Pareto-improving unequalizing move might be accepted on grounds other than justice, that, indeed, Rawls's own case for it is not really one of justice, was made, persuasively, by David Lyons in his 'Nature and Soundness of the Contract and Coherence Arguments', in *Reading Rawls*, ed. Norman Daniels (Oxford: Blackwell, 1975), pp. 152–3.
10 Rawls, *A Theory of Justice*, p. 65.
11 Although, as I have said, I am in sympathy with the first part of the argument, I also have reservations about it. Rawls's use of the motif of moral arbitrariness is subjected to (as yet) largely unanswered searching criticism by Robert Nozick in his *Anarchy, State, and Utopia* (New York: Basic Books, 1974), pp. 213–27.
12 'The Basic Structure as Subject', in *Political Liberalism*, p. 281, and see 'A Well-Ordered Society', in *Philosophy, Politics, and Society*, 5th series, eds Peter Laslett and James Fishkin (New Haven: Yale University Press, 1979), pp. 15–16.
13 G. A. Cohen, 'Incentives, Inequality, and Community', in *The Tanner Lectures on Human Values*, vol. 13, ed. Grethe B. Peterson (Salt Lake City: University of Utah Press, 1992).
14 Rawls, *A Theory of Justice*, p. 72.
15 Ibid., p. 72.
16 Thomas Nagel's defence of utilitarianism against Rawls is relevant here: see 'Equality', in his *Mortal Questions* (Cambridge: Cambridge University Press, 1979), p. 119 [p. 71 in this volume].
17 As I indicate in note 20 below, I do not believe that Rawls construes libertarianism in the suggested strained fashion.
18 Barry, *Theories of Justice*, p. 222.
19 Rawls, *A Theory of Justice*, p. 64.
20 In the foregoing paragraphs I present the movement from natural liberty to equality as an entirely immanent one, each of its first two sub-stages yielding to its successor because the latter is more faithful to its predecessor sub-stage's rationale. I believe, without being certain, that Barry intends to ascribe precisely such an argument to Rawls, but I am certain that the structure of the argument Rawls himself presents (See *A Theory of Justice*, sections 12 and 13) is in one way different from the structure of the one that I have constructed, which is based on pp. 218–20 of Barry's *Theories of Justice*.

Rawls proceeds as follows. He cites the principles of 'natural liberty', 'liberal equality' and 'democratic equality' as affording three readings of the ideal of equality of opportunity. Natural liberty is rejected because of its complacency about the influence of natural and social luck on shares. Because liberal equality aims to suppress social luck, it is commended, but it is then criticized, on the ground that there is no difference between social and natural luck that would justify exclusive preoccupation with the former.

Accordingly, the movement from liberal equality to democratic equality is indeed an immanent one, but the movement from natural liberty to liberal equality is not. Natural liberty is not rejected by Rawls because of any internal incoherence of the sort that Barry gestures at but because it fails to resist the morally arbitrary.

21   Barry, *Theories of Justice*, p. 224.

22   Different egalitarians believe that different things should be equalized, so they would endorse and condemn different outcomes, but that does not matter here: the phrase 'outcome that egalitarians would endorse' can be treated here as a variable, since the argument we shall examine is for inequality no matter what conception of equality is embraced.

23   If, as Barry says, true equality of opportunity amounts to equality of outcome, then stage two of the Pareto argument, in asking us to abandon equality, also asks us to abandon true equality of opportunity. I doubt that Barry was fully alive to this aspect of his position, which implies that 'the *most* just society' (*Theories of Justice*, p. 217, my emphasis, and cf. p. 234) lacks equality of opportunity.

24   Strictly, of *social* primary goods, but, as Rawls himself does, I shall abbreviate to 'primary goods' where misunderstanding is unlikely. Primary goods are 'things that every rational man is presumed to want' since they 'normally have a use whatever a person's rational plan of life'. The 'social primary goods' are the primary goods 'at the disposition of society', to wit, 'rights and liberties, powers and opportunities, income and wealth', and the social bases of self-respect. 'Other primary goods such as health and vigor, intelligence and imagination, are natural goods; although their possession is influenced by the basic structure, they are not so directly under its control' (Rawls, *A Theory of Justice*, p. 92). Will Kymlicka argues that Rawls has no good reason for restricting his index of well-being to the social primary goods: see his *Contemporary Political Philosophy*, (Oxford: Oxford University Press, 1990), pp. 70–3. Thomas Pogge's defence of what he calls Rawls's *semi-consequentialism* (see his *Realizing Rawls* (Ithaca: Cornell University Press, 1989)) supports Rawls's restriction of the purview of justice to social primary goods.

25   To, that is, the worst off: better off people gain immediately from *in*equality. The idea is that we withhold from the poor in order to give more to the rich and, as a result, the poor end up better off, later.

26   Rawls, *A Theory of Justice*, p. 151.

27   Ibid., p. 546.

28   Ibid., p. 62.

29   Ibid., p. 101, and see ibid, pp. 15, 75, 79, 102, 179, and, decisively in favour of the interpretation of Rawls given in the present paragraph, 'A Well-Ordered Society', pp. 16–17.

30   Rawls, *Justice as Fairness: a Briefer Restatement* (Harvard University typescript, 1989), p. 57, and see ibid., pp. 56, 89.
    In my interpretation of the passages cited in this and the previous note, the constraint placed on how far ahead the talented may get depends on its being good for them that they have more talent. In a suggested counter-interpretation, Rawls says that talent endowments are morally arbitrary, so no one may benefit from them as a matter of desert, but, if the well endowed benefit from their talent in ways that also help the untalented, then the benefit redounding to the former is

acceptable. In the counter-interpretation, it is immaterial to Rawls's argument that, as he mentions, talent is a good thing.

The counter-interpretation argument may be both coherent and Rawlsian (for there is more than one argument in Rawls), but, for two reasons, I rest with my own interpretation of the cited passages. First, the counter-interpretation does not account for the rhetorically strategic placement of the repeated reminder that talent is beneficial. Second, and perhaps more importantly, Rawls is in my interpretation readily seen to be addressing an intuitively grounded protest against superior emolument to the talented, a protest that such emolument follows the notion that 'to them that hath shall be given': see the reference to Mill at n. 31 below. Rawls is naturally interpreted as replying: that is fine, provided that those who hath *not* also benefit.

As I have pointed out elsewhere ('Incentives, Inequality and Community', note 6), there is ambiguity in Rawls with respect to which inequalities are permitted. Many texts, such as those cited above, permit only inequalities that help the worst off. Other texts, those, for example, in which the leximin principle is affirmed, also permit inequalities that do not harm them. The counter-interpretation argument corresponds to the less egalitarian leximin principle. Unlike my interpretation, it does not explain why maximin might take a restrictive form, and that is the form in which maximin appears in the cited passages.

31 John Stuart Mill so describes higher reward to the talented in section 4 of chapter I of book II of his *Principles of Political Economy*: see *Collected Works of John Stuart Mill*, ed. J. M. Robson (Toronto: Toronto University Press, 1965), vol. 2, p. 210. For an adverse contrast between Rawls and Mill on this issue, see the final page of my 'Incentives, Inequality, and Community'.

32 Rawls, *A Theory of Justice*, p. 62.

33 For related points, see Ronald Dworkin, 'Equality of Resources', *Philosophy & Public Affairs*, vol. 10, no. 4 (Fall, 1981), p. 343.

34 As Michael Lessnoff pointed out, it was inconsistent with Rawls's understanding of justice as a matter of 'the proper distribution of the benefits *and burdens* of social cooperation' (*A Theory of Justice*, p. 5, emphasis added) that he omitted labour burdens from the index of social primary goods. ('Capitalism, Socialism and Justice', in *Justice and Economic Distribution*, eds William Shaw and John Arthur (Englewood Cliffs: Prentice-Hall, 1978 edition), p. 143.

Later, Rawls contemplated including leisure time among primary goods: see his 'Reply to Alexander and Musgrave', *Quarterly Journal of Economics*, vol. 88 (Nov. 1974), p. 654 [pp. 38–9 in this volume], and 'The Priority of Right and Ideas of the Good', *Philosophy & Public Affairs*, vol. 17, no. 4 (Fall, 1988), p. 257. And Thomas Pogge is quite definite: 'the index must also include *leisure time* as a distinct social primary good. This good can be defined simply as the inverse of time worked, which is a burden of social cooperation' (*Realizing Rawls*, p. 198). This is not entirely satisfactory since, if 'time worked' is a burden, it is one that varies importantly in size with the character of the job and the make-up of the person (cf. John Baker, 'An Egalitarian Case for Basic Income', in *Arguing for Basic Income*, ed. Philippe Van Parijs (London: Verso, 1992), p. 125, n. 4). And it makes matters more difficult still that some people find their fulfilment in their work. Is it a *burden* of social cooperation for them too?

Nineteen years after the publication of 'Reply to Alexander and Musgrave', Rawls sustains his non-commitment on the matter of whether leisure should be included among the primary goods (see *Political Liberalism*, pp. 181–2). I believe that this fence-sitting reflects the fact that labour is a burden (and, sometimes, benefit!) of social cooperation (so it should be a primary good) that fails the test of public checkability (see *A Theory of Justice*, p. 95) laid down for primary goods (so it should not be one).

Henceforth, when I speak of 'labour burden', I mean to refer not only to the quantity of a person's labour but also to its character in the sense of how burdensome or oppressive it is. Notice that, even if *A Theory of Justice* had included leisure time as a primary social good (or labour time as a primary social bad), we should still have been in the dark not only about the character but also about the mere quantity of people's labour inputs in D1.

35 *A Theory of Justice*, p. 62: see the text to n. 28 above.

36 See n. 4 above. D2 and D3 are Pareto-incomparable because in each some are better off than they are in the other.

37 For some readers, the following tabular presentation of the above array of comparisons may be helpful:

	D1		D2		D3
Talented	W	$<$	Wt	$>$	We
	$=$		$>$		$=$
Untalented	W	$<$	Wu	$<$	We

('$<$' means 'is less than', '$>$' means 'is greater than', and '$=$' signifies equality).

38 See my 'Incentives, Inequality, and Community', section VII, for an extended discussion of, in effect, this issue.

39 Which is to say that their labour supply curve is in the relevant region vertical. It could also be backward-bending, in which case they would produce more at We than they do at Wt.

40 It might therefore be suggested that they be paid less than others. But I shall not pursue that suggestion here: I am deconstructing an argument for inequality, not sketching a complete egalitarian theory.

41 Rawls, *A Theory of Justice*, p. 15.

42 Ibid., p. 75.

43 See, respectively, ibid., pp. 151, 78.

44 This holds whether or not D1 itself turns out, after further required specification, to be an equal distribution: that would partly depend on comparative labour burdens in D1, which were not specified in section III above.

Note that, had we specified earned income equality in D1 as wage per unit output (as opposed to, as we did, as wage per unit time), we should then have been unable to represent D1 as a state of equality without stipulating that the talented carry special labour burdens, since, for morally arbitrary reasons, they would then have been earning more per hour than the untalented. By stipulating equal wage per hour, we concealed, up to now, the labour burden issue.

Ex hypothesi, the talented get the same primary goods as others at D1. If leisure is a primary good, then they work as many hours as others, therefore produce more, but get the same income. If leisure is not a primary good, and payment is per unit output, then they get more leisure and/or more primary goods, and not, in general, the same basket of primary goods, thus specified, but just the same rate of primary goods per unit output. It would be hollow to call that a society of equality, as Rawls's own (curiously unconsummated – see n. 34 above) inclination to acknowledge leisure as a primary good betrays. If talented people should not get more just because they are talented, they should not get more leisure in the initial equality.

45   For splendid fine-grained criticisms of the penultimate draft of this article, I thank Ellen Paul. If she is as deft with others as she was with me, then her disciplining interventions help to explain the high quality of the volumes she edits. I am also grateful to the following for excellent written commentary on earlier drafts: Richard Arneson, Gerald Barnes, Joshua Cohen, John Gardner, Keith Graham, Christopher Morris, Jan Narveson, Michael Otsuka, Jeffrey Paul, John Roemer, Robert Shaver, Martin Wilkinson, Andrew Williams, Jonathan Wolff, Erik Wright and Arnold Zuboff. I am sorry that I cannot remember the names of all who gave oral help and criticism at various meetings where versions of this was read, but Gregory Kavka and Samuel Scheffler were particularly penetrating at San Diego.

8
Liberalism, Distributive Subjectivism, and Equal Opportunity for Welfare*

Richard J. Arneson

Should distributive shares be tailored to people's preferences? That is, if my preferences are more expensive to satisfy than yours, is this a good (though perhaps not conclusive) reason for society, striving to achieve distributive justice, to lavish more resources on me than on you? The most sweeping 'No' to this question rests on the claim that the fact that one person's tastes are more easily satisfiable than another's is never in and of itself a good reason, from the standpoint of distributive justice, to assign a larger share of resources to either person. A possible example of a principle that meets this taste invariance requirement is the Rawlsian difference principle regulating individual shares of primary social goods.[1] Several of the considerations that spring to mind in support of this taste invariance requirement are practical in nature. Doubtless it would be extremely costly and difficult, perhaps impossible, to set up institutions that could effectively gather and deploy the information that would be needed to tailor distributive shares to preferences. Hoping to bring about an increase in their distributive shares, individuals would have an incentive to present false information about their preferences to these share-setting institutions. One pictures a bureaucratic

* An ancestor of this article was read at the Pacific APA meeting in March 1985. I am grateful to Holly Smith for helpful criticism on this occasion. I also want to thank the editors of *Philosophy & Public Affairs* for instructive criticisms of various drafts of this article. Research for this project was supported by a University of California President's Research Fellowship in the Humanities.

nightmare. I ignore these practical feasibility issues in this article except for a brief discussion in the [final] section. In the rest of the article I assume that correct and full information regarding people's preferences is available at no cost to whatever institutions we establish to implement the principles of distributive justice that we accept.

Imagine an agency charged with the task of upholding some principle of distributive justice in the following way. The agency scans the situation of individual citizens in order to determine their holdings of various resources singled out by the principle and to develop an account of how they came to hold these resources couched in terms the principle stipulates as pertinent. If citizens' holdings diverge from what the principle prescribes, the agency is empowered to redistribute resources to bring the actual distribution into closer conformity with that norm.

The claim I wish to defend is that for purposes of determining what should count as fair shares from the standpoint of distributive justice, the appropriate measure of a person's resources is some function of the importance those resources have for that very person as weighted by her conception of her own welfare (perhaps corrected to accommodate the conception she would hold if she reflected with full information and full deliberative rationality). Following Thomas Scanlon, I will call this claim about the appropriate measure of fair shares *distributive subjectivism.*[2] Here 'distributive subjectivism' labels the position that for the purposes of a theory of distributive justice the correct account of nonmoral value is one according to which the good for a person is the fulfillment of his (corrected) tastes and values. This is a claim about what is good insofar as what is good partially determines what is fair. Whether fairness requires maximizing the good, maximining the good, providing equal (or some other appropriate set of) opportunities for the good, requiring equality of the good at as high a level as possible, tailoring people's shares of the good to some notion of what they deserve, or instituting some mix of the above policies or an altogether different one is left entirely open.

For the most part I defend distributive subjectivism by working out one specific version of it, coupling that to a partial explication of fairness as provision of opportunities, and showing that the resultant position is capable of meeting several recent apparently powerful criticisms of subjectivist approaches to distributive justice. Among the criticisms I discuss are influential objections raised by John Rawls, and Ronald Dworkin. [. . .]

Both Rawls and Dworkin argue against the desirability in principle of any account of distributive justice that holds that an individual's fair share of resources varies with that individual's preferences. Their criticisms focus on the proposal that the proper measure (so far as distributive justice is concerned) of the share of resources of any given individual is the degree to which those resources in fact make a contribution to the individual's welfare, understood as the satisfaction of her preferences. Rawls, generalizing from the practice of religious tolerance, holds that liberal theory deems the various individual conceptions of the good pursued by citizens to be incommensurable, so as a matter of principle the state should make no attempt to rank citizens' differing levels of achievement of their good on a common scale in order to mold these achievement levels into some desirable overall pattern.[3] In a similar spirit, Dworkin identifies the political doctrine of liberalism with commitment to a conception of equality that supposes that 'government must be neutral on what might be called the question of the good life'.[4] From the standpoint of neutrality urged by Dworkin, even the austere theory that the good consists of people getting what they want is condemned as unfairly partisan. According to Rawls and Dworkin the proper job of the state – so far as economic distribution issues are concerned – is to secure a fair share of resources for each individual in an environment that allows each to develop and pursue her own conception of the good. What, if anything, citizens do with these resources is their own business, not the government's proper concern. [. . .]

Preference

One may prefer something for its own sake or as a means to further ends; my concern is with the former.

In a broad sense of 'prefer', one may prefer x over y owing to a moral or religious commitment or one's sense that x is best from an impersonal standpoint though bad for oneself. In what follows I restrict the discussion to self-interested preferences – what one prefers insofar as one seeks one's own advantage. I take it to be obvious that, all things considered, a person may prefer to do what he believes to be morally required or what is nonmorally best from an impersonal standpoint while being perfectly aware that this course is not in his own interest. Of course, in other cases, such as a parent acting on behalf of his child, it may be difficult to disentangle to what extent one is acting for one's own sake rather than for the sake of another. The test of self-interested preference is what a person would prefer if she were to set aside her sense of what is morally required or morally supererogatory, her altruistic concern for others, and her concern for what is nonmorally good from an impersonal standpoint.[5]

I suppose that preferences involve behavioral dispositions, feelings or desires of a certain sort, and judgments of personal value, these three elements being conceptually independent of one another but often found together. Normally, when I prefer x to y it is true of me that (a) I am disposed to choose x over y, all else being equal, when presented with a choice between them, (b) when the issue is on my mind I feel that I want x more than y, other things being equal, and (c) I judge that x would be more valuable for me than y. We feel most confident in ascribing preferences when a person's choice behavior, felt desires, and verbal judgments are all consonant. But in cases of conflict among (a), (b), and (c), I stipulate that (c) has priority: the criterion of preference is sincere judgment of what is best for oneself, provided there is behavioral evidence of a weakness-of-will explanation of the discrepancy between one's choice behavior and feelings, on the one hand, and one's evaluations, on the other.[6] The ascetic mounted on his pillar may experience strong waves of desire to dismount yet attach no value to dismounting. If he dismounts yet shows clear signs of regret or sadness at his own behavior, we may credit his claim that he really prefers staying on his post to abandoning it.

Why call such judgments preferences? Are value judgments not personal opinions as to what is objectively valuable?[7] I believe that the judgmental component of preference, which implies that error is possible, has to do with the gap between actual preferences, which may be ill-considered, and the preferences one would have after more careful consideration. Personal value judgments do not claim intersubjective validity. In advancing a personal value judgment one does not make a claim one must retract if other persons fail to converge toward agreement with the judgment as the ideal of reasonable deliberation with full information is approached.

On this account, the preferences that serve as the measure of an individual's welfare are hypothetically ideally considered preferences – those the individual would have if he were to engage in ideally extended deliberation about his preferences with full pertinent information, in a calm mood, while thinking clearly and making no reasoning errors.[8] (We can also call these ideally considered preferences 'hypothetical rational preferences.')

The obvious difficulty with taking a person's actual preferences as the measure of her welfare is that actual preferences may be based on irrational belief. It seems strained to count the satisfaction of such preferences as enhancing welfare, for not only would the person disavow the preferences once she was enlightened, she also might deny that satisfying them would have had value even had she stayed unenlightened. But the equally obvious difficulty with the proposal to take hypothetical rational preferences as the measure of a person's welfare is that the person may never affirm these preferences and may in actual fact attach no value to their satisfaction. When my hypothetical rational preference is for champagne, it does not seem that you improve my welfare by seeing to it that I drink champagne even though my actual preference, steadfastly maintained until my death, is to guzzle beer.

A clarification of the idea of hypothetical rational preference may help. What determines the value of the satisfaction of any actual preference of mine is the valuation I would assign it after ideal deliberation. From this enlightened standpoint, *ex hypothesi* I would prefer champagne to beer. But from this standpoint, I might also prefer drinking beer with unenlightened gusto to drinking champagne with no appreciation of its subtle delight, so if these two options are the only ones available, from the enlightened standpoint I can make the second-best judgment that the better option for me is beer with gusto. It is my enlightened judgment of my perhaps unenlightened preferences that determines their value.[9] [. . .]

Responsibility for ends

Rawls urges that to expect that a just government tailor individual shares of social benefits to individual variations in preferences is to regard citizens merely as 'passive carriers of desires', incapable of assuming responsibility for their goals. In contrast, 'implicit in the use of primary goods is the following conception: since we view persons as capable of mastering and adjusting their wants and desires, they are held responsible for doing so (assuming the principles of justice are fulfilled).'[10]

Setting aside hard determinist worries, we note that the idea that persons are responsible for their preferences invites the response that as a matter of empirical fact, social circumstances and accidents of birth that are beyond the individual's power to control shape individual preferences to a very considerable degree. Surely social and biological factors influence preference formation, so if we can properly be held responsible only for what lies within our control, then we can at most be held to be partially responsible for our preferences. The division of responsibility between society and individual that Rawls proposes needs more justification than he supplies.

The tack I shall follows avoids engagement with these empirical issues. A natural response to the claim that subjectivist accounts slight the importance of individual voluntary choice is the suggestion that we should measure each person's distributive share not by the contribution to his welfare it in fact makes but rather by the opportunities for increased welfare it provides. An opportunity standard of distribution leaves room for final outcomes to be properly determined by individual choices for which individuals are responsible, so that some inequalities of welfare are not even prima facie injustices because the inequalities arise by way of individual voluntary choice from an initial situation in which opportunities for welfare are fairly distributed. (In this formulation, talk of 'opportunity' is a stand-in for whatever factors affecting preference formation we decide should be treated as matters of individual responsibility.) To see the import of developing a subjectivist conception of fair distribution in terms of an opportunity for welfare standard, I adopt the simplifying assumption that fairness just equals equality, and I work out an equal opportunity for welfare principle.

Whatever its ultimate metaphysical and empirical backing, it is a commonsense claim that individuals can arrive at different welfare levels owing to choices they make for which they alone should be held responsible. Individuals who otherwise would have identical expected welfare may voluntarily engage in a game of pure chance with each other with a lot of money riding on the outcome. One wins, the other loses, and thereafter their welfare expectations are very different. The winner prudently invests her winnings and the loser never recoups his losses. But surely this inequality in expected welfare does not create any prima facie case for society to correct the inequality by transfer of resources. The same would be true if the two individuals could reach the same lifetime welfare level by trying equally hard to maximize their welfare, but one chose instead to devote his life to the care of the sick and dying, or to the preservation of aesthetically pleasing wilderness vistas, or to any cause viewed either as morally desirable or nonmorally valuable from an impersonal perspective – in the process willingly sacrificing his personal welfare on behalf of this chosen cause. Or consider Rawls's example of the individual who voluntarily and freely chooses to cultivate an expensive preference, and who for that reason alone needs more wealth to sustain the same preference satisfaction level as persons who have frugally refrained from such cultivation. The norm suggested by these examples is that distributive justice does not recommend any intervention by society to correct inequalities that arise through the voluntary choice or fault of those who end up with less, so long as it is proper to hold the individuals responsible for the voluntary choice or faulty behavior that gives rise to the inequalities. Notice that the judgment that it would be inappropriate to transfer resources to restore equality of welfare in the three examples mentioned need not involve any claim that the individuals making choices that generate inequality are behaving unreasonably. No imperative of practical reason commands us to maximize our personal welfare. The judgment is rather that the duty of the just state is to provide a fair share of opportunity to each citizen, not to guarantee the attainment of a particular pattern of outcomes.

An opportunity is a chance of getting a good if one seeks it. A first step toward seeing what equal opportunity for welfare might amount to is marking Douglas Rae's helpful distinction between prospect-regarding and means-regarding equality of opportunity. According to Rae, the former version of equality of opportunity holds that two persons 'have equal opportunities for X if each has the same probability of attaining X'. The means-regarding version holds that two persons 'have equal opportunities for X if each has the same instruments for attaining X'.[11] Neither version quite serves our purpose of carving out a space for individual choice to determine outcomes consistently with equality. Suppose a government had the policy of deciding by a fair random process what welfare level each citizen should reach and then arranging matters so that each person reached exactly that randomly determined level. Such a policy satisfies the standard of prospect-regarding equality of opportunity for welfare. But this policy that implements prospect-regarding equality of opportunity leaves no room for outcomes to be legitimately affected by individual voluntary choice. My lifetime welfare level is fixed by the outcome of a lottery that is independent of any choices I might make in my life (so if I make choices that, left uncorrected, would affect my lifetime welfare, government policy is to take exactly counterbalancing steps so that ultimately my randomly determined welfare is reached).

On the other hand, if personal characteristics, such as your problem-solving ability and my strong back, are not counted as instruments, then means-regarding equality of opportunity for welfare could be satisfied in a situation in which individuals have vastly different abilities to deploy given instruments in order to produce welfare for themselves.

In contrast to both of these suggested interpretations, the ideal of equal opportunity for welfare is roughly that other things equal, it is morally wrong if some people are worse off than others through no fault or voluntary choice of their own.[12]

For equal opportunity for welfare to obtain among a number of persons, each must face an array of options that is equivalent to every other person's in terms of the prospects for preference satisfaction it offers.[13] The preferences involved in this calculation are ideally considered second-best preferences (where these differ from first-best preferences). Think of two persons entering their majority and facing various life choices, each action one might choose being associated with its possible outcomes. In the simplest case, imagine that we know the probability of each outcome conditional on the agent's choice of an action that might lead to it. Given that one or another choice is made and one or another outcome realized, the agent would then face another array of choices, then another, and so on. We construct a decision tree that gives an individual's possible complete life histories. We then add up the preference satisfaction expectation for each possible life history. In doing this we take into account the preferences that people have regarding being confronted with the particular range of options given at each decision point. Equal opportunity for welfare obtains among persons when all of them face equivalent decision trees – when the expected value of each person's best (most prudent), second-best . . . nth-best choice of options is the same. The opportunities persons encounter are ranked by the prospects for welfare they afford.

To illustrate, suppose that you and I have exactly two life options. Each of us could become either a banker or a missionary. The welfare we could expect from each of these options is the same for both of us, and known with certainty. If you become a banker and I become a missionary, you gain (say) high welfare and I gain low welfare, but equality of opportunity for welfare is satisfied, whichever choice either of us makes. But suppose instead that under your missionary option, you can choose Alaska (no mosquitoes) or Africa, whereas all of my missionary options involve mosquitoes

and there are no other relevant differences between your missionary options and mine. In this case, equality of opportunity for welfare
is violated, because on our second-best option path you have the
option of mosquito-free missionary life, which I lack.

The criterion for equal opportunity for welfare stated above is
incomplete. People might face an equivalent array of options, as
above, yet differ in their awareness of these options, their ability
to choose reasonably among them, and the strength of character
that enables a person to persist in carrying out a chosen option.
Further conditions are needed. We can summarize these conditions
by stipulating that a number of persons face *effectively equivalent*
options just in case one of the following is true: (1) the options
are equivalent and the persons are on a par in their ability to 'negotiate' these options, (2) the options are nonequivalent in such a
way as to counterbalance exactly any inequalities in people's negotiating abilities, or (3) the options are equivalent and any inequalities
in people's negotiating abilities are due to causes for which it is
proper to hold the individuals themselves personally responsible.
Equal opportunity for welfare obtains when all persons face effectively
equivalent arrays of options. When persons enjoy equal opportunity for welfare, any actual inequality of welfare in the positions
that they reach is due to factors that lie within each individual's
control and hence is nonproblematic from the standpoint of distributive justice. The norm of equal opportunity for welfare is distinct
from equality of welfare only if some version of soft determinism
or indeterminism is correct. If hard determinism is true, the two
interpretations of equality come to the same thing. [. . .]

Equality of resources versus equality of welfare

Dworkin's case against equality of welfare includes his suggestion
that a better standard than welfare for the measurement of fair shares
is at hand: a resources standard.[14]

To illustrate the intuitive attraction of a resources ethic Dworkin
constructs an expensive preferences example. Dworkin imagines a
Jude who initially possesses few resources in a society that has
achieved equality of welfare. Despite the paucity of his resources,
Jude enjoys an average level of welfare because his wants are few
and easily satisfiable. It is further stipulated that he then comes to
believe that his life would be richer if he cultivated an expensive
taste for bullfighting, and does so. But suppose that even if Jude
were given an extra allotment of resources to help him satisfy his

new expensive taste, he would still have less than an equal per capita share of society's assignable resources. Now imagine an exactly parallel case involving Louis, who initially possesses a resource share that is far above average in a society that has achieved equality of welfare. Louis now cultivates a new expensive preference, like Jude's for bullfighting. Unless Louis is given an even greater share of resources to compensate for this new expensive preference, he will have a lower level of welfare than everybody else in society. If we wish to give Jude, but not Louis, the money he needs to satisfy his expensive preference, the reason can only be, Dworkin asserts, that we are inclining toward allegiance to the ideal of equality of resources. Whether a person's preferences are expensive or cheap does not in and of itself affect what he is justly entitled to in the way of a fair share of privately held resources.[15]

The example first of all raises preference formation worries. If we suspect that Jude's initial preferences are somehow distorted by his stingy resource holdings, we may endorse his liberation from these distorted preferences. This factor will distinguish our response to Louis, whose initial holdings are generous. Stipulating that Louis and Jude differ in amount of wealth possessed tends to carry further connotations. So Dworkin may be wrong to think that a response favoring Jude over Louis can be explained only by acceptance of an equality of resources ethic.

We can eliminate the preference distortion issue from the example by stipulating that Jude's initial preferences are formed in an environment just as favorable to preference formation as the environment in which Louis's initial preferences germinate. Suppose that initially equality of opportunity for welfare is satisfied – Louis and Jude (the one with expensive, the other with cheap preferences) initially face arrays of options that offer them the same welfare prospects. Jude then acquires an expensive preference, which will cause his welfare to plummet unless he is compensated for it. Should he receive compensation? From an equal opportunity standpoint, the answer turns on whether the preference was acquired in a substantially voluntary or a substantially involuntary way. If the expensive preference was deliberately chosen by Jude, or if his acquisition of it was a foreseeable by-product of a voluntarily chosen course of action, there is no case for redistribution, because equal opportunity for welfare is fulfilled, not violated, by the example thus described. Preference changes are just components of some of the options among which people choose in planning a life. If the option sets are ratified by an equal opportunity principle, then so far as that principle is concerned we ought to let stand the results of any voluntary choice of one or another option. Suppose, on the other hand, that Jude gains the preference by a chain of events for which he is in no way personally responsible. A chance event occurs which could not have been insured against. A meteor fragment hits Jude on the head, and his preferences unpredictably change in the course of his convalescence. Equal opportunity for welfare then demands compensation. Intermediate cases will be harder to resolve, but the point should be clear that the Louis/Jude variations on the expensive preferences theme do not provide any reason beyond the supposed voluntariness of preferences for rejecting a welfare standard of measurement of shares for purposes of a theory of just distribution. As we have seen, the claim that preferences can be voluntary gives reason not to reject all subjectivist views but to accept equal opportunity for welfare.

Why compensate for expensive preferences?

Quite apart from doubts about the propriety of compensating people for voluntarily cultivated expensive preferences, many will feel that it cannot be fair to grant more resources to those with expensive tastes even if they are in no way personally responsible for those tastes.[16] This objection directly challenges the root idea of the distributive subjectivism I have been concerned to defend. The objectors might allow that a theory of distributive justice could legitimately recommend special compensation for individuals who are burdened with physical handicaps such as the lack of usable arms or legs. Compensation for physical disability may well be acceptable, but (the objection goes) it would be perverse to extend compensation to those who suffer from 'preference handicaps' such as a taste for expensive champagne rather than cheap beer. From the fact that an individual is not rightly held morally responsible for having certain expensive preferences it of course does not follow that society is morally responsible for guaranteeing their satisfaction (or compensation in the event of their frustration).

The assertion that someone is not responsible for her preferences could mean either (1) that she is not responsible for their formation, although she might now be able to take steps to alter or eliminate them, or (2) that she is not responsible for their formation and that the preferences now are fixed, unalterable by anything she might do.[17] A further distinction is that someone might not be responsible for presently having an expensive preference either because (a) she is not responsible for having the preference or (b) she is not responsible for having a preference that has now become expensive. An example of type (b) nonresponsibility would be voluntarily cultivating a preference for spending one's leisure hours driving about in one's car at a time when gas is cheap, when it is unforeseeable that the price of gas will later skyrocket.

Recall that distributive subjectivism is the view that for purposes of a theory of distributive justice the proper measure of a person's goods or resources is the welfare level that these resources enable him to reach. Of course there would be no use for such a measure unless society – or a government acting as agent for society – was sometimes rightfully in the business of distributing resources to individuals and redistributing resources among individuals in order to achieve fair shares for all. My discussion presupposes that some government redistribution along this line is legitimate, so that there is some validity to the question of what measure of interpersonal comparison of people's resource shares is appropriate.

One way to measure the disparate resources held by various individuals is by market value – the price that each individual's goods would fetch if offered for sale to others. (This is the measure of resources that is in play when we characterize a person's preferences as expensive or cheap.) On this view, people would be deemed to hold equal resources if their resource holdings were of equal monetary value. The obvious objection to this way of measuring resource shares is that if Smith and Jones are accorded sets of resources that are equal in monetary value (for simplicity, just suppose they are given equal amounts of money) and Smith has normal eyesight and no other disabilities while Jones is afflicted with bad eyesight and must spend all his resources to purchase expensive eyeglasses to correct the condition, the 'equality' of their resources shares intuitively seems illusory.[18] In these circumstances Jones has an involuntary expensive preference for normal vision, and true equality requires that he be given extra resources to compensate for the expense of correcting his vision. The point here is not just about distributive equality but about the appropriate measure of resource shares. We might hold that Smith is far more deserving than Jones and that distributive justice requires that Smith get a resource share that is greater in proportion to his greater deservingness. Still, the right measure of the resources they get, from the standpoint of distributive justice, is the extent to which they are enabled to fulfill their aims with these resources. In a nutshell, the case for distributive subjectivism involves a generalization from this particular example involving physical handicap to all other expensive preferences that individuals are not plausibly regarded as bearing any personal responsibility for.

This generalization is bound to encounter resistance. Intuitively it does seem to be more plausible to compensate people for physical disabilities such as blindness than for expensive preferences such as a taste for fancy champagne over cheap beer. To some extent, I claim, this intuition rests on the fact that these examples encourage the presumption that the individual can reasonably be held personally responsible for the taste, but not for the handicap. (If the person became blind through deliberate and fully informed participation in a dangerous sport that often gives rise to injuries that result in blindness, it becomes questionable whether compensation is owed for the handicap.) But to pursue the argument, let us suppose that both the handicap and the expensive taste of a given person are due entirely to a congenital condition. Beyond differential association with voluntary formation, an expensive taste for normal eyesight differs from an expensive taste for fancy champagne in that the former is more widely shared and likely to be comprehended and approved by more persons. Everyone can appreciate that eyesight is immensely valuable in the pursuit of a great many different life plans that all of us regard as worthy and sensible. In contrast, a taste for fancy champagne is more idiosyncratic and will strike people as more of a fluke. People need good eyes, but they do not need a high-status alcoholic drink.

Interestingly, some of the considerations just mentioned would count as good reasons from a distributive subjectivist standpoint for a public policy that compensates for handicaps but not for expensive tastes. These considerations that are reconcilable with distributive subjectivism point to the immense difficulties that any actual state agency would encounter in gathering accurate information about the nature, relative strength, and likely stability over time of any given individual's preferences. (These are factors that I have been ignoring in this article up to this point.) If people are almost sure to continue to want normal eyesight throughout their lives, but are likely to change their tastes, this is a perfectly good subjectivist reason for giving more weight to whether someone's resource bundle enables him to approximate normal vision than to whether it enables him to satisfy a taste of the moment. Also, if virtually everybody wants normal eyesight, but only some have fancy tastes, one is less likely to be making a mistake if one takes at face value an individual's claim to want normal vision compared to a claim to want exotic beverages. In many contexts of practical importance the best an agent of society can do in order to determine what a particular person prefers is to impute to that person the preferences that most people share. (Imagine a proposal to alter the federal income tax return by adding the following: 'Do you like beer or champagne? Check one. [If you check champagne, your tax liability for the year will be lowered by $100.00.]')

My claim is that if we abstract from questions regarding the personal responsibility of individuals for their predicaments and from issues regarding the feasibility of social measurements, the idea that having more expensive preferences entitles one to a larger share of social resources is not counterintuitive. But it is hard to focus on the right questions, at the appropriate level of abstraction. It may be useful to consider the distribution of resources within families, because it is reasonable to assume that family members know a great deal about how any single preference of another family member fits into the overall economy of her preference ordering. Suppose that Sally is a child who very much wants to devote her spare hours to playing baseball and that to do this she requires a mitt – at a cost of five dollars. Her sister Judy has a similarly strong desire to play the piano, and to carry out this activity she needs a piano – at a cost of eight hundred dollars. Their parents provide each child the means with which to carry on her chosen avocation and each child gains a comparable benefit from this parental gift. In the example as described each child has been given equal consideration; it does not seem unfair that one child gets more because her preferences happen to be more expensive to satisfy. (In an alternate terminology, each child gets the same resource provision, because the right measure of resources provided is the contribution they make to one's welfare.)

The relevance of this example might be subject to doubt on the ground that distribution by parents to their children need not answer to any principles of distributive justice. I think the doubt is misplaced and that it is easy to think of examples in which the parents' allocation of scarce family resources among family members is grossly unfair. Be that as it may, one can find social justice examples in which variations in individual preference plausibly ground variations in treatment. Suppose that we know that workers who entered the steel industry and became dependent on its prosperity by developing firm-specific and industry-specific skills could not have predicted that world market conditions would eventually result in a large, sudden, and permanent contraction of employment within the industry. These workers who valued stable employment highly and made prudent career choices with a view to securing it are now faced with the prospect of long-term unemployment in their chosen field and the necessity of making a painful switch to some new career. The question arises whether the extent to which the objective circumstance of unemployment has a negative impact on a given individual's preference satisfaction prospects affects what society might owe to that individual by way of compensating him for this loss. Of course tailoring unemployment benefits to the full detail of a given worker's fundamental life aims is hopelessly impractical. But suppose we discover good psychological evidence for the assertion that middle-aged workers, 40 to 55 years of age, tend to experience far more distress from sudden permanent job loss than either younger or older workers when objective features of their plight such as duration of unemployment and loss of income are held constant. On a subjectivist view, this is a good reason for an unemployment compensation policy that provides extra support to middle-aged beneficiaries.[19]

If we put aside practical difficulties about information-gathering and measurement of hypothetical rational preferences, what further good reasons could there be for treating involuntary expensive preferences due to handicaps differently than involuntary expensive preferences due to tastes? Practicalities aside, a subjectivist view insists on parity of treatment: Compensate for expensive preferences of either sort to the same extent. Surely the mere fact that one type of preference is widespread among citizens while another type is less common cannot in and of itself warrant favoring those whose preferences are more popular. Nor could the fact that one type of preference is more widely accepted and approved than another type justify (though it might well help explain) society's greater willingness to make good any deficits in the satisfaction of the more generally approved type of preference. The fact that more citizens admire chess than checkers (or the reverse) is not a good reason for the state to bring it about that devotees of one or the other pastime reach higher welfare levels.

The evaluation of a person's preferences by citizens generally rather than by the person who has the preferences can be a sensible basis for public policy only if we take the general evaluation to be

a (perhaps rough) indicator of the objective worth of those preferences. To be justifiable, differences in the treatment by society of
different categories of expensive preferences must then rest on perfectionist judgments. In other words, if we could discover a viable
perfectionist theory that enabled us to assign points to any fundamental aim of a person according to the contribution its fulfillment
would make toward her achievement of an objectively worthwhile
life, we would then have good grounds for discounting those preferences (whether cheap or expensive) that are subjectively overrated
by the persons whose preferences they are. We could perhaps distinguish between expensive preferences due to physical handicaps
and expensive preferences due to fancy tastes on the ground that
satisfaction of the former contributes significantly to an objectively
good life whereas satisfaction of the latter does not. We might hold
that the objective value of intoxication at social gatherings is equally
served by cheap beer or expensive champagne, so a preference for
fancy drink per se does not give rise even to the slightest prima
facie obligation on the part of society to supply the devotee of
fancy drink the means to satisfy her specialized desire.[20]

In tracing the source of the intuition that just having an expensive preference does not give society any reason at all to lavish
more resources on a person than he would otherwise be entitled to
have, we are led back to a vast project of uncertain status: the
construction of a perfectionist theory of worthwhile human life
that is fit to serve as part of a theory of distributive justice in modern
liberal society. I do not wish to be prejudicial in judging the prospects
of such a project. It might prove viable.[21] But it is uncontroversially
the case that we presently lack anything close to a viable theory of
this kind and that a good deal of contemporary thought about the
moral foundations of liberal society – by such writers as Rawls,
Dworkin, and Bruce Ackerman[22] – self-consciously seeks to eschew
any reliance on perfectionist doctrine. The 'don't compensate for
expensive preferences' intuition thus rests upon a large promissory
note that contemporary moral theory has not redeemed and that
may ultimately prove unredeemable. The conviction that mere
preferences are analytically distinguishable from true human needs
may prove to be illusory.

The reader may be unmoved by this argument owing to conviction
that there is conceptual space for a viable position intermediate
between perfectionism and subjectivism that will be congenial to
liberal theories of distributive justice. The subjectivist view holds

that for purposes of determining fair shares we should measure a person's resource holdings by the level of self-interested preference satisfaction that they enable the person to reach. The perfectionist view holds that the proper measure of a person's resource holdings is the level of objective well-being that they enable the person to reach. Of course there are other possible positions. One could hold that the proper measure of persons' resource shares is a broad social consensus as to what the resources are worth.[23] But we have already challenged the appropriateness of using social consensus to determine what counts as the fair share of an individual who dissents from this consensus and embraces idiosyncratic evaluations of his resource share. The liberal theorists mentioned in the previous paragraph have not so far succeeded in articulating an intermediate position on how to measure resources for purposes of applying principles of distributive justice.

The measurement problem can be posed simply. Various goods will qualify as resources the distribution of which ought to be fair (according to whatever principle of distributive justice we accept). Presumably having more of one resource can be balanced by having less of another. But how is the measurement of an individual's overall resource share to be done? If Smith has a nice house, a clunky car, access to the beach, and a PhD from Yale, whereas Jones has a spectacular house, a Jaguar, no beach access, and a high school diploma, who has the greater resource share? Ackerman abstracts from this issue by supposing that distributive justice is concerned with the allocation of a homogeneous 'manna,' an all-purpose resource.[24] Rawls proposes primary social goods as the basis of interpersonal comparison. Primary social goods are goods that are both distributable by society and such that every rational person wants more rather than less of them, whatever else she wants. According to Rawls there are several such primary social goods, so to determine people's primary social good shares an index is needed, but in none of his writings to date does he make any proposal as to how to construct such an index. Pending a proposal for constructing a primary social goods index, we lack a Rawlsian solution to the measurement problem.[25] The case of Dworkin is more complex, and I lack space to give his proposal adequate treatment here, but I wish to note and to endorse a conclusion reached by several of his critics: 'Dworkin's attempt to jettison welfare as the concern of distributive justice and to replace it with resources is a failure.'[26] To mention one other attempt to find a viable midway position, consider Amartya Sen's recommendation that for purposes of distributive justice the appropriate basis of interpersonal comparison of persons' situations is not the amounts of resources they hold, but rather the functionings of various sorts that they are enabled to achieve via these resources.[27] For example, distributive principles should be sensitive not to the individual's available food stock, but to the extent that the food enables him to be well-nourished, not to the instruction expended upon the individual, but to whether it enables him to read and write and do arithmetic, and so on. But Sen's proposal (as he recognizes)[28] does not suffice for interpersonal comparisons, because a given batch of resources at the disposal of an individual will always generate an indefinitely large number of functioning capabilities of various kinds, and the question arises how to amalgamate these various discrete functioning scores into an overall score that registers the overall functioning capability that the batch provides for that individual. I see no way to construct such an index except either in terms of the person's subjective rating of his various functioning capabilities (which brings us back to distributive subjectivism) or in terms of a perfectionist rating of those functioning capabilities (in which case the viability of a perfectionist doctrine is once again presupposed). [. . .]

Notes

1 I say this is a 'possible' example because in recent writings Rawls seems to treat the notion of a primary social good as relativized to people's fundamental interests in modern democratic societies. See John Rawls, 'Kantian Constructivism in Moral Theory: The Dewey Lectures 1980', *Journal of Philosophy* 77 (1980): 515–72.

2 In 'Preference and Urgency,' *Journal of Philosophy* 72 (1975): 655–69, Thomas Scanlon defends objective criteria of judgments of well-being for use in deciding issues of distributive justice: 'By an *objective criterion* I mean a criterion that provides a basis for appraisal of a person's level of well-being which is independent of that person's tastes and interests, thus allowing for the possibility that such an appraisal could be correct even though it conflicted with the preferences of the individual in question, not only as he believes they are but even as they would be if rendered consistent, corrected for factual errors, etc.' (p. 658).

3 See John Rawls, *A Theory of Justice* (Cambridge, Mass.: Harvard University Press, 1971), p. 94; 'Fairness to Goodness', *Philosophical Review* 84 (1975): 536–54, esp. pp. 551–3; 'A Kantian Conception of Equality', *Cambridge Review* 96 (1975), 94–9; 'Social Unity and Primary Goods', in *Utilitarianism and Beyond*, ed. Amartya Sen and Bernard Williams (Cambridge: Cambridge University Press, 1982), pp. 159–86; and 'The Priority

of Right and Ideas of the Good', *Philosophy & Public Affairs* 17, no. 4 (Fall 1988), 251–76.

4 Ronald Dworkin, 'Liberalism', in *Public and Private Morality*, ed. Stuart Hampshire (Cambridge: Cambridge University Press, 1978), p. 127.

5 Cf. John Stuart Mill, *Utilitarianism*, in *Collected Works*, ed. J. M. Robson (Toronto: University of Toronto Press, 1969), 10:213. The suggested test of self-interested preference does not rule out the possibility that prior moral training may causally affect what an individual now wants, setting morality aside.

6 This stipulation does not settle what to say when a person's judgments of personal value are in conflict with her choice behavior and feelings of desire but she does not experience herself as divided. As Gary Watson points out in a related context, 'When it comes right down to it, I might fully "embrace" a course of action I do not judge best; it may not be thought best, but is fun, or thrilling; one loves doing it, and it's too bad it's not also the best thing to do, but one goes for it without compunction' ('Free Action and Free Will,' *Mind* 96 [1987]: 150).

7 On this issue see Amartya Sen, 'Well-being, Agency and Freedom: The Dewey Lectures 1984,' *Journal of Philosophy* 82 (1985): 189–90.

8 See Richard B. Brandt, *A Theory of the Good and the Right* (Oxford: Oxford University Press, 1979), pp. 110–29; David Gauthier, *Morals by Agreement* (Oxford: Oxford University Press, 1986), pp. 21–59; and Derek Parfit, *Reasons and Persons* (Oxford: Oxford University Press, 1984), pp. 493–9.

  On the definition of *hypothetical ideally considered preference* in the text, a preference based on more full information and greater deliberative rationality than the preference it supplants is not necessarily superior to it. What determines the value of satisfying a preference is the attitude the agent would adopt toward it after ideal deliberation.

9 In this paragraph I attempt to solve a difficulty noted by James Griffin in 'Modern Utilitarianism,' *Revue internationale de philosophie* 36 (1982): 334–35. See also Amartya Sen and Bernard Williams, 'Introduction' to *Utilitarianism and Beyond*, p. 10.

  We should distinguish between 'first-best' and 'second-best' hypothetical rational preferences. First-best preferences are what one would want for oneself, to make one's life go best, after fully informed ideal deliberation, on the assumption that the results of this hypothetical deliberation can determine one's actual preferences. Second-best preferences are what one would want for oneself, to make one's life go best, after fully informed ideal deliberation, where full information includes knowledge about the real-world costs of changing one's actual preferences, the likelihood that attempts at change will be successful, the likelihood that such attempts will be made in one's actual life, and so on.

10 Rawls, 'Fairness to Goodness', p. 553. The phrase 'passive carriers of desires' is from 'Social Unity and Primary Goods', p. 169.

11 Douglas Rae, Douglas Yates, Jennifer Hochschild, Joseph Morone, and Carol Fessler, *Equalities* (Cambridge, Mass.: Harvard University Press, 1981), p. 81.

12 Cf. Parfit, *Reasons and Persons*, p. 26.

13 This paragraph and the second and third paragraphs following it are borrowed from my 'Equality and Equal Opportunity for Welfare,' *Philosophical Studies* 56 (1989), 77–93.

14 Ronald Dworkin, 'What is Equality? Part 2: Equality of Resources', *Philosophy & Public Affairs* 10, no. 4 (Fall 1981), 283–345.

15 Dworkin, 'What Is Equality? Part 1,' pp. 228–40.

16 The Editors of *Philosophy & Public Affairs* called my attention to the need to respond to this criticism. See also Scanlon, 'Preference and Urgency', pp. 663–7, and 'The Significance of Choice', in *The Tanner Lectures on Human Values*, ed. Sterling M. McMurrin (Salt Lake City: University of Utah Press, 1988), 8, 149–216. For a clear statement of the antiresourcist position, see Paul Samuelson, *Foundations of Economic Analysis* (New York: Atheneum, 1965), p. 225.

17 If someone finds himself with an expensive preference for which he is nonresponsible in sense (1), but which he can now alter if he chooses, would he not properly be held responsible for continuing to hold the preference (which he can now see puts a strain on scarce social resources)? Yes and no, according to the norm of equal opportunity for welfare. This principle requires that opportunities for welfare be initially equal, such that any later welfare inequalities will be traceable to choices and conduct for which it is fit to hold individuals responsible. But at the initial canonical moment my opportunities – including my opportunities to alter my expensive preferences – are to be evaluated from the standpoint of prudence, as explained above in the text. So if initially I have an expensive preference, which by dint of effort I could gradually replace with a cheaper preference, but I now evaluate that cheaper preference as worthless (it might be counting the grass on courthouse lawns), the option of exchanging the expensive preference for this cheaper preference will count for nothing.

18 On this point, see my 'Equality and Equal Opportunity for Welfare,' p. 78.

19 This example is decisive only against the position that welfare deficits per se should never affect what people are owed under principles of distributive justice. Another possible position – which I do not address – is that preference satisfaction is a component of any reasonable conception of objective value and should count in distributive justice calculations to the extent that the satisfactions in question are ratified as significant in an adequate objectivist (perfectionist) view. See Scanlon, 'Preference and Urgency', p. 658, and Amartya Sen, 'Equality of What?' in his *Choice, Welfare and Measurement* (Oxford: Blackwell, 1982), pp. 363–4.

20 Notice that a perfectionist doctrine supports the 'don't compensate for expensive preferences' intuition only to the extent that the doctrine judges that satisfying fancy tastes is no more objectively valuable than satisfying comparable unfancy tastes. 'Perfectionism' labels the view that for purposes of distributive justice theory, objective knowledge of human good (what constitutes a good human life) is attainable, that institutions should be organized so as to give all citizens a fair share of the good, and that a person's resource share should be measured by the extent to which it enables that person to have a good life, a life exemplifying human perfection.

21 See, for example, Joseph Raz, *The Morality of Freedom* (Oxford: Oxford University Press, 1986), for a perfectionist approach to the issues discussed here.
22 Bruce Ackerman, *Social Justice in the Liberal State* (New Haven: Yale University Press, 1980).
23 See Scanlon, 'Preference and Urgency,' p. 668.
24 Ackerman, *Social Justice in the Liberal State*, pp. 24, 188–89.
25 See Rawls, 'Social Unity and Primary Goods'; Larry Alexander and Maimon Schwarzschild, 'Liberalism, Neutrality, and Equality of Welfare vs. Equality of Resources', *Philosophy & Public Affairs* 16, no. 1 (Winter 1987), 89–90; and my 'Primary Goods Reconsidered', *Nous* 24, 1990, 429–54.
26 Alexander and Schwarzschild, 'Liberalism, Neutrality, and Equality of Welfare', p. 109. (Alexander and Schwarzschild do not endorse equality of welfare, however.) For related criticisms of Dworkin, see John Roemer, 'Equality of Talent', *Economics and Philosophy* 1 (1985), 151–86; Roemer, 'Equality of Resources Implies Equality of Welfare', *Quarterly Journal of Economics* 101 (1986), 751–84; my 'Equality and Equal Opportunity for Welfare'; and G. A. Cohen, 'On the Currency of Egalitarian Justice', *Ethics* 99 (1989), 906–44.
27 Sen, 'Equality of What?'; 'Well-being, Agency and Freedom', pp. 185–203; and 'The Standard of Living: Lecture I.'
28 Sen, 'Well-being, Agency and Freedom', p. 200.

9

Justice in the Distribution of Health Care

Ronald Dworkin *

I

You might think it very odd that, living as I do half the year in Britain and half in the United States, I've come to Canada to talk about justice in the distribution of medical care. In both those countries, the Canadian structure for the distribution of health care is taken by many people to be a model of success. Your Dean mentioned my former colleague at University College, Oxford, who is now my President. Under his administration, and under the supervision of his wife, the United States is now, as you know, engaged in a massive re-examination of health care. Almost every day an article appears in the American press about the Canadian plan, which is widely proposed as a model for Americans to follow. Nevertheless, strains on your system of health care are beginning to become evident. There's talk of rationing, and more people go south of the border to seek medical care. Doctors in negotiation with the provincial authorities claim with greater stridency that they are seriously underpaid. The system, nevertheless, is producing more Canadian doctors than economists think wise. You, too, will face the problems I'll discuss this evening. You too must worry about justice in the distribution of health care when it comes – and I'm sure it will come – to rationing health care explicitly.

Some people, particularly in America now, say there is really no need to ration health care. They agree that medical expense already

* This lecture was delivered on 17 March 1993 at the Faculty of Law, McGill University, as the Inaugural Lecture of the McGill Lectures in Jurisprudence and Public Policy.

203

constitutes an alarming proportion of the American economy, and that, even though America spends that much in the aggregate, forty million Americans are wholly uninsured or without any adequate health care, which is intolerable. But they deny that correcting these deficiencies will require some form of rationing: they say that there is so much waste and inefficiency in the health care system that, if these were eliminated, we could save enough money to insure that everyone had all the medical treatment he needed. We know what they mean. The administrative inefficiency of United States medical insurance companies and carriers is legendary. American doctors' salaries are large and, according to many people, inflated. The average medical salary two years ago in the United States was over $160 000 – the *average*. Nevertheless, a series of recent studies suggests that even if administrative efficiency were greatly improved, and even if doctors' salaries were capped at some reasonable level, rationing of health care would still be inevitable, because by far the biggest cause of the explosion in health care costs (not only in the United States, but, I believe, in Canada as well) is a massive supply of new technology. It isn't that we're paying all that much more for what we formerly bought cheaper; it is that we now have so much more to buy.

Many politicians and some doctors say that much of the new, expensive technology is 'unnecessary' or 'wasteful' or 'inappropriate'. But if you look to see what they mean, you find they have in mind techniques that are (as it's often put) 'low yield', which is not the same as 'no yield'. They point, for example, to massive mammography screening of women under the age of fifty, or to the heavy use, in some medical facilities, of magnetic resonance imagining. A society that spends a great deal of money on routine screening or expensive diagnostic equipment may not save *many* more lives than a society that does not. But it will presumably save *some* more lives, and that means that we cannot appeal just to efficiency as an abstract value to justify saving the cost. We cannot recommend eliminating 'inappropriate' medical care without deciding what medical care is appropriate, and why, and that, in turn, depends upon how we answer the question: 'how much medicine *should* a society provide?'

That question can usefully be divided into two more specific ones. The first is the question of a community's *aggregate* health care budget. Money spent on health care (I include not just acute care but also preventative medicine, care of the chronically sick or disabled, and so forth) is money that might be spent on education, or on economic infrastructure that will produce more jobs. How much of the overall budget should be devoted to health care instead of other plainly valuable projects, like these? The second question, though it's really part of the first, is the question of distribution. Once it's established what a society should spend overall on health care, then it must also be decided who should have that care, and on what basis it should be allocated. Of course, nations struggling with health care costs must resolve many issues beyond these twin questions of justice. There are economic questions – what are reliable predictors of how much a particular health care plan or structure will cost? There are administrative issues: what is the most efficient organization for administering any particular plan? There are medical questions: what is the likely impact of a particular program on morbidity and mortality? Above all, there is the political problem: what plans will a particular democracy in fact be willing to accept and pay for? I don't mean to denigrate the importance of these various problems, or to deny their evident connections with the problems of justice. But I shall concentrate on the latter. To repeat: In all justice, how much should a decent society spend on medical care, broadly described? In all justice, how should that society distribute what it does spend – who should get what? Behind these two questions lies a more explicitly philosophical one. What is the right standard to use in answering these questions? What should we take as our ideal of justice in medical care?

II

I begin by describing an ancient and attractive ideal that many people instinctively accept, which I shall call the ideal of *insulation*. It has three features. The first argues that health care is, as René Descartes put it, chief among all goods: that the most important thing is life and health and everything else is of minor importance beside it. The second component of the insulation ideal is equality. The ideal supposes that even in a society which is otherwise very inegalitarian – indeed even in a society in which equality is despised as a general political goal – medical care should nevertheless be distributed in an egalitarian way so that no one is denied care he needs simply because of an inability to pay. The third component (it really flows from the other two) is the old principle of rescue, which holds that it is intolerable when people die, though their lives could have been saved, because the necessary resources were withheld on grounds of economy.

This ideal of insulation has exerted great power throughout history. Hospitals have always been paradigm examples of appropriate charities, and religion has, from ancient days, always been associated with them. Contemporary political philosophers – I have Michael Walzer in mind, for example – say that the provision of medicine constitutes a separate sphere of justice, and that in that sphere decency, community, solidarity, and equality must reign. The power of the insulation ideal is so great that people often think that though the administrative, medical, economic and political problems I described are intellectually daunting, the questions of justice are not: that it is clear what the ideal of justice demands in health care, and that our only problem is that we are unwilling to live up to that ideal. That is, I believe, a serious mistake. The crisis in health care includes a crisis in our conception of what a just health care system would be – what answers we should give to the questions of justice I set out. We face that intellectual crisis because it has become clear that the insulation ideal, for all its ancient popularity, is now irrelevant. Consider the first question I posed: the problem of the aggregate expense a decent society will commit to health care, as against competing needs and values. What advice does the ideal of insulation give? It says a society should spend all it can on health care until the next dollar it spends would buy no gain in health or life expectancy at all. Of course no society ever did organize its affairs in that way, any more than any sane individual organizes a plan of life with the goal of making that life as long and as healthy as possible. In past centuries, however, there was not so significant a gap between the rhetoric of the insulation ideal and what it was medically possible for a community to do. It was possible to give lip service to the ideal, and charge social failure to live up to it to collective moral shortfall. But now – when technology continues to produce more and more ways to spend great sums on medical care – it is self-evidently preposterous that a community should treat health as lexicographically prior to all other values. Any community that really tried to do so would secure for its citizens marginally longer lives, perhaps, but these would be lives barely worth living. Once, however, this suggestion of the ancient ideal is rejected as incredible, the ideal has nothing more to say. It has, as it were, no second best or fall-back level of advice. It simply falls silent.

In fact, as a result, philosophers, theorists and medical specialists who nominally subscribe to the ideal of insulation all despair of attacking the first question. After some discussion, they announce that the size of the overall medical budget will be 'decided in politics', which is an academic way of saying that abstract considerations of justice have nothing much to contribute to this part of the health-care discussion. I believe that that is a mistake; if I am right, then the dominance of the insulation ideal has been a hindrance, and not just not a positive contribution, to achieving justice in health care.

Now look at the second question, the question of distribution. When the theorists finish saying that politics will set the overall health-care budget, they quickly add that justice will require that that budget, whatever it is, be spent in a fair way. But how does the insulation ideal help us to define a fair distribution? It tells us something negative and undoubtedly important: that how someone is medically treated should not depend, in our society, simply on ability to pay. It tells us that if rationing is necessary, the principle of rationing should not be, as it now largely is in the United States, the pocket book. But we need more positive advice. What should the principle of rationing be, if it is *not* to be money? Once again, the ancient ideal has very little to say. The egalitarian impulse of the ideal seems to recommend that medical care be distributed according to some principle of efficacy and need. And so people committed to the ideal speak about rationing according to cost-effectiveness or according to some principle that requires money to be spent where it will do the most good.

As many of you know, the state of Oregon established a commission some time ago to try to give structure to that idea, to try to describe what rationing health care in accordance with effectiveness would mean. The difficulty, of course, as that commission discovered, is that the concept of doing the 'most good' (or, in more academic terms, of maximizing welfare, or utility, or well-being, or happiness, or capability) is systematically and multiply ambiguous. These various terms, when properly used, do not name psychological concepts. Or medical or, in my view, economic ones. They name contested ethical concepts: the proposal that health care money should be spent to do the most good means that it should be distributed in whatever way will make the lives of citizens better lives to have lived, and that goal cannot be restated, without controversy, as the goal of making lives more pleasant, or economically more productive, or socially more beneficial. Whenever you attempt to describe in more detail what making the lives of citizens better actually means, you enter the kind of controversy that it was the promise and hope of the insulated ideal to avoid, and it would be sheer disaster to try to reduce that ideal to something mechanical enough to be measured by a computer. The Oregon commission discovered this. It developed mechanical measures of the cost-effectiveness of various sets of treatment matched to various kinds of disease, typed these metrics into a computer, typed in a great deal of further information, and watched the computer produce a ranking of cost-effectiveness that ranked capping a tooth higher in social priority than appendectomy. It's perfectly true, the computer said, that you will die if you have appendicitis and don't have your appendix removed. But it costs four or five thousand dollars to do that and dentists can cap a great many teeth and prevent a massive amount of toothache if you spend that five thousand dollars on dentistry instead. Well, of course, as soon as that result appeared, the commission saw that its algorithms were hopeless, re-rigged its operational definitions, and produced something at least less implausible than that. But the story indicates the character of the problem I have in mind.

So the old ideal of insulation fails to answer our second question as well as our first. Its proposal, that health care should be distributed according to need, or so as to do the most good, or so as to improve overall welfare, is fatally ambiguous, and becomes evidently unattractive when the ambiguity is resolved by defining success in terms of some utilitarian reading. We have not, after all, settled the question of what justice in health care means, and that philosophical problem stands beside the economic, medical and administrative problems we know we face, and it may be at least equally daunting.

III

This evening I shall try to construct, at least in very broad outline, an alternate approach to justice in health care, which is based not on the insulation of health care as a separate sphere of justice or activity, but, on the contrary, on the *integration* of health care into competition with other goods. I shall describe an approach that, I believe, is more instructive about the two great issues of justice I named. I can state the central idea in advance: we should aim to make collective, social decisions about the quantity and distribution of health care so as to match, as closely as possible, the decisions that people in the community would make for themselves, one by one, in the appropriate circumstances, if they were looking from youth down the course of their lives and trying to decide what risks were worth running in return for not running other kinds of risks.

At some point (as those of you who have read any political philosophy written after the Middle Ages know) an imaginary story gets told. My story has the virtue of being less imaginary than some others, but it will nevertheless require you to exercise your imagination. Suppose that your community were to develop and change in the following three ways.

First, *per impossibile*, suppose it developed into a society in which the economic system provided 'fair equality' in the distribution of resources. I mean that government recognized its inevitable responsibility to choose amongst economic and tax structures, and chose a structure that treated all members of the society with equal concern. I have my own idea about what that means in practice, and I've tried to spell this out in a series of articles.[1] I said (this is a very crude summary) that an economic structure treats all members of the community with equal concern when it divides resources equally, measured by the opportunity costs of each person owning a particular resource, and then leaves each member free in principle to spend those resources designing a life that each believes appropriate. That conception of equality will not make people equal in the amount of money or goods each has at any particular time; still less will it mean that everyone will lead the same kind of life. Some people will have invested and some people will have consumed. Some will have spent early and some will have saved for late. The result will nevertheless be egalitarian, because the choices people will have made will answer to their own conceptions of what life is right for them.

These are my views about what a just economic system would be like, but I offer it only by way of illustration. You may – you probably do – have a different conception of what economic structures genuinely treat all people with equal concern; if so, your view of how that community would have changed, in order to meet my first condition, will be different from mine. That does not matter for the present exercise: I merely ask you to assume that it has changed, in whatever way you think justice and equal concern require.

Second, imagine that your community is also different in that all the information that might be called, roughly, state-of-the-art knowledge about the value and cost and side-effects of particular medical procedures – everything, in other words, that very good doctors know – is known generally by the public at large as well.

Third, imagine that no one in your community – including insurance companies – has any information available about the *antecedent* probability of any particular person contracting any particular disease or infirmity that he or she does not evidently already have. No one would be in a position to say, of himself or anyone else, that that person is more or less likely to contract sickle-cell anemia, or diabetes, or to be the victim of violence in the street, than any other person. So no information exists about how likely it is that young blacks, as distinguished from people generally, will die in violent fights, for example.[2]

The changes I am asking you to imagine in your community are heroic. But they are not, I think, beyond the reach of imagining, and I am not inviting you to imagine other changes. Indeed, I am asking you not to: I want you to assume that your preferences and ethical convictions, and those of other members of your community, have remained constant in spite of these changes. Very well. Suppose that your community is indeed changed in those three ways, and then also suppose that health care is simply left to individual market decisions – in as free a market as we can imagine. Medical treatment is not provided by the government for anyone, as it is for everyone here and for some people in America. Nor are there any government subsidies for health care – in particular, the premiums people pay for health care insurance are not, as they are now in the United States, tax-deductible. If people choose to purchase such insurance, they do so as they buy anything else: out of post-tax funds.

What kind of health care arrangements would develop in such a community? How much of its aggregate resources would end up devoted to health care? How would medical treatment in fact be distributed among its members? Well, of course, it is hard to say; indeed it is impossible to say with any precision, though I shall offer you some speculations in a moment. But I'm anxious to make two claims in advance of any such speculation, to show you why the question of what such a society would do is important. The first is that *whatever* the society I've just described spends as its total health-care budget, which means simply the aggregate of what individuals spend, would be the just and appropriate expense for that society. The second is that *however* health care is distributed in that society would be a just distribution of health care for that society. I must qualify those two dramatic claims to some degree, but the qualifications I need are not major, and I'll relegate them to a note.[3] So I shall proceed on the flat assumptions just stated: nothing that society does, by way of health care arrangements, is open to objection on grounds of justice, though of course what it does might be questionable or objectionable in many other ways.

If so, then it is indeed important to consider what health care arrangements our society would make if it were changed in the ways I described, because, as I shall argue, what they would do through independent decisions can serve as a guide to what we should do, in whatever way we can, to improve justice in our own circumstances. So speculation seems worthwhile. It seems likely that even though the members of the imagined community – our community transformed – would perhaps begin by making individual insurance decisions, they would soon develop, through these individual decisions, collective institutions and arrangements; it also seems likely that progressively more and more people would join those collective arrangements. They would develop very large cooperative insurance plans, or very large health maintenance organizations which provide stipulated categories of medical care for a stipulated advance contract price, or both, for example. As such plans became larger, and more efficient, it would become progressively more and more expensive, relatively, for people to make wholly personalized, individual medical arrangements for themselves, and progressively fewer and fewer people would do so. (Remember that in this society wealth is much more equally distributed than it is in our society now, and though some people are relatively rich there, they are mainly people who have decided to concentrate on saving.) So the number of people who could and would turn their back on the economies of scale and administration of the collective provisions will be few, and, as the process continues, fewer still. The result of the process might very well be something functionally very close to the single, comprehensive health care provision scheme that you have reached here in Canada. Large insurance cooperatives or health maintenance organizations might negotiate a basic scheme of provision that would be much the same for everyone. If so, however, the community would probably also develop a secondary insurance market: people would be free to negotiate specialized insurance in *addition* to that basic insurance package. What form that secondary market would take, and how large a market it would be, would, of course, depend on factors we cannot sensibly predict. But even in a much more egalitarian society, some people would be able and willing to make provision for queue-jumping, or elective cosmetic surgery, or other benefits that the basic provision made available through general collective schemes would not provide. (In a more egalitarian society, the cost of some of these special benefits might well be lower than it is now – since doctors' salaries, for example, would presumably be lower, specialized services might be available at lower cost.)

We need not dwell on the character of that secondary market: it is more important to consider the basic, standardized coverage packages which I'm assuming that the large cooperative institutions would provide. What would be the character of those packages? Well, of course, that would depend upon the mix of preferences and convictions. But we can speculate with some confidence about what would *not* be covered in such a plan. Some private insurance decisions would be plainly irrational in the imagined community: they would be what the economists might call *dominant* mistakes, by which I mean they would be mistakes, even in retrospect, no matter what happened in the future, including the worst. I'll give you one or two examples: they are extreme, but of course they would be, given the claim I've just made about them.

Almost no one would purchase insurance that would provide life-sustaining equipment once he had fallen into a persistent vegetative state, for example. That would be a dominant mistake: the substantial sum spent year-by-year in insurance premiums to provide that coverage would be at the expense of training or experience or culture or investment or jobs that would have enhanced real life. Even someone who lived only a few months after purchasing the insurance before he fell into a vegetative state would have made, in retrospect, a mistake, giving up resources that could have made his short remaining conscious life better to buy a longer unconsciousness. My second suggestion might seem more controversial. I suggest that almost no one would purchase insurance providing for expensive medical intervention, even of a life-saving character, after he entered the late stages of Alzheimer's disease or other forms of irreversible dementia. Almost everyone would regard that decision, too, as a dominant mistake, because the money spent on premiums for such insurance would have been better spent, no matter what happens, making life before dementia – life in earnest – more worth while.

Now I come to a further suggestion, more controversial still. In most developed countries, a major fraction of medical expense – in the United States it approaches forty percent of the health care budget – is spent on people in the last six months of their lives. Of course, doctors don't always know whether a particular patient will die within a few months no matter how much is spent on his care. But in many cases, sadly, they can say, with considerable confidence, that he will. I believe that if people reflected on the value of buying insurance that would keep them alive, by heroic medical intervention, four or five more months, in the condition in which most such patients undergoing that intervention live, compared with the value the premiums necessary to purchase that insurance could add to their earlier lives if spent in other ways, they would decide that buying that kind of insurance was not a wise investment. That is not to say, of course, that most people would not want those additional months, no matter in what state or condition they spent them. Many people want to remain alive as long as possible, provided they remain conscious and alert, and provided the pain is not too great. My point is rather that they would not want those additional months at the cost of the sacrifices in their earlier, vigorous life that would be necessary if they had to make that choice. They would think the money better spent, earlier, on job-training or education or investment or on something else that would benefit their lives as a whole more than just taking on a few months of very limited life at the end. I cannot quite make the claim here that I made about persistent vegetative state or advanced-stage Alzheimer's disease: that purchasing insurance for costly procedures extending life a few months would be a dominant mistake. We can imagine circumstances – someone falls fatally ill the day after buying a policy providing for such care – in which, in retrospect, the decision to buy it turned out to be a good one. But most people would agree, I think, that in the circumstances we are imagining – in which, remember, no one knows he is more likely than anyone else to contract a disease not already evident – that decision would be an *antecedent* mistake.

How much further can we go down this road? How much more insurance can we be reasonably confident people would not buy in the circumstances we are imagining? I'm not sure, and anyway have no time to explore other examples now. But I do want to raise, at least, one further issue which, as I suggested to you earlier, is already of crucial importance and will become even more critical in the next decades. How far would people in the imagined community make provision for access to the ultra-expensive medical equipment now in use, or which is being developed, or is still over the horizon?

I came here from attending a meeting at the Harvard Medical School in which new advances in technology were being described. You ain't see nothin' yet. I've already mentioned advances in diagnostic radiology: expensive magnetic resonance imaging, for example. Much of the talk at this meeting was about molecular biology: about, for example, promising research into treating cancer by creating monoclonal antibodies specific for each patient, from the patient's own genetic material, at stupendous cost, and new, very expensive, blood tests that marginally – very marginally – improve the accuracy of a diagnosis of heart disease. Each of these examples illustrates, though in different ways, how technology might come to be regarded as 'low yield' relative to its large cost. Both would undoubtedly save some lives. But at a cost, in development and production, that might seem very high when we consider how a community might use the funds in other ways that would enhance the economy and provide more jobs and a higher standard of living for more people.

Would people in the imagined society, ultimately deciding for themselves how to allocate their resources, provide for expensive and/or speculative technology? People informed and reflective might make distinctions along the following lines. They might pay to provide life-saving techniques for diseases that tend to occur relatively early in life, particularly when these techniques have a high probability of success. But they might not spend to insure for technology that is very speculative, even though it will save some lives, or for technology whose main results benefit people in relatively old age. Paying all our lives to secure the latter kind of technology, if we need it, might seem a poor decision when it means that we run a higher risk than we need to run of unemployment or an otherwise less satisfactory life. I won't pursue these speculations further. I hope I've given you some idea of the kind of choices that people in the conditions we're imagining would have to make, and of how they might be tempted to make them.

IV

Do you resist my claim that whatever such a society spent, through collective institutions governed by individual decisions of this character, would be just, and that the distribution of health care such a society achieved would also be just? You will not, if you accept a conception of social justice that assigns individuals responsibility for making the ethical choices for their own lives against a background of competent information and a fair initial distribution of resources. If you accept that vision of a just society, then you will accept my claim – though, as I said, you may well have a different conception of what a fair initial distribution of resources would be like, and how unjustified inequalities should be remedied, than I do – in which case your understanding of the conditions I described will be correspondingly different from mine.

So I will assume that you do agree with my main claim: that whatever our imagined society achieves, by way of health care arrangements, cannot be faulted on grounds of justice. I suggested, earlier, that we might therefore make practical, political use, for our own communities, of at least our less speculative conclusions about what people in the imaginary community would provide for themselves. There is a natural way in which we might be tempted to do this. Almost all government-sponsored or supervised health schemes now in existence, and almost all of those that have been proposed as vehicles of reform in the United States, define a basic health-care package of benefits that must be made available, at responsible cost, to everyone, and supplied without charge to those who cannot pay that responsible cost themselves. We might use our speculations about the imaginary society to help us to define what should be in that basic package, and what that responsible cost should be.

In one way, at least, the imaginary story might be helpful for countries, like the United States, who have not settled on a particular structure for health care reform. As I said, many people in America believe we should follow your example in constructing a single-payer arrangement in which government, not private insurance firms or health care providers, decides what medicine to offer and at what price. But others think the United States should adopt what is called a scheme of 'managed competition', in which private insurers compete to offer a basic package stipulated by government, and government supervises their performances and premium structures. As of this evening, at least, most commentators predict that a managed competition scheme will be adopted, primarily, they say, because it is better suited to the political culture of the United States than a single-payer scheme would be. But our imaginary story might be helpful in guiding the choice between the two forms of scheme, in the following way. The decision might turn, among other things including suitability to the political culture, on the degree of confidence we have in our speculations about what people would choose in the imaginary community. If we were reasonably confident that we knew roughly what such people would buy – what the dominant collective arrangements they would reach would provide – then that would argue for trying to set in place a single-payer system like yours or like the National Health Service in Britain. Government can more effectively guarantee people what it is persuaded justice demands that they have if it is free to provide it itself, in some such way. To the degree we are uncertain about what people in the imaginary world would decide, however, that argues for a scheme of managed competition with enough flexibility to allow different people to choose different packages all meeting a common stipulated standard. The choices that actual people make among such schemes would provide a self-regulating mechanism that would bring us closer to the just distribution of the imagined world.

But of course whether the United States ultimately chooses a single-payer scheme like yours or, as seems more likely, a scheme that includes private competition, is more likely to depend on considerations other than justice. Nor, I think, is justice decisive of that issue one way or the other. Both types of scheme include the idea of a basic package (or set of such packages) of insurance made available to all, and the main issues of justice consolidate in the question of what should be in that basic package or set of packages. That is the question, as I suggested, that is most directly responsive to the exercise I've been imagining. I offered you reasons for thinking that certain kinds of insurance or health organization contractual provision would be rare in the community we imagined, and that, I now submit, is a good reason why that kind of provision should *not* be part of the basic package that will be the heart of any reform in the United States and any readjustments here in Canada. Since those are expensive provisions, this is an important result. But it is a negative one, and the exercise must be conducted on the other side as well. I have little doubt that people in the imagined community would insist on provision for standard prenatal care, for example, and on the kinds of primary medical care, including relatively inexpensive routine examinations and inoculations that poor people in the United States so conspicuously lack. It follows, from the argument I have been making, that these are essential elements in the basic package that any responsible health care reform would establish.

V

I have been exploring ways in which practical health care administration and reform could be guided by the exercise I hold out: trying to imagine what health care people in the imaginary circumstances I described would provide, out of their own pockets, for themselves. It is past time, however, for me to consider the drawbacks and pitfalls of my overall argument. One danger is evident: my suggestions about how people would behave in the imaginary society are speculative, and even though some of these speculations seem very plausible, we cannot test them by asking how everyone actually behaves in communities as they are now constituted. Resources are unjustly distributed among us: Canada is not as bad in this respect as is the United States, but even Canada is very far from ideal justice in economic distribution. We obviously don't have a society in which people enjoy state-of-the-art information about medicine. On the contrary, people's medical ignorance is often cited as one reason why medical expenses continue to rise. And, of course, our insurance companies do know that risks are higher among certain groups within the community than others, and the curse of experiential rather than community rating for premiums has dogged attempts to make commercial medical insurance fair.

But it doesn't follow that our speculation about what people would want under very different, and fairer, circumstances must remain just speculation. The choices Americans of average income make about their employee insurance package in wage negotiations, for example, can offer some guidance. And research and publicity can provide better guidance. Not only government but private organizations – large medical schools, for example – could help design a few sample paradigm insurance protocols representing different insurance strategies. Some of these would provide for catastrophic care or transplant surgery in circumstances in which others denied it, for example. The protocols could be accompanied by the medical information of the kind that is crucially missing from public awareness now: by some realistic expert opinion of the expected consequences for mortality and morbidity from a public commitment to each protocol, together with, for each, some estimate of its total cost and consequent macro-economic effect. If information of that sort were put into the public domain, and challenged and debated there, the resulting discussion would be at least minimally informative about how much people value what kind of care, and might be very informative. When we think of the kind of opinions that pollsters examine now, and that feature on television discussion shows and radio phone-ins, we might welcome a shift to the kind of discussion I'm now imagining.

A second difficulty is potentially much graver, however, at least conceptually. I've imagined a utopian (in some respects) society and I've then suggested that we set out to copy one feature of that utopian society: the provision it would make for medical care. An economist will remind me that, when the first best is impossible, the second best is not always achieved by mimicking the first best *partially*. That may, indeed, make matters worse than the *status quo*, and it is not difficult to see this possibility as a threat to my argument. Suppose, for example, that we decide that if our community were just, and different in the other ways I imagined, the standard medical package nearly everyone would purchase through collective insurance arrangements would include a particular set of benefits. If we decide, therefore, that that set of benefits should make up the basic package that must be made available to everyone in our own community, some relatively low-income people may end up paying a higher share of their actual income for medical care (for themselves and, through taxes, for others) than they would have chosen to pay in a just society. Or, to put the matter the other way around, they may have less left over for other expenses than they would have chosen in those circumstances. That may not seem, particularly to them, an improvement in justice.

I do not want to minimize the problem this hypothetical example illustrates. But the possibility that the test of justice I propose *might* produce unjust results is not, in itself, a sufficient argument against accepting that test; someone who objects must show a strong likelihood that the result would in *fact* be worse, from the point of view of justice, than using some other defensible standard for designing the basic package of protection. This is not a question of who has the burden of proof. If it is true that if our economic structure were just, everyone would be able to and nearly everyone would purchase a particular medical provision, that supplies a very strong even if not decisive argument that our structure would be closer to a just one if we made sure that everyone had that provision now. We should act on that strong argument unless we have some positive reason, not just the bare possibility, that it is mistaken.

It is true, however, as the example I just gave demonstrates, that the new model of health care provision and distribution I am proposing will work more dependably as the community's tax system grows more just. If relatively low-paid workers pay much more than their fair share of taxes, because the tax structure is insufficiently progressive to be fair, then any governmental program that relies on the redistribution of tax proceeds to improve justice for those with scarcely any income at all will be compromised for that reason. It will involve an unjustified transfer to the worst-off group from the almost-worst-off-group. That reflection provides a strong reason why tax reform must be at the centre of any general campaign to improve social justice. It would be ironic and disappointing, however, if the point were stood on its head, and if those who resisted redistribution to the very poor were able to point to imperfections in the tax structure as justification for doing nothing, and retaining their own privileges under the *status quo*.

We must next consider a very different kind of issue, which I must not evade, though my views on that issue, I fear, will disappoint many of you. Suppose that everything I've been describing as possible came to pass. Suppose that, after the right kinds of collective consultation, after meetings and discussions and polls and electronic politics and all the rest, we settled on a particular basic program of medical care that we collectively thought government should, in one way or another, make available to everyone. That basic package, as my earlier argument suggests, will not include some treatment that rich people are now in a position to buy for themselves. I said earlier, for example, that the test I proposed would very likely rule out ultra-expensive marginal diagnostics or extraordinarily costly treatments that have some but very little prospects for success. Some people in Canada and America now have the money to buy health care that would be excluded from the basic package. They have the money to buy a liver transplant when the odds are very small but nevertheless real that the procedure would save their lives. In England, people are standardly denied even renal dialysis on the National Health Service when they are sixty-five. So people of that age die if they cannot afford to pay for dialysis themselves.

If we adopted the kind of scheme that I'm describing, in our admittedly imperfect society, and took no steps to forbid people buying more expensive care than the basic package provides, some people would have better medical care – some people would live longer and healthier lives – only because they had more money. In most cases, since the basic economic structure would continue to be unjust, because they unjustly had more money. Should we therefore take steps to prohibit or constrain the private market in medicine? Should that be part of any respectable campaign to improve justice in health care? Of course, we couldn't actually abolish the private market in health care altogether: we would end by producing back street dialysis. But should we do what we can, aiming to prevent anyone from buying better medical care than the basic package provides, so far as that is possible?

The insulation model of medical justice I began by describing, if taken seriously, would insist that we should, and I believe many people here this evening would agree. Solidarity is compromised, they think, when some people can live while others die only because the former have more money. That seems to me the wrong answer, however. The spirit of the argument I have been making suggests that no one can complain *on grounds of justice* that he has less of something that someone else does, so long as he has all he would have if society were overall just. And, of course, in the circumstances we are now considering, people whose basic provision does not include liver transplants, and cannot afford to buy such an operation for themselves, are by hypothesis not denied what they would have if economic justice were perfect.

Some of you will hate that argument, as I said: you will think it intolerable. May I remind you, however, that the hypothetical inequality in medical care I'm now considering is, in one important respect, relatively benign compared to other inequalities in our society. If health care were rationed in the way we are contemplating, then everyone would have at least the medical care he would have in a just society, and that would not be true in most other departments of resource allocation. In education, employment, culture, recreation, travel, experience and a host of other goods and opportunities that for most of us make up the value of being alive, the poor would continue to have much less than they would if we had reformed not just health care but our economic and social life more generally. If we somehow manage to succeed in providing the poor with the medical care that justice requires, it would be perverse, given that a rich man can spend on more comfortable housing or better education for his children, not to allow him to spend on more expensive health care. We would do better to put an excise tax on

special health care, and use the proceeds of that excise tax to improve public education, or the economic infrastructure, or to reduce
public debt that blights employment prospects, or in some other
ways that would make the community distinctly more egalitarian.

VI

I will offer you no final summary of my somewhat discursive remarks; I shall try, instead, to broaden the argument in closing it. I
began by criticizing the insulation model, as I called it, and you
may think I've been undermining that criticism in the last part of
the lecture. I've been arguing how we might make our communities better in just one respect, and that goal seems to assume, with
the insulation model, that health care is special, 'chief' among goods.
But my special interest in medical care is largely practical. Medicine is now a problem for people so high up in the economic scale
– well up into the middle, fat part of the economic diamond where
the votes are. People generally, not just the poor, agree that government should take a larger role in structuring, controlling and financing
the provision of health care. We can seize on this opportunity to
make the distribution of health care more just as well as more efficient.

But if America does make new progress in that direction, as Canada
already has, then the lesson might be of more general political
importance. For one thing, it might teach us that the bad press the
ideal of equality has had for some time is unjustified. There is a
rap against equality: that accepting equality as an ideal, even one
among others, means levelling down and requiring everyone to live
the same kind of life. But the conception of equality I've been
relying on has quite the opposite character: it is dynamic and sensitive to people's differing convictions about how to live.

I end with this further observation: the question of health-care
reform in America, including politically acceptable and fair health-
care rationing, is ideologically leveraged. If we find, after all the
fuss, that politically we can't do much to make the distribution of
medical care more just, in spite of the apparent present opportunities to do so, then a pessimistic conclusion may be irresistible: we
may abandon hope for any more widespread or general democratic
concern for social justice. But if we do now make substantial and
recognizable political progress in this one urgent matter, we may
learn more, from the experience, about what justice itself is like,
and we might find it to our taste, so that we can steadily, bit by

bit, incrementally, fight the same battle in other areas. So the war against injustice in medicine that you have been fighting so well here, and that we are about to take on in America, is indeed a crucial one. Health might not be more important than anything else – but the fight for justice in health might well be.

Notes

1 The central article, for purposes of this lecture, is 'What is Equality? Part II', which appeared in *Philosophy & Public Affairs*, Fall 1981.

2 I am ignoring an important issue that I will have to consider in a subsequent full presentation of this material. Is it right, in the hypothetical exercise I am constructing, to exclude information relating risk of disease to voluntarily chosen behaviour? Should insurance companies be in a position to charge cigarette smokers or mountain climbers higher premiums, for example? If so, then what counts as voluntary behaviour? Should sexual behaviour of a particular kind be treated as voluntary for this purpose? Should insurance companies be able to charge active male homosexuals higher premiums because they are more likely to contract Aids?

3 Some paternalistic interference with individual decisions about health care insurance, particularly those people make early in their lives, might be necessary out of fairness to people who might make imprudent insurance decisions when young. And some constraints and requirements might be necessary in the interests of justice toward later generations.

Further Reading

General

E. Anderson, 'What is the Point of Equality?', *Ethics* 109.2 (1999), pp. 287–337.
S. Darwall (ed.), *Equal Freedom* (Michigan: University of Michigan Press, 1995).
A. Mason (ed.), *Ideals of Equality* (Oxford: Basil Blackwell, 1998).
J. Roemer, *Theories of Distributive Justice* (Cambridge, Mass.: Harvard University Press, 1996).
L. Temkin, *Inequality* (New York: Oxford University Press, 1993).

Equality and priority

D. Brink, 'The Separateness of Persons, Distributive Norms, and Moral Theory', in R. G. Frey and C. Morris (eds), *Value, Welfare, and Morality* (Cambridge: Cambridge University Press, 1993).
B. Barry, *Theories of Justice* (Berkeley: University of California Press, 1989), ch. 6.
J. Cohen, 'Democratic Equality', *Ethics* 99.4 (1989), pp. 727–51.
W. Glannon, 'Equality, Priority and Numbers', *Social Theory and Practice* 21.3 (1995), pp. 427–55.
S. Kagan, 'Equality and Desert', in L. Pojman and O. McLeod (eds), *What Do We Deserve?* (Oxford: Oxford University Press, 1999).
D. McKerlie, 'Equality and Priority', *Utilitas* 6 (1994), pp. 25–42.
J. Rawls, *A Theory of Justice* (Cambridge, Mass.: Harvard University Press, 1971), secs. 11–13, pp. 60–83.
J. Raz, *The Morality of Freedom* (Oxford: Clarendon Press, 1986), ch. 9.
S. Reibetanz, 'Contractualism and Aggregation', *Ethics* 108.2 (1998), pp. 296–311.
T. M. Scanlon, *What We Owe to Each Other* (Cambridge, Mass.: Harvard Univeristy Press), ch. 5.
T. M. Scanlon, 'Contractualism and Utilitarianism', in A. Sen and B. Williams (eds), *Utilitarianism and Beyond* (Cambridge: Cambridge University Press, 1982).
T. M. Wilkinson, 'Raz on Equality', *Imprints* 3.2 (1998), pp. 132–55.

Equality and sufficiency

H. Frankfurt, 'Equality as a Moral Ideal', *Ethics* 98.1 (1987), pp. 21–43, and *The Importance of What We Care About* (Cambridge: Cambridge University Press, 1988).
J. Kekes, 'A Question for Egalitarians', *Ethics* 107.4 (1997), pp. 658–70.
J. Rawls, *A Theory of Justice* (Cambridge, Mass.: Harvard University Press, 1971), secs. 29 and 49.
A. Rosenberg, 'Equality, Sufficiency, and Opportunity in the Just Society', *Social Philosophy and Policy* 12.2 (1995), pp. 54–71.

J. Waldron, 'John Rawls and the Social Minimum', *Journal of Applied Philosophy* 3 (1986), pp. 21–33, and *Liberal Rights* (Cambridge: Cambridge University Press, 1993).
D. Wiggins, *Needs, Values, Truth* (Oxford: Basil Blackwell, 1987), ch. I.

Equality and self-ownership

R. Arneson, 'Property Rights in Persons', *Social Philosophy and Policy* 9.1 (1992), pp. 201–30.
G. A. Cohen, *Self-Ownership, Freedom, and Equality* (Cambridge: Cambridge University Press, 1995), chs 3, 4, 9 and 10.
M. Gorr, 'Justice, Self-Ownership and Natural Assets', *Social Philosophy and Policy* 12.2 (1995), pp. 267–91.
R. Nozick, *Anarchy, State and Utopia* (New York: Basic Books, 1974), pp. 167–74 and pp. 228–31.
M. Otsuka, 'Self-Ownership and Equality: a Lockean Reconciliation', *Philosophy and Public Affairs* 27.1 (1998), pp. 65–92.
P. Vallentyne, 'Review of *Self-Ownership, Freedom, and Equality*', *Canadian Journal of Philosophy* 28.4 (1998), pp. 609–26.
P. Vallentyne and H. Steiner (eds), *Left-Libertarianism and Its Critics* (Palgrave, 2000).

Welfare egalitarianism

R. Arneson, 'Equality and Equal Opportunity for Welfare', *Philosophical Studies* 56 (1989), pp. 77–93.
T. Christiano, 'Difficulties with the Principle of Equal Opportunity for Welfare', *Philosophical Studies* 62 (1991), pp. 179–85.
R. Dworkin, *Sovereign Virtue* (Cambridge, Mass.: Harvard University Press, 2000), chs 1, 6, and 7.
E. Rakowski, *Equal Justice* (Oxford: Clarendon Press, 1991), pp. 43–72.
J. Rawls, 'Social Unity and Primary Goods', in A. Sen and B. Williams (eds), *Utilitarianism and Beyond* (Cambridge: Cambridge University Press, 1982).
J. Roemer, *Equality of Opportunity* (Cambridge, Mass.: Harvard University Press, 1998).
T. M. Scanlon, 'Equality of Resources and Equality of Welfare: a Forced Marriage?', *Ethics* 97.1 (1986), pp. 111–18.

Resource egalitarianism

C. Arnsperger, 'Envy-Freeness and Distributive Justice', *Journal of Economic Surveys* 8.2 (1994), pp. 155–86.
G. A. Cohen, 'On the Currency of Egalitarian Justice', *Ethics* 99.4 (1989), pp. 906–44.
R. Dworkin, *Sovereign Virtue* (Cambridge, Mass.: Harvard University Press, 2000).
C. MacLeod, *Liberalism, Justice, and Markets* (Oxford: Oxford University Press, 1998).

E. Rakowski, *Equal Justice* (Oxford: Clarendon Press, 1991), chs 4, 5, 6 and 7.
J. Roemer, *Egalitarian Perspectives* (Cambridge: Cambridge University Press, 1994), pt. II.
P. Van Parijs, *Real Freedom for All* (Oxford: Clarendon Press, 1995), ch. 3.
J. Wolff, 'Fairness, Respect, and the Egalitarian Ethos', *Philosophy and Public Affairs* 27.2 (1998), pp. 97–127.

Capability and functioning

J. Cohen, 'Review of *Inequality Re-Examined*', *Journal of Philosophy* 92.5 (1995), pp. 275–88.
N. Daniels, 'Equality of What: Welfare, Resources or Capabilities?', *Philosophy and Phenomenological Research* (1990, Supplement), and *Justice and Justification* (Cambridge: Cambridge University Press, 1996).
T. M Scanlon, 'The Moral Basis of Interpersonal Comparisons', in J. Elster and J. Roemer (eds), *Interpersonal Comparisons of Well-Being* (Cambridge: Cambridge University Press, 1991).
A. Sen, 'Equality of What?', *Choice, Welfare and Measurement* (Oxford: Basil Blackwell, 1982), and S. McMurrin (ed.), *The Tanner Lectures on Human Values*, 1 (Cambridge: Cambridge University Press, 1980), and S. Darwall (ed.), *Equal Freedom* (Michigan: University of Michigan Press, 1995).
A. Sen, *Inequality Re-Examined* (Oxford: Clarendon Press, 1992).
A. Sen, 'Justice: Freedom versus Means', *Philosophy and Public Affairs* 19.2 (1990), pp. 111–21.

The site of distributive justice

G. A. Cohen, 'Incentives, Equality, and Community', in G. Petersen (ed.), *The Tanner Lectures on Human Values*, 13 (Salt Lake City: University of Utah Press, 1990), and S. Darwall (ed.), *Equal Freedom* (Michigan: University of Michigan Press, 1995).
G. A. Cohen, 'Where the Action Is: On the Site of Distributive Justice', *Philosophy and Public Affairs* 26.1 (1997), pp. 3–30.
J. Cohen, 'Review of *Justice, Gender and the Family*', *Canadian Journal of Philosophy* 22.2 (1992), pp. 263–86.
L. Murphy, 'Institutions and the Demands of Justice', *Philosophy and Public Affairs* 27.4 (1998), pp. 251–91.
S. M. Okin, *Justice, Gender and the Family* (New York: Basic Books, 1989).
T. W. Pogge, 'On the Site of Distributive Justice: Reflections on Cohen and Murphy', *Philosophy and Public Affairs* 29 (2000), pp. 137–69.
J. Rawls, *Political Liberalism* (New York: Columbia University Press, 1993), Lecture VII.
J. Rawls, 'The Idea of Public Reason Revisited', *University of Chicago Law Review* 64.3 (1997), pp. 765–73 and 787–94.
A. Williams, 'Incentives, Inequality, and Publicity', *Philosophy and Public Affairs* 27.3 (1998), pp. 226–48.

Index*

---

* The editors are grateful to David Stevens for preparing the index.